Shakespeare
and the Art of Humankindness

Shakespeare and the Art of Humankindness

the essay toward androgyny

Robert Kimbrough

HUMANITIES PRESS INTERNATIONAL, INC.
New Jersey ◇ London

First published 1990 by Humanities Press International, Inc.,
165 First Avenue, Atlantic Highlands, N.J. 07716 and
3 Henrietta Street, London WC2E 8LU

First paperback edition published 1992

Photo credits: Venus and Cupid (c. 1573) by Luca Cambiaso (1527–85) (courtesy *The Art Institute of Chicago*), "Cupid Chastised" (c. 1608) by Bartolomeo Manfredi (1587–1620), and "Holy Family" (c. 1615) by Peter Paul Rubens (1577–1640) (courtesy *The Art Institute of Chicago*). © 1988 The Art Institute of Chicago. All Rights Reserved.

Library of Congress Cataloging–in–Publication Data

Kimbrough, Robert.
Shakespeare and the art of humankindness : the essay toward androgyny / Robert Kimbrough.
p. cm.
Includes bibliographical references.
ISBN 0–391–03669–6 ISBN 0–391–03767–6 (Pbk.)
1. Shakespeare, William, 1564–1616—Criticism and intepretation.
2. Sex role in literature. 3. Androgny in literature. 4. English literature—Early modern, 1500–1700—History and criticism.
I. Title.
PR3069.S45K5 1990
822.3′3—dc20 89–29698
CIP

British Library Cataloguing in Publication Data

Kimbrough, Robert
Shakespeare and the art of humankindness : the essay toward androgny.
I. Title
822.3′3
ISBN 0–391–03669–6
ISBN 0–391–03767–6 (Pbk.)

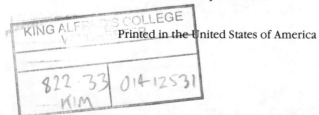

Printed in the United States of America

PRINTED WITH SOY INK

for
Phyllis

I may, of course, have deluded myself. I may not have earned a place among those writers who entered the vast room of their androgyny and calmly generated a large portion of literature's enduring characters—characters who have taught us a large part of what we know about love and tolerance in the actual world of sight and touch. If my own attempt fails, still I assert the original claim.

The most beautiful and fragile of our birth gifts is an entire humanity, an accessibility to all other members of our species—all shades of gender and private need. The gift lies not primarily in our sexuality but in something simpler and more complex—an early comprehension of the *means* of human life, packed as they are so lovably, transparently, delicately, frighteningly in bodies and minds called male and female but deeply kin. It's in our power—writers and readers—to take the next step, back and forward, to a common gift: our mutual room.

Reynolds Price
Book review, *New York Times*, 11/9/86
On his novel, *Kate Vaiden*

Contents

Illustrations

Plates

Figures

Preface

During the composition of this book, three others appeared which gave me great encouragement. Because none of them receives its full due in what follows and because taken together they provide a philosophical and theoretical context for my work, I should like to acknowledge their existence and to claim a touch of consanguinity.

In 1979 Dorothy Koenigsberger published *Renaissance Man and Creative Thinking: A History of Concepts of Harmony 1400–1700*, which has almost nothing to do with any sixteenth-century English literature, but which posits a theory of dynamic modes of mental comprehension, apprehension, and projection all based on traditional, received models of medieval thought. The process of discovery that she describes gave me confidence, for my description of Sidney's invention of fiction is quite similar. I greatly admire her encyclopedic talent and seeming ease of expression.

In 1985 A. J. Smith published *The Metaphysics of Love: Studies in Renaissance Love Poetry from Dante to Milton*, an elegant and eloquent example of how tracing the history of an idea can be complemented by a series of discrete, acute, engaging close-readings of creative writing. I wish I had his in-born grace and achieved learning.

In 1986 Stevie Davies published *The Idea of Woman in Renaissance Literature: The Feminine Reclaimed.* In her Introduction, Davies discusses some of the same authors and topics that I do, and some different ones, and finds, as I do, that there is emergent in the sixteenth century in England a feminism clad in androgynous garb; I envy the economy of her presentation. Her subsequent proofs are found in sensitive readings of Spenser, Shakespeare, and Milton.

A fourth book, John S. Mebane's *Renaissance Magic and the Return of the Golden Age: The Occult Tradition and Marlowe, Jonson, and Shakespeare*, appeared in 1989 after this work had gone to press. I had benefitted from an earlier article by him, and was glad to find that I was not all alone treading what are sometimes dangerous waters.

I have had a long acquaintance with Sir Philip Sidney, so was pleased to discover upon completion of this book that I had followed the example of my friend's *A Defence of Poetry* both in genre and in method. Mine, too, is a "Defence" in the simple sense that it attempts to make a case for the presence of androgyny in Shakespeare. Furthermore the argument is presented, as is Sidney's, cumulatively; that is, the whole thesis is partly present in each part—what is said in small in the first section is reiterated and elaborated in all of the other sections. Indeed, motifs are introduced in the beginning in order that they may be developed later, even as late as the last chapter.

Although I have been selective in my discussions of Shakespeare's plays, I have touched on nearly all of them, except the history plays which tend not to turn inward in their explorations (except for *Henry V*, which may be why this was Shakespeare's farewell to a genre which he more than any other playwright had defined and practiced). Even though I have not been exhaustive, I believe that the approach to Shakespeare which I advocate can be followed in profitable exploration of aspects of all of his plays.

My aim, overarching all else, has been to put into writing a working definition of humankindness and to suggest that one can, in turn, try to incorporate such a definition in one's own living, even if only tentatively. Both attempts take effort—each is an essay. For this reason, I have put my subtitle entirely in the lower case in order to call to mind the French *essai* with its deeply embedded triple-meaning: a written discourse, endeavor, and provisionality. In all three instances, an essay should stretch us.

Acknowledgments

The Art Institute of Chicago granted permission to use photographic prints of Peter Paul Rubens, "The Holy Family with Saints Elizabeth and John the Baptist"; Luca Cambiaso, "Venus and Cupid"; and Bartolomeo Manfredi, "Cupid Chastised."

The Kröller-Müller Foundation (Amsterdam) granted permission to use a photographic print of L. Cranach de Oude, "Venus en Amor als honing-dief."

The Bibliothèque Nationale granted permission to use a photographic print of a small wood-panel painting of Françoise le Premier by Niccolò da Modena.

The British Library granted permission to use the twelve photographic prints which appear, with sources given, in Appendices II and IV.

Art Resource (NYC) granted use of their photographic prints of Botticelli, "Birth of Venus" and "Primavera."

The Western Humanities Review, *Shakespeare Quarterly*, and *Shakespeare Studies* gave me permission to use and revise three articles (see Bibliography).

The Graduate School Research Committee of the University of Wisconsin-Madison gave me gifts of time off from teaching.

Librarians within the Memorial Library of the University of Wisconsin-Madison, The Newberry Library (Chicago), the Cambridge University Library, The British Library (London), and the University of Warwick Library (Coventry) have provided much-needed assistance over the years.

June Jordan kindly allowed me to reprint her "DeLisa Questioning Perplexities."

Carolyn Heilbrun and Susan Stanford Friedman encouraged me during the formative stages of this project; Leah Marcus fit into her packed schedule the time to read and comment on an abbreviated draft of this work; and Annis Pratt has offered continuous collegial support.

The secretaries in the Department of English at Wisconsin during the various stages of this project have carefully deciphered (no easy matter) and accurately translated my manuscript into typescript via the mysteries (to me) of word-processing.

Kathy Dauck, Mary Ann Ford, and Lynne Roberts prepared disks of the penultimate draft. Barbara Bosold typed the preface and index.

Deidra M. Hewitt of Coventry came to my rescue when none of my disks would function in England, which forced a retyping of the whole project, old material and new, from beginning to end, during the spring of 1989.

All of these, anonymous and named, and many more unnamed, my students and my friends, have helped me to maintain my faith in humankindness, even in an ever darkening world.

1

Introduction: Discovering Humankindness

We can never know with precise accuracy how Shakespeare actually perceived (through metaphor) both natural phenomena and cultural phenomena—nor would Shakespeare have been able to have guessed in what ways we would come to create models both of life and of stimulus and response. What was once felt awareness becomes for us textbook awareness—the "Great Chain of Being," an "Elizabethan World Picture," "Renaissance Self-Fashioning." Paradigms shift. But essential human nature has not shifted: across Time and through Time that one touch of Nature still makes the whole world kin. We still share our humanity with Shakespeare—and he, surely, his with us. We can "feel" that this is so when we come away from his theater enriched, pleased with life, more open to nuance, with heightened self awareness—for better or ill—and, perhaps, better *if* ill. (That "one touch of Nature" has always woven mingled yarn, the good and ill together.)[1]

Today, cultural change is rapidly accelerating through the intervention of science and technology within the various contexts of our various environments. Yet, paradoxically, natural change within humanity (biological evolution, natural selection, adaptation) has been slowed because the brain in creating artificial (non-natural, un-natural) human environments has finally fitted us, internally and in numbers, to survive in spite of nature. (Whether we have created collectively from within a culture which so spites nature that it will not allow us to survive, and whether the mindless, nearly exponential, natural replication of our numbers will not allow us to survive, are essential questions that must be faced more directly in other forums, although they are addressed indirectly here.) Cultural selection has taken over the work of natural selection.[2] Thus, today, we can recognize more clearly than ever that we are still and always have been children of Dame Nature—that mythic, androgynous, hermaphroditic figure who dwells in the bosom of Sabaoth, but who each year recreates on Arlo Hill. Our kind descends from her; we partake of her sapience and her generative powers. That wisdom informs our life and gives us hope through learning, but those generative powers which form our life also brought death into the world and all our woe. Thus we live in two worlds: the ideal world of sapient nature and the actualized world of a fallen nature.[3] Although the model is outdated, Sir John Davies' summation should still stir the soul:

> I know my body's of so frail a kind,
> As force without, fevers within can kill;
> I know the heavenly nature of my mind,
> But 'tis corrupted both in wit and will.
>
> I know my Soul hath power to know all things,
> Yet is she blind and ignorant in all;
> I know I am one of Nature's little kings,
> Yet to the least and vilest things am thrall.
>
> I know my life's a pain and but a span,
> I know my Sense is mock'd with everything:
> And to conclude, I know myself a MAN,
> Which is a proud, and yet a wretched thing.[4]

Davies and Shakespeare took the measure of reality by using the same construct of that reality, the medieval model of the world. Yet the one writer is essentially in tension and is pessimistic, the other is in resolution and is optimistic. While Shakespeare's plays are built on tension and reek of pessimism—their dark underbellies are swelled by subversion—their effect is one of reassurance and hope. No more than could Montaigne, could Shakespeare reject the inherited paradigm of the Renaissance, but unlike Montaigne he fully embraced the implications of the philosophy of humanity which evolved within that paradigm as it shifted from a static to a dynamic model, from a theological to a secular.[5]

Shakespeare holds a mirror up before our human nature which reflects honestly, in depth, the good and ill together. But his act of holding a mirror before us stems from his assumption, shared with Bacon, that human nature is essentially good, has a potential of positive fulfillment.[6] Shakespeare did not hesitate to confront us with existent evil and present ugliness, but he was not fixated by them; rather, he worked through the seamy to locate the potentially good and essentially beautiful. His impulse is to help us overcome the limitations imposed by everyday actuality as experienced in nature and society. While one hopes that the ultimate, long-range effect of Shakespeare's art is external (that is, social, political), the impulse for liberation appeals to the individual, and any degree of realization remains within the individual, within our humanity.[7] Shakespeare, saying farewell to his theater, modestly said his aim was but to please, and please he does because his appeal is to our "better part," that aspect of our nature nurtured by "the milk of human kindness." Shakespeare has pleased many and pleased long because his art is the art of humankindness.

What Shakespeare was like matters not at all. Keats got it right: Shakespeare led a life of allegory and his works are its record. We do not need the testimony of his friends Heminge and Condell: we can sense in his work that Shakespeare's artistic accomplishment came easily to him. The native skill and the practiced effort that make art, as in a Picasso, seem to be a mere toy and a simple joy. But art does take skill and effort. Ben Jonson, in his prefatory poem in the First Folio, praised Shakespeare's skill (wit) in imitating nature:

> Nature her selfe was proud of his designes,
>   And joy'd to weare the dressing of his lines!
> Which were so richly spun, and woven so fit,
>   As, since, she will vouchsafe no other Wit.

But Jonson goes on to praise the art as well:

> Yet must I not give Nature all: Thy Art,
>   My gentle *Shakespeare*, must enjoy a part.

And being Ben Jonson, he is compelled to add regarding poetic invention:

> For though the Poets matter, Nature be,
>   His Art doth give the fashion . . .
> For a good Poet's made, as well as born.

Sidney, too, had stated that the potential artist is born, but that art itself is produced through the cultivation and interaction of learning and personal energy. With Shakespeare, Poet of Nature and of Art, as example and text one can learn the art of humankindness, can undertake the essay toward androgyny.

The concept of androgyny can frighten and perplex because discovery that the potential for androgyny is part of our essential human nature can cause shock waves which disturb the arrangement and display of our surface sexual selves, our genders. Coleridge located the radical placement of androgyny when he casually remarked on September 1, 1832 (in *Table Talk*), "The truth is, a great mind must be androgynous," a truth beautifully acknowledged by Virginia Woolf in *A Room of One's Own*, during which she returns again and again to Shakespeare's "unity of mind" as the great example of androgyny realized.[8]

Elaboration will come; for now, androgyny may be defined as fully realized humanity. Because this is a state of mind rarely attained and, when achieved, nearly impossible to maintain, androgyny is an ideal goal—a vision of unity and harmony within the confines of the human. It is an end to be essayed.

Some radical feminists such as Mary Daly and Janice Raymond, and most traditional masculinists such as Robert May, resist and reject this basic humanist position (see Appendix I). Both groups, for different reasons, wish to maintain a rigid socio-sexual segregation—separate but not equal. Each sees the other sex as the enemy, the destroyer. To them, that each one of us comes into the world with one pair of chromosomes out of twenty-three either X–X or X–Y is not just an initial, but is the ultimate, fact of human development.

However, to advocate an artificial (that is, a cultural) division of humanity is to deny not only social justice but also the process of nature. Robert Frost was consciously stating a biological truth when he wrote in "Mending Wall": "Something there is that doesn't love a wall,/That wants it down." All life is cellular, with constant breaking and bonding. But the idea is not just scientific; it expresses as well the essential aim of the humanities to understand the structures of humanity, the self and the other(s). For this fundamental, basic reason, androgyny, both in Shakespeare's day and in ours, is a subject appropriate for study within the humanities—that record of lore, art, and science which, collectively and in parts, tries to show ourselves to ourselves. The humanities are our mirror up to nature.

Androgyny is one of the earliest and most pervasive images of humanity to be found within racial history, for the idea of an at–one–time uni-sexual human-wholeness can be found within the creation myths of all cultures. In western culture this myth of spherical integrity has pretty much been flattened out by linear/literal post-Renaissance/pre-Jungian thought. To be an androgyne is to be a wimp—a limp, unenergized, sexless twerp, usually male. Carolyn Heilbrun, however, gave the concept of the potential for human growth beyond single-sex identity a new vibrancy in her pioneering, provocative *Toward a Recognition of Androgyny* (1973).

Writing in *Women's Studies* the next year, Heilbrun stated that she was happy neither with the effect of, nor the need for, the word. But she realized that something with more impact than merely "human" is needed to take us beyond the present division of experience, to use the phrase from the title of

Marilyn French's book, into male/female, masculine/feminine. Radical feminists (with clever help from male fifth-column "feminists" such as Daniel A. Harris) attacked the concept of androgyny as just another age-old patriarchal device of control: after all, this seeming gesture toward equity, and even unity, put male (*andro*) before female (*gyne*).[9]

Driven from the feminist movement in the late 1970s before fully explained and explored, androgyny in the 1980s landed half-understood in the pop-music culture of MTV; Boy George even made it to the cover of that ultimate establishment journal, *Harvard Magazine* (January–February 1985). The esoteric details of androgyny may be blurred and misunderstood but the impulses are there: the urge of a person rooted in a sex to grow beyond gender realization to a more encompassing experience of human realization. The process is organic, not sequential; it embraces "all of," does not move "from, to." Androgyny seeks radical growth, not radical change.

When Heilbrun's small book appeared, I was in the midst of sorting through what seemed to be disparate ideas about Shakespeare's attitudes toward the roles people are forced to play or choose to play, how roles provide modes of moving toward identity while at the same time they provide restrictions on growth and development. Caught in a dualistic, either/or frame of reference, I was freed by Heilbrun's organic paradigm of androgyny. Won by her casual definition—"Androgyny seeks to liberate the individual from the confines of the appropriate" (p. x)—and encouraged by what she called her "few fugitive observations" about "Shakespeare's androgynous vision" (28–29), I was able to organize my thoughts under a new rubric: the art of humankindness.

As did Heilbrun then, I believe that Shakespeare's plays are filled with signs of the androgynous vision which was slowly coming into focus during the high Renaissance in England.[10] On the social plane, when a woman laments that she wished she had the prerogative of men and could speak out in matters of love, or when a man self-consciously states that he is being weak and effeminate if he shows disgust with fighting or a bit of fear, each is trying to break out of the frustrating confines of what society has labeled appropriate gender behavior for a woman or a man. What triggers these kinds of response may be a simple frustration with societal limitation, but what informs that frustration, what gives it purpose, is the sense of something better, something figuratively larger—something like Caliban's dream, which is an androgynous vision of the potential for achieving unity, wholeness, harmony, and perfection even within the confines of the human. Androgyny reaches widely and deeply, running a scale from the personal/societal to the psychic/mythic, and the works of Shakespeare encompass the full range.

Although the original wholeness of each human as Man, Woman, or

Androgyne in Plato's *Symposium* and the Gnostic traditions of God, Adam, and Christ as androgynous were known throughout medieval and renaissant Europe; although the concept of androgyny was reemphasized within the renewed interest in the fifteenth and sixteenth centuries in Neoplatonism, the Cabala, Hermeticism, and alchemy; and although the spirit of androgyny was everywhere abounding in late sixteenth-century thought and expression—medicine, mathematics, magic, music—the term is rarely used.[11] Shakespeare, in fact, never uses the word in any direct form. The closest he comes is in "The Phoenix and Turtle" when he refers to "Single nature's double name": Dame Nature is an andro(man)gyne(woman). William W. E. Slights has pointed out that we hear an echo from the *Symposium* when Antonio asks Sebastian in the concluding action of *Twelfth Night*: "How have you made division of yourself?/An apple cleft in two is not more twin than these two creatures" (5.1.215–17).[12]

Shakespeare could have defined androgyny and given examples. He would have recognized that androgyny is a word which exists above and beyond the words male and female, both as nouns and adjectives. As nouns, male and female designate sexual identity; as adjectives, they designate gender attributes which we tend to ally with one or the other of the two sexes. Androgyny is a word which embraces all of humanity—the shared and the unshared biological characteristics together. Shakespeare's word is "kind." Androgyny is the acceptance of our kind-ness.

Like the word human ("belonging to the earth"), kind means belonging to nature: kind, kindred, kin all mean related through nature: hence, "One touch of Nature makes the whole world kin" (*Troilus and Cressida* 3.3.175). In fact, although Shakespeare uses the phrase, "human kindness" was still a redundancy in his day because, simply, to be kind was to be human. Because we are kin we must be kind. Humanity's nobility and gentility are expressed in natural acts of kindness. Shakespeare touches the deep reaches of androgyny, using his own terms, when, in *As You Like It*, Oliver says that "*kindness*, nobler ever than revenge/And *nature*, stronger than his just occasion," made Orlando give battle to the lioness threatening the "unnatural" Oliver (4.3.122–129, emphasis added). Oliver is "unnatural" because his despicable treatment of his younger brother even to the point of seeking Orlando's death has been in defiance of nature, a denial of the bonds of nature, as would be the act of revenge in a just cause, for "revenge" and "justice" are essentially social, ethical, man-made concerns, which are overridden by "kindness" and "nature," by nurtured nature, human nature, man kind, natural goodness—kindness, the androgynous overcoming of human tendency to settle in partiality.

The action taken (or *not* taken) by Orlando represents what I shall call an androgynous moment, a moment of allegiance to a larger concept of self than merely self, a moment that includes self but includes more than self, whether other or others. Such a moment occurs in *Othello* when Emilia finally comprehends her husband's guilt and refuses to keep quiet and to leave the room: "Tis proper I obey him, *but not now*" (5.2.197, emphasis added). By society's laws, a woman's silence and a wife's obedience are "proper," but the context of the presented instance is larger than the petty embrace of man-made regulation: the acts of Othello and of Iago are outrages against humanity. Emilia obeys the dictate of a greater law than society's when as a woman she refuses to be quiet and as a wife she refuses to leave.

It matters not whether Emilia consciously realizes fully the philosophical assumptions and implications of her words and actions—Shakespeare makes his point through her (and no actress should or would hit, hold, and highlight that line at that moment within the rushing final action of the play). In *Hamlet*, Laertes is surely not intended to be aware of the androgynous assumptions and implications of his words which follow Gertrude's report of Ophelia's death:

> Too much of water hast thou, poor Ophelia,
> And therefore I forbid my tears; but yet
> It is our trick; *nature her custom holds*,
> Let shame say what it will. When these are gone,
> The woman will be out. Adieu, my lord.
> I have a speech o'fire, that fain would blaze
> But that this folly drowns it.
>
> (4.7.184–90; emphasis added)

To Laertes, tears are merely womanly, are folly. But to be a fool is to be fully human, as Erasmus pleads in his praise of folly, and as Shakespeare demonstrates through clown and king, through Bottom and Lear. Public betrayal of manhood may be shame-ful, but an instinctive urge of nature, the expression of sorrow, has a prior, deeper claim on Laertes's manhood: his humankindness. Indeed, "It is our trick."

Laertes again sounds this sense of a divided allegiance between private "nature" and public "name" in the final act when Hamlet appeals to Laertes's "most generous thoughts" in asking for forgiveness. Laertes replies:

> I am satisfied in nature,
> Whose motive in this case should stir me most
> To my revenge. But in terms of honor
> I stand aloof, and will no reconcilement

Till by some elder masters of known honor
I have a voice and precedent of peace
To keep my name ungored. But till that time
I do receive your offered love like love.

(5.2.233–40)

That Hamlet would appeal to Laertes's "most generous thoughts" can remind us that Hamlet, even at this moment of readiness to carry out an "appropriate" act of son-for-father revenge, still talks like a student of the Renaissance from Wittenburg, where we know he has read Giovanni Pico della Mirandola: that word "generous" gives him away. Generous, from: *genus* (pl. *genera*), meaning "kind"; and -ous, meaning "having the qualities of"; therefore, generous means "having the qualities of kind," which leads naturally to generous meaning magnanimous, noble-minded, open and free. Hamlet is appealing to Laertes's essential self, his better part, not his socially induced surface-self. Yet, Laertes hedges about in his response: he speaks of the greater good—nature and love—but holds to his need of the lesser good—honor and name.

Hamlet's very first line in the play is a punning aside which can almost serve as prologue to the through-line of his own interior play: "A little more than kin, and less than kind." Ophelia is right: during the play we witness the overthrow of a noble mind, a mind trained and encouraged at Wittenburg in all the fresh excitement of Renaissance thought, the dignity of man, metaphysical inquiry: What is "kind"? But in Elsinore, all is society's custom: no, not "kind"; just a stepfather and a usurping king. At university, Nature's lore; at court, social roles: loving child, dutiful son, rejected lover, revenger. At Wittenburg, Hamlet had undertaken an essay toward androgyny; at Elsinore, he is blocked.[13] Even in his cursing of Claudius, Hamlet's education shows through: "Remorseless, treacherous, lecherous, kindless villain" (2.2.566). And in his last words to Horatio before Osric comes in to arrange the fatal fencing match, Hamlet observes that "a man's life is no more than to say 'one'" (5.2.74), which Ralph Berry paraphrases, "a man's life is a quest for unity of self and situation."[14] *Hamlet* in small, although greatly, represents, then, the thesis of this present work: that Shakespeare's plays contain the theme of an androgynous vision.[15]

After this present introductory chapter of definitions and summary, the rest of the work is divided into four parts. In the next chapter, the first within Part I—"Androgyny: 'Single nature's double name'"—I define androgyny both in terms of myth and in terms of modern biology and social psychology. In each context, the same essential movements can be traced: because androgyny first went from unity to division, *division must be removed before wholeness can be experienced.* Here Plato's version of the myth (*Symposium*, 189d–193d) is particularly helpful; Jerome Schwartz in "Aspects of Androgyny in the Renaissance" aptly summarizes:

> Let us recall briefly Aristophanes' speech in the *Symposium* in which he attempts to account for the origins of love, both homosexual and heterosexual. "The sexes were not two but three, man, woman, and the union of the two, called 'Androgynous'." As punishment for their arrogance, Zeus cut them in two, causing each half to yearn for reunion with the other half, man with man, woman with woman, and the Androgyne with its opposite. Love is thus defined by Aristophanes as a pursuit and desire of that original wholeness. (121)

In the Renaissance, education informs that "pursuit and desire of that original wholeness": we still speak Aristophanically of the educated person as well-rounded, and of how "love made me whole."

At the center of education was the Renaissance philosophy of man, the subject of chapter 3; by the sixteenth century, the aim was Faustian, the seeming paradox of wanting to become and be "a spirit in form and substance." A material spirit is a paradox; but to be as fully as possible *like* a spirit is not. And *this* is the dominant note in the philosophy of the late Renaissance. This philosophy is not Hermetic, Gnostic, cabalistic, alchemic, or Platonic, but can seem to be each and all, for the eclectic methods of the new philosophy searched in each, and searched in all.[16] This is not mere relativism because at the extreme reach of philosophy is theology, Christian theology, the unstated assumption of which is the simple, plain, direct "God Is."[17] For this reason, the various kinds of sixteenth-century "occult" philosophy do not spring up on the fringe of thought, but stem from the center. For example, magic is not found outside, above, or below nature, but *within*, and was called "natural magic."[18] So also, the secular salvation of mankind is not found outside, above, or below, but *within*—specifically, as Sidney said, "within the zodiac of [one's] own wit." Secular salvation is achieved through the fulfillment of human potential by the overcoming of the fruits of the Fall through education. Milton, whom the late Douglas Bush was fond of calling the last Elizabethan, echoes this humanist theme: "The end then of learning is to repair the ruins of our first parents by regaining to know God aright, and out of that knowledge to love him, to imitate him, to be like him, as we may the nearest by possessing our souls of true virtue, which being united to the heavenly grace of faith, makes up the highest perfection," where "true virtue" means, in Renaissance terms, the full strength of human worth.[19] The fall of Adam and Eve is one form of a necessary myth which explains the discord, division, destruction, and despair which mark human existence. But everywhere in the world can be found another myth which antedates those such as the one of the Fall: the myth of androgyny is the myth of "highest perfection."

Sidney, Spenser, and Shakespeare began to sense that the highest possible perfection, the sixteenth-century ideal of *humanitas*, could not be reached until the complete humanity of women was first accepted, even to the point that men learned to embrace some of the "female graces"—such as pity, fear, compassion, remorse—along with the traditional male virtues as part of their own human development or education. Although the situation is ringed in irony, Buckingham publicly praises Richard: "Well we know your tenderness of heart/And gentle, kind, effeminate remorse" (*Richard III* 5.2.49). Filled with sorrow at the loss of Viola and with gratitude for Antonio's rescue and pledge of loyalty, Sebastian can only say: "Fare ye well at once. My bosom is full of kindness, and I am yet so near the manners of my mother that, upon the least occasion more, mine eyes will tell tales of me" (*Twelfth Night* 2.1.35–37). Such tears would be, by definition, "manly drops" as are those of Salisbury in anguish over the plight of England. Lewis praises them and him:

> A *noble temper* dost thou show in this,
> And *great affections* wrestling in thy bosom
> Doth make *an earthquake of nobility*.
> O, what a noble combat has thou fought
> Between compulsion and a brave respect!
> Let me wipe off *this honorable dew*,
> That silverly doth progress on thy cheeks.
> My heart hath melted at a lady's tears,
> Being an ordinary inundation,
> But this effusion of such *manly drops*,
> This shower, blown up by *tempest of the soul*,
> Startles mine eyes, and makes me more amazed
> Than had I seen the vaulty top of heaven
> Figured quite o'er with burning meteors.
>
> (*King John* 5.2.40–53; emphasis added)

Old ideas die hard, or hardly at all; but increasingly during the sixteenth century in England the note is sounded that within the trappings of her sex woman had a mind that was itself without sex, for the mind is the dwelling place of the soul which is without sex. The soul is the divine within the human because God, in order to create humanity in the divine image, breathed his essence into Adam and Eve, and that androgynous essence informs the mind, making it capable of higher knowledge and, hence, greater power than the rest of living animals are capable of. In order to accept woman as an equally capable human being, man first had himself to realize that such traditional questions as "the choice of Hercules" and "love versus friendship" did not really offer living alternatives, only prevented full human growth and development.[20]

Sidney, the subject of chapter 4, provides both theory and example. The theory came from his explorations while reading and translating Philippe du Plessis de Mornay's *On the Truth of the Christian Religion* and while writing *A Defence of Poetry* where he discovered the nature of organic human growth. The two versions of his *Arcadia* give the example. In each version the two princes, who are travelling the world to learn how to be knights and rulers, must go into disguise or role-reversal—one as an Amazon (man to woman), one as a shepherd (noble to commoner)—to begin to be able to look inward. Sidney puts his emphasis on individual choice and inner growth, in distinction from the idea of romance that identity comes from outer, social achievement alone.

In chapter 5, I trace the dual aspect of androgyny—that one must first stop dwelling in the restricted suburbs of self in order to enter the inner circle, or sphere, of self—which can be found in Spenser's *The Faerie Queene*, both in the plot lines of the seven books and in the constantly informing androgynous presence of Queen Elizabeth.

In Part II, "Undertaking the essay," I offer a transition from definitions to demonstrations, first, in chapter 6, through study of three Ovidian pieces, and, in chapter 7, through a play. Primarily using the device of role-reversal, Spenser, Marlowe, and Shakespeare move beyond the question of gender division to reach the primordial origins of the myth of androgyny by making their own myths. In Spenser's "Venus and Adonis" of Book III (1590) of *The Faerie Queene*, Ovidian role-reversal moves into examination of behaviors. Spenser's Venus is the keeper/wooer; Adonis, the kept and adored—but their functions re-create the paradigm of androgynous creation myths. Marlowe, too, in "Hero and Leander" reveals a "mythic awareness"—in fact parodies the myth of creation by reversing male and female descriptions and by coining a secular myth out of the power of Hero's nude beauty. Shakespeare in his "Venus and Adonis" shows full awareness of androgynous creation myths, and he fully reverses roles in order to question the socially appropriate, customary roles of men and women. Shakespeare implies that humanhood embraces manhood and womanhood.

By way of transition to Shakespeare's plays in the rest of the book, in chapter 7 I discuss *A Midsummer Night's Dream*. Shakespeare sensed that so long as one remains exclusively female or exclusively male, one will be restricted and confined, denied human growth. One will be the prisoner of gender, not its keeper.

Part III, "The Stages and Ages of Androgyny," begins with chapter 8, which centers on the controversial topic of girl-actors dressed as boys.

Because a woman dressed as a man has simultaneously two genders, the theatrical device of girl-into-boy disguise provided Shakespeare with a kind of laboratory testing-ground where he could isolate moments of heightened, broadened androgynous awareness. As "men" Shakespeare's women are able to display a broader range of human thoughts and emotions than they could as women only; they are liberated from the confines of socially appropriate gender behavior.

Reaching further into our humanity are the attempts to cross gender barriers found in *Julius Caesar*, *Othello*, and, especially, *Macbeth*, the main subject of chapter 9. From the outset we know that the relationship between Lord and Lady Macbeth has been one of mutuality and sharing; yet they are prevented from attaining and maintaining a full range of human character traits because of cultural attempts to render some exclusively feminine and some exclusively masculine. But this is only a base-level statement, for the drama of *Macbeth* contains a fierce war between gender concepts of manhood and womanhood played out upon the plain of humanity. In a metaphoric sense, as well as in the final dramatic siege, Macbeth loses the battlefield.

Chapters 7 and 8 are concerned with the androgynous stirrings in youth; chapter 9 is concerned with those mature in years; chapters 10 and 11 move on to those of older age, Lear and Prospero. Here we add to the private roles that stem from being girl and boy, and to the private roles that stem from being wife and husband, those private roles that stem from parenthood, the generation of generations. Whether or not this movement through "the ages of man" is a reflection of Shakespeare's own movement through the years we can only guess. Yet certain it is that Shakespeare's last plays—the four romances—most fully contain aspects of the myth of androgyny. But the threshold to the androgynous message of the romances, the connecting point between them and the tragedies, is found at the end of *King Lear*, where manly Lear crying with dead Cordelia in his arms is an emblem of androgyny.[21] In *The Tempest*, Prospero, the teacher, learns from Miranda and Caliban, but mainly from Ariel, that living Renaissance paradox, a spirit in form and substance. At the end, Ariel vividly describes how Prospero's "prisoners" are painfully confined in a nearby grove and concludes matter-of-factly: "That if you now beheld them, your affections/Would become tender." Prospero is obviously taken back: "Dost thou think so, spirit?" Then follows one of those moments which can only be called Shakespearean: "Mine would, sir, were I human." Ariel the non-human has observed that to be human includes tenderness, mercy, remorse, sympathetic tears. Prospero, with some amazement and wonder, learns his lesson:

> Hast thou, which art but air, a touch, a feeling
> Of their afflictions, and shall not myself,

> *One of their kind*, that relish all as sharply
> Passion as they, be *kindlier* moved than thou art?
>
> (emphasis added)

Lear and Prospero learn the lesson of androgyny, the art of humankindness.

Part IV, "End Matter," contains the conclusion, chapter 12, a summary view of Shakespeare's androgyny; six appendices which are illustrations, verbal and visual, of points raised in the text; the notes to the chapters, which are not required reading in order to understand the cumulative argument of the text, but which do support the argument and offer further reading; and the bibliography, which is full, but far from "complete"; I have had to limit myself to what is almost entirely a list of works cited in the text and in the notes.

Shakespeare's last plays celebrate the myth of androgyny because in the romances gender and generational differences are overcome through merger and synthesis into "something rich and strange." In Shakespeare's day "something rich and strange" had deep connotations of wonder, of the marvelous, of the "super" natural. Today, something rich and strange suggests Michael Jackson or Prince. Indeed, the word androgyny is having a rough time getting accepted and established because we tend to think of androgyny as Dr. Johnson thought of a metaphysical conceit: the violent yoking together of disparate elements. But androgyny is not just a coming together; it is an overcoming of separation. Androgyny is accommodation—accommodation not as compromise and diminishment, but in the fullest, most positive sense of taking in, digesting, understanding, embracing, encompassing, building, growing.[22]

PART I

Androgyny: "Single nature's double name"

2

Hermaphrodite and Androgyne: Myths of Sex and Gender

Long before "conscience was born of love," the human species had inherited a mammalian sub-division into sex, female and male, nature's way of providing generation and continuity of our species. Before mammals, and yet so in many other kinds of life, all generation was a unisexual operation. Post-conscience-ness sensed as much with its invention of the myths of the Hermaphrodite and the Androgyne to account for lost wholeness and goodness. Deep in the dark/light, yin/yang of mythic history, hermaphrodeity and androgyny were joined in physical and psychic unity. In the Judeo-Christian version of this doubled myth, God the Creator is both a hermaphrodite and an androgyne, and humanity is created in the image of that unisexual androgyny.[1] With the division of humanity into separate sexes, the concepts of hermaphrodeity and androgyny suffer an attendant anthropological division.

In spite of the evolution of two sexes within humanity, the internal and external physical differences between female humans and male humans remain infinitesimally small; yet these small differences loom large because of the evolution of conscienceness, or mind. With the evolution of mind, differences between females and males became ground-plots for constructs of conscienceness, both of self and of other. Thus, female and male differences are, for the most part, matters of mind. These evolved and evolving attitudes of mind which stem from and are directed toward sex became matters of gender.[2]

Sex is genetically determined. Gender is not.[3] While gender is allied to sex through secondary characteristics, the effective determinants of gender differentiation between female and male are psychological, social, and cultural. Nevertheless, even though what we call "male" and "female" roles, and "feminine" and "masculine" behavioral characteristics, are derivative and attributive, the power of sex and the nature of the division of tasks which was at one time (in pre-history) required for human survival, led to an artificial separation of humanity (especially during the period of Industrial Society) into what has appeared to be two types, each with its own prescribed rules of behavior.[4]

Even by Shakespeare's day, the division of humanity within the evolving world of mind had reached a state, as Marilyn French has forcefully argued, of an almost absolute division of humanity, *not* into sub-types of *one* species, but into separated types, each treated as if it were itself a separate species. Two worlds had evolved, two cultures had been created, masculine and feminine—not in a parallel relationship but hierarchical: masculine first, feminine second—as we are reminded not only by French but also in books (in order) by Juliet Dusinberre, Coppélia Kahn, Irene Dash, Linda Bamber, Lisa Jardine, Linda Woodbridge, Marianne Novy, Peter Erickson, Carol Thomas Neely, Marilyn Williamson, Diane Dreher, and Stevie Davies.[5] Yet, these scholars also remind us that there is a tendency in Shakespeare, although they disagree in the size and strength of its presence, to want to break down the barriers between the sex-genders.[6] As other writers have shown, such a breakdown is necessary in order to allow humanity to inhabit a freer space in the circle of androgyny.[7] In her far-ranging survey, *Androgyny: Toward a New Theory of Sexuality*, June Singer notes that androgyny "in its broadest sense can be defined as the one which contains the Two; namely, the male (*andro-*) and the female (*gyne-*)," and she goes on to state that "androgyny is an *archetype* inherent in the human psyche . . . [and] may be the oldest archetype of which we have any experience" (20). Whether or not one shares Singer's Jungian assumption about the origin of symbols, the evidence from anthropology makes clear that the concept of androgyny is both pervasive and ancient.

Joseph Campbell remarks in *The Hero With a Thousand Faces*:

> Awonawilona, chief god of the pueblo of Zuni, the maker and container of all, is sometimes spoken of as he, but is actually he-she. The Great Original of the Chinese chronicles, the holy woman T'ai Yuan, combined in her person the masculine Yang and the feminine Yin. The cabalistic teachings of the medieval Jews, as well as the Gnostic Christian writings of the second century, represent the Word Made Flesh as androgynous—which was indeed the state of Adam as he was created, before the female aspect, Eve, was removed into another form. And among the Greeks, not only Hermaphrodite (the child of Hermes and Aphrodite), but Eros too, the divinity of love (the first of the gods, according to Plato) were in sex both female and male. (152–53)

I cite Campbell not as a final authority, but only as representative of anthropological scholarship. Indeed *as do all* who write on androgyny (be it in connection with Gnosticism, alchemy, Platonism, Hermeticism, the Cabala, deep myth, or established ritual—whatsoever), Campbell goes on to quote Genesis: "So God created man in his own image, in the image of God created he him; male and female created he them" (1:27). The confusing syntax and confused sex are rooted both in the translated language, Hebrew, and in the message being conveyed, androgyny. Rabbinical commentary—in spite of its male, patriarchal bias—is clear: "When the Holy one, Blessed be He, created the first man, He created him androgynous" (*Midrash*, Rabbah 8:1). The removal of the female into a separate form marks the move from perfect physical unity and psychic harmony to duality and tension. It also, so to speak, gives birth to both the hermaphrodite and the androgyne.

Androgyny is, then, a harkening for a lost state of ideal psychosomatic wholeness. Because life as experienced is fragmented, androgyny, situated in duality, must look "back" to that mythic time when human personhood experienced innate wholeness and harmony—a time "back there," "once upon a time," "in the beginning"—rather, *before* the beginning of his-story.[8] Such a proposition may have been deduced in time—in "time after"—when social beings in general felt individually divided and incomplete, or it may stem from the roots of our essential structural origins (see Appendix VI)—the theories are many. Regardless of how they came about, dreams of a symbolic state of unity figure within and inform the myths of our world; Shirley Weitz, in *Sex Roles: Biological, Psychological, and Social Foundations*, sums up the matter: "Perhaps the most persistent symbolic sexual theme in myth and ritual is that of androgyny" (169). The androgynous vision is the human desire to reach a sense of human wholeness, and the potential for that state resides in the individual. Androgyny, like alchemy, is the microcosmic attempt to discover and imitate the macrocosm, the *uni*-verse (see Appendix II).

But a plain observable fact of the late Middle Ages and early Renaissance is that the lines of social division, conflict, and subjection between the sexes were rigidly drawn. The seeming inferiority of women and the socially induced gender roles of appropriate behavior for each sex were well agreed upon. So the question arises: If there was such division and inequality between sexes, how could a concept of androgyny begin to take hold? We could answer mysteriously (and mischievously) with Robert Frost: "Something there is that doesn't love a wall./That wants it down." But the fact is the wall would not start to come down unless and until some men either on their own, or in response to a few angry female voices, undertook the initiative. With the spread of humanistic doctrine (especially with regard to education), with the impact of the emphasis on the individual expressed in the Reformation, and with the image and example of Elizabeth on the throne, by the late sixteenth century in England accepted ideas on the differences between the sexes and their relationships to each other were beginning to be debated. In the fifteen years since Joan Kelly-Gadol asked the question, "Did Women Have a Renaissance?" many answers have been contributed, coming from many fields (for a main strength of women's studies has been, from the beginning, its interdisciplinary commitment). As a result, most fields of study have themselves been subjected, to some degree, to a feminist corrective, and all fields of study should include a feminist perspective until male-sex-favoring is no longer the major shaping force within the definition of culture.

But, to return to England, to the sixteenth century, and to the culture of literature. Within this specific context, Kelly-Gadol's question can be answered, "Some few"—some few received a humanist education, some few encouraged literary production, and some few produced literature: translations, moral essays, prose fiction, and poetry.[9] So, some few did participate in the English literary Renaissance but not enough for us to be able to say that women collectively had a renaissance in the sixteenth century in England. But a larger question, what was labeled "The Woman Question" in the nineteenth century, was raised within the general movement of Renaissance thought with its focal concern on the mind of man. Since the mind of man is the mind of God, and since the mind of God is androgynous, the subversive question arises: Does it not follow of necessity that the mind of woman is the same, *in potens*, as the mind of man? Although the question was greatly ignored, still the question was asked, and, once asked, the question received various kinds of answers, from both men and women. The very fact that there is what Linda Woodbridge calls "the formal controversy" is itself proof of an emergent feminism within sixteenth-century England.[10]

Stevie Davies, whose assumptions are startingly different from Woodbridge's, has convincingly demonstrated how the idea of woman was central to the seemingly esoteric philosophies of the Renaissance, reaching strong expression in the art of Spenser, Shakespeare, and Milton (to which list I would add Sidney, Marlowe, and Donne).[11] On a less elevated plane than that of *formal* literature, the question was pursued directly in what we used to call, most inadequately and inappropriately, the "courtesy literature" of the sixteenth century.[12] My examination of the fine, chronologically catalogued collection in the Newberry Library of all Elizabethan books and pamphlets, both translations and original treatises, allowed me to sort out those which touch on the woman question. First of all, the vast amount of concern over the question, regardless of answers, demontrates the presence of a feminist issue in the sixteenth century which culminated in the controversial celebrations of Elizabeth's presence and achievements. But the *kinds* of answers given also support this observation. Those who denied the equality of women felt compelled to *strongly* deny it.[13] Further, a great many male writers were not just silently neutral on the issue, but were *openly* neutral, which in itself acknowledged the existence of a woman question.[14] A good many hedge about: "Yes . . . but," as, for example, Richard Mulcaster, who intends the education of both boys and girls when he talks about the elementary education of "children"; indeed, he even advocates continued education for girls beyond the elementary because "God, the Lord of nature," created in woman an inclination toward education which is a "treasure . . . bestowed on them by *nature*, to be bettered by nurture."[15] Yet, he ultimately says that most attention should be paid to boys.

Nicholas Breton states outright that "Women have wit [reason] naturally" and that both men and women are the same "natural kind."[16] And Alexander Barclay, translating Dominicus Mancinus, states that all virtues come from "natural reason": prudence, justice, magnanimity, temperance—all of which are androgynous virtues because they are human virtues.[17] Andrew Willet boldly states that a woman can be said to be a virgin if her mind is pure; virginity of the soul is more important than virginity of the body.[18] And there were others.[19]

In spite of these last, clear voices, no more than at present did sixteenth-century England achieve an attitude of parity with regard to both sexes. But the woman question had been raised publicly and had been openly debated. Signs of a positive feminism can be found in the works of Sidney, Spenser, Marlowe, Shakespeare, and Donne. The way had been prepared, in part, by the atmosphere created by Erasmus, More, Colet, Elyot, Hoby (as translator of Castiglione), Bruno, and Protestant reformers as diverse as Calvin and Hooker.[20] For the first time in western tradition, as experienced in England, man was being prepared philosophically, theologically, practically, and psychologically to accept woman as equally human, one of the same kind. To embrace woman, man had himself to embrace those aspects of humanity usually restricted to woman if he was to fulfill himself as a human being. And man could not be fully liberated until he allowed, permitted, even encouraged woman to fulfill herself as a human being. But this he was disinclined to do.

Here the example of Elizabeth serves to illustrate male reluctance: she was allowed to claim androgyny of soul—she was not merely a woman. Yet, she was only allowed this claim at the cost of giving up her womanhood. Hence her androgyny was a perversion, was not natural, for she was not allowed to express her androgyny as a maturing from and growing beyond, but still embracing, her sexual identity. She was forced to sever the roots to her sex. Her ever-increasing compensatory reliance on the trappings of gender enhancement as she got older, her elaboration of dress and make-up, is a sight sad to behold.

Nevertheless, Elizabeth as an educated female monarch was the most complete sixteenth-century example of the myth of the androgyne. Françoise le Premier had had his portrait painted as an androgyne (see Appendix III), but his male-based sex works against visual presentation of the female virtues he sought to embrace. Both monarchs sought to be living examples of the Renaissance concept of *humanitas* as fulfilled humanity, humanity created in the Divine Image, which allows an emphasis on the mental and psychic over the purely physical. Here Elizabeth's sex is to her advantage, for it suggests that she is both hermaphrodite and androgyne, having both a physically generative power without need for or use of sexual organs and characteristics of beneficence, strength, wholeness, wisdom, goodness, knowledge, integrity, beauty, power, contentment, containment, and truth.

From this emphasis on what the Renaissance would call "the rational" derives the current use of the word androgyny as a socio-psychological concept which has received rebirth and renewal mainly in the literature of Jungian therapy, humanistic psychology, and the women's movement. In spite of its widespread presence (or possibly because of it) androgyny is still dismissed by some as merely a trendy literary-critical term resurrected from Coleridge through Virginia Woolf. Others seek to avoid the term because it provides a deeply probing psychological threat. But to those who are seeking for a socio-sexual liberation that includes both men and women, present interest in androgyny can be attributed to a growing awareness that human being is more than sex identification and the attendant attribution and development of gender.

Androgyny understood in this "new" sense is essentially a humanistic concept, as old as Plato, Aristotle, and the Renaissance (to stay just within the western humanities). Nevertheless, no matter their heritage and innocence—as Leslie Fiedler has observed in *Freaks: Myths and Images of the Secret Self*—the terms androgyny, androgynous, and androgyne stir up sexual fears because they conjure up images of physical hermaphroditism and homosexuality. In fact, much of the recent literature on androgyny has been confused and muddled because of the simple inability to distinguish between the fact that *androgyny is a mythic concept* which represents an inner, psychic state of experience available to all human beings, whereas hermaphroditism is an objective, physical state of being forced on a limited few.

Strictly speaking, however, *there is no such thing as a hermaphrodite within human nature*—that is, a person with two sets of fully developed and differentiated sex organs. Only in a fiction such as Alan Friedman's *Herma-*

phrodeity can the fully developed and functioning male organs of a person impregnate the female organs of the same person and lead to a birth. The vast majority of humans are born with simply and purely either an X–X or an X–Y as their twenty-third chromosomal pair; only in a minute number of cases is there a *variation* of one *or* the other of these two pairings, but *never* can both pairings appear together. Each person is, then, born into the world as either an essential male or as an essential female, chromosomally determined, and verifiable within all of the cells of the body from birth to death, even in those proportionally few cases where unusual chromosomal bonding and not-normal, un-usual, hormonal stimulations lead to ambiguous surface confusions (which can lead to gender confusions). The absolute division of humans by sex is illustrated through the ease with which sex-identification of athletes is carried out by merely scraping surface skin cells for microscopic examination.[21]

To complicate matters, the hermaphrodite is still too often mistakenly called an androgyne, and in the eighteenth and nineteenth centuries androgyne was a term used for an "effeminate" man, a term defiantly cherished by Oscar Wilde and friends. As Marie Delcourt has pointed out in *Hermaphrodite: Myths and Rites of the Bisexual Figure in Classical Antiquity*, the hermaphrodite may be used to symbolize an androgynous moment (as is the case at the end of Book III of Spenser's *The Faerie Queene* as published in 1590, when Scudamore and Amoret in sexual embrace are observed by Britomart), but hermaphroditism and androgyny embrace different realms of human apprehension. Furthermore, because an androgyne is simply a person who is untroubled by having both "male" and "female" qualities within, androgyny is only secondarily related to a person's being a man or a woman, or having a personal orientation that is homo- or bi-sexual; celibate, onanistic, platonic, orgiastic; or any combination thereof. We may come into this world deeply etched as woman or man, but we need not be limited to a sexual identity. The whole of humanity is greater than the power of its parts.

Nature defines and binds each species of humanity through a set of twenty-three chromosomes, twenty-two of which are identical. That the "so-called"[22] twenty-third genetic pair of chromosomes is either X–X or X–Y leads to the division of humanity into two sexes: female and male. Because of the elemental role and power of sex in life, and because of the resultant cultural emphasis on sexual identity, we tend to ignore the great abundance of shared organs and identical physical characteristics within the human species when we talk of humanity. Our ignorance is potentially fatal.

Culture joins Nature at the moment the sex of a new infant is identified ("It's a . . .") because attitudes of parents, relatives, and friends ("Is it a boy, or a girl?"—usually asked in that order) begin to shape the development of a *gender identity* for the infant, which grows along with and interacts with the initially established *sexual identity*. For the man, the primary characteristics of sexual identity are the ability to produce and launch fertile sperm; in a woman, the ability to produce and place in receptivity fertile eggs; to conceive, gestate, and give birth; and to provide mammary nourishment. The secondary sexual characteristics run from the voice level and pelvic structure through size and shape of penis and breasts, to varying amounts and location of body hair.

Two aspects of secondary sexual characteristics must be emphasized: gender identity is expressed through the way a person talks, walks, covers the body, and treats body hair, and, secondary sexual characteristics are not really sexual. For example, body hair is a fact of human identity shared by men and women, so much so that on the scale of the human species, some X–Y's will have less body hair than some X–X's, which in no way affects the functioning of the primary sexual characteristics. The same applies to voice, gait, and grooming—sex can be emphasized or muted but cannot be changed. In fact, as John Money has remarked, "if you were to grade a random sample of men and women in the world on each of the generally accepted sex differences and then plot the results, you would find complete division by sex only on the graph dividing those who can impregnate from those who can menstruate, gestate, and lactate . . . You would find that in muscular strength, breast development, and all the rest of the characteristic sex distinctions, except the basic four, the difference between one normal man and another, and between one normal woman and another, can be, and often is, much greater than the average difference between men and women collectively. It's not hard to find a normal man who is more like the average woman than like the average man on any count except the basic four, or to find a normal woman who is more like the average man than the average woman in this or that respect. In other words, within-group differences, even when it comes to the secondary sex characteristics, may be as great and are often much greater than the between-group differences."[23]

Biology, then, is the point of departure for the journey toward gender identity. Chromosomes establish basic sex and hormones help to produce sexual organs. After birth, hormones help to develop physical characteristics related to one's sex, and, after puberty, help to stimulate some behavior related to sexual function. But biology does not in itself shape gender identity; rather, one's *attitude* toward one's sex organs, secondary characteristics, and stimulations shape gender identity. But only in part—for the attitudes of others, individually and collectively, also play their shaping roles. Nature is not in itself destiny. In fact, one could say that nature's role is quite simple: the separation of all humanity into one of two complementary categories. After that task is accomplished, the possibilities after birth for gender development are as myriad as humanity is varied.

In humanity, the brain is the bridge between sex and gender, nature and nurture. Within that multifold process simplistically called natural selection, behavior within the so-called "lower" forms of life is so biologically programmed that only changes in environment can force changes in that behavior. But, as Robert May has observed, "simple and automatic hormonal control of behavior decreases as one ascends the evolutionary scale";[24] that should be reversed: cerebral control of behavior increases as one ascends the scale. Mammals became dependent on their brains for survival and continuity, and in Homo sapiens, reliance on the brain has become so marked that biologically governed natural selection now plays only a slight role in survival. Furthermore, within evolution, male and female mammals developed separated modes of activity to insure continuity and survival within, and because of, the bi-polarity of sexual function.

This mammalian division of roles seems in the abstract and in the large to be reinforced by hormonal influence of behavior—masculine linear projections versus feminine circular conservation, or what we call male and female tendencies. The bigger and more complex the brain, the more pronounced these tendencies become—and uniquely so in humankind because only humans exist within cultural evolution. In "early man" behavior became both nurture and nature, which tended to act in consort to encourage within "natural selection" those kinds of genetic/hormonal development which would facilitate the separated modes of behavior needed for survival and continuity: the hunting and hauling of men versus the nursing and nurturing of women.

The brain is the bridge between sex and gender because hormones functioning through the pituitary gland influence human development, including the hypothalamus, which affects the development of the brain and the central nervous system.[25] Hormones do not essentially change the brain or central nervous system, but have *influence* upon certain behaviors, both organic and conscious, but not *all* behavior whether organic and/or conscious. Although hormones flow through it, the brain becomes a nearly self-contained unit, capable of controlling hormone flow and capable of controlling behavior without dependence on hormonal flow. As the brain and central nervous system in "higher" mammals became increasingly more highly organized and complex, the cerebral cortex began to control behavior more and more, giving humanity the power of thought, speculation, memory, calculation, and choice, which began to play the more significant part in behavior and development than had the merely natural aspect. So much so that the realm of nurture begins to play what seems to be an almost separate function from the natural. Ideas which can affect/effect behavior can be transmitted from person to person, laterally in present space and vertically through time.

Seen in the light of modern brain research and theory, the Renaissance concept of the "Rational Soul" need not seem so strange or quaint. The human brain has evolved to a point of human separation from other mammals. No matter how many methods can be devised to communicate with chimps and dolphins, no chimp or dolphin has yet devised a method of teaching us the language system of chimps or dolphins. As in the Renaissance, the rational separates humankind from beast. To Aristotle as to Shakespeare, humankind is a rational animal, and to Shakespeare the rational soul resides in the brain. The unity of rational soul and brain is caught by Richard II in an androgynous/hermaphroditic conceit: "My brain I'll prove the female to my soul,/My soul the father" (*Richard II* 5.5.6–7). From Plato through Pico, the mind separated the human kind from the merely animal kind. The production of thought has become the most powerful vector in terrestrial evolution. Richard II continues his meditation on the brain and soul: "These two beget/A generation of *still-breeding thoughts*" (emphasis added).

Just as "earlier" in evolutionary time, nurture of the crudest sort affected evolutionary change and development (more clothes led to less body hair), so also "now" in evolutionary time, the presence of "abstracted nurture," ideas, is returned back in, on, into, nature and evolution. The uncovering of the "double helix" story, the capability of human intervention and manipulation within the process of DNA/RNA replication, and the development of computers as extensions of the brain all emphasize the unique aspect of human evolution: while a sword or a missile may be just another phallus, only a brain can conceive and produce a book.

Even though we have all sorts of evidence inside us and all around us that the brain is "human environment," we still do not know all the why's and how's of neural development and cognition, in spite of the massive strides taken toward answers in the past decade. But out of this new research has come the death knell for one of the longest-lived theories of the brain, that of sex-linked differences between the brains of X–X's and X–Y's. Sex functions through the brain (internal and/or external hormonal stimulation and flow), but the brain itself has no sex. The same kind of circular thought that researchers into animal sexual behavior have found themselves unscientifically guilty of has permeated the discussions of the right and left hemispheres of the brain.[26] Because each side of the brain *seems* to make a certain kind of contribution to the unity of the human mind, and because those functions resemble in part the socially observable, separated functions of women and men, one side of the brain gets labeled masculine and the other side feminine. Because a label gets used before full description and analysis can be carried out, the label acts as a coloration factor in that description and analysis. What we are coming closer to realizing is that a brain is a brain is a brain and must be treated and understood as such.[27]

Sex is on one side of the brain-as-bridge and gender is on the other, because gender is an attitude that gets developed in the brain. Gender is what we and the onlooking world take our sex to be. But the process of building a gender identity, which leads to a conception of a gender role to be expressed through gender behavior, starts in society—"It's a . . ."—and this kind of imprinting is elaborated. By the time we come to our own awareness of gender and take over its cultivation, parents, relatives, family friends, random members of society ("Oh, what a cute little . . .") have managed to establish a formidable base upon which we are left to build and shape our own gender identity.

Our own concept of and attitude toward our gender takes on detail and definition as we begin to tabulate behavioral characteristics that we link to our sex, and develops into an actual gender role as we enhance, emphasize, and embellish those behaviors with learned, nurtured (artificial as distinguished from natural) behavior—the wearing of muscle-shirts or make-up. The process of genderization, then, tends to separate the human species into bipolar sub-categories because it is sex-linked. When functional difference leads to attitudinal absolute division, the purpose of evolution, survival and continuity, becomes thwarted. Unchecked genderization has the tendency to isolate the sexes with the result that, in the extreme, disharmony and division occur not just between the sexes but within the members of each sex (i.e., alienation, hysteria, paranoia, schizophrenia, obsessions). Furthermore, genderization so emphasizes sex-linked essential and surface differences that the vast body of natural and nurtured *human* characteristics and behavior tend to be ignored. When the full range of human potential is not brought within the sphere of consciousness and allowed to play through and affect the whole person—male or female—gender can be seen to have blocked essential development at the expense of surface development.[28]

Simply put, humanization is a *trans*-sexual process.[29] Transsexual does not mean one's being above sex, as in "transcend" in order to leave behind. It means the accepting of one's genetic sex as the base-level upon which to build one's conception of self. It means that "humanity" runs through or across the sexes, as in "transect."

Gender is an inevitable and necessary concept, if only because of the presence at this stage of human evolution of fairly pronounced secondary sexual characteristics. But after a certain point, consciousness and enhancement of those characteristics can become destructive to self and society. Extreme genderization—the intense and exclusive cultivation of the aspects and behaviors of one gender only, even to the point of consciously marginalizing all aspects and behaviors of the other gender—leads not just to polarization and separation of individuals of different sex, but also to polarizations and separations between peoples, both within cultures and between cultures. Macho behavior can be protective and saving but it can also be destructive and rejecting. Yes—make peace, not war. Yes—take the toys away from the boys. Societies can limit movement by binding feet or toddling along on stiletto heels. Cultural genderization carried to the extreme prevents the human, social bonding that is now necessary for the continuance of life, a bonding that at this stage of human evolution is more important than the sexual bonding that is necessary for replication of the species. Individually and collectively we need to cultivate a resolving, balancing "third gender," one which destroys artificial barriers, that wants them down. There is no need to invent a term; one exists within the oldest creation myths of all cultures. Androgyny joins the two sexes within one kind: humanity. It recognizes sex difference, but says a human person is more than a sex.

An androgyne is a full human—one who in "gender" is both male and female, though only of one sex (even when in apparent degrees of physical hermaphroditic, or neuter, or muted sex). I put "gender" in quotes not just because my use is literally a non-sense, but because gender, while a necessary term, is ultimately a limited term. What we call masculine or feminine characteristics are actually *human* characteristics, more noticed by society in "men" or "women" because of sex-linked behavior tendencies: men are tough, women are soft. But any one behavior is not an exclusive characteristic of one sex only. At this stage of evolution and culturalization, behavioral characteristics may seem exclusively of one sex or another, but common sense should tell us otherwise. That we easily accept today that it is all right for men to cry or to be nurses and for women not to hide their intelligence or to be carpenters are steps toward androgyny—small steps, to be sure. We have not come very far and we have a long way to go.

The move of an individual toward the awareness of androgyny involves two phases, which do not just happen one before the other: there must come the recognition that there exists a point in the development of a personal gender identity where enhancement and elaboration based on genetic sex cease to be healthy, at the same time that there must come the recognition that full development of self comes, must come, in spite of, because of, one's genetic self. This is the pattern of movement in Shakespeare: first must come the recognition that to seek one's identity outwardly through adherence to sexual social role (male, husband, father, king) is, literally, self-limiting; and then can come the recognition that one must seek one's full identity within—within one's humanity, within the circle of one's self, within the recognition of the common origin of our species.

Male and female coming together create life: one plus one equals one. This is not a paradox; it is the fact of life. As a fact of life, it becomes the basis of valid metaphor. Androgyny is not the "one plus one"; it is the "one" in which the "one plus one" exists. We may be born as male or female, *but*, for a split second, we are born without gender: we are born androgynous. Androgyny, then, is the metaphor of a created whole. The source is in the individual once created; the potential for wholeness is realized in living. While Dame Nature's ways no longer include the possibility of a return to Hermaphrodeity, Androgyny is still a living myth.

3

Locating Androgyny in Sixteenth-Century England

At the center of Renaissance thought is the *human* kind, mankind, the paragon of animals, but the lowest of divine creatures, almost cut off from the creator because of what happened in Eden. Yet, the Renaissance reveled in the proposition that nature and nurture come together in humankind. Man is kin and kind, a creature of nature, but humankind is different from other merely natural kinds because humankindness through the rational soul directly partakes of, and participates in, the divine.[1] Indeed, the rational soul is divine because it is the mind/soul which is created in the image of God, not the body.[2] Embodied man is born a creature of kind, but the essence of humankindness can be cultivated to grow toward divine perfection.[3] Human nature can be nurtured; but humankindness does not blossom automatically. Our nature is a compound of earth, air, fire, and water, and must remain so, but within our nature there resides the potential of a fully realized fifth element: *in esse* humankind has in it to become the quintessence of dust. The shaping place of this potential culture is in the mind, or brain, "Which some suppose the soul's frail dwelling-house" (*King John* 5.7.3). The brain is the Philosopher's egg, or vessel of Hermes, wherein the quintessential truth can be discovered. But the rational soul, or wit, needs the helping hand of the serving sciences ("Else a great prince in prison lies"). As Sidney said, "as the fertilest ground must be manured, so must the highest-flying wit have a Daedalus."[4]

The cultivation of humankindness is an art, but not just another of all those arts in the Renaissance: it is *the* art of the Renaissance. It is the art of learning. In sixteenth-century terms, the art of humankindness is the microcosmic attempt to discover and imitate the macrocosmic ideal of unity and harmony—in short, androgyny. In a light vein, when Romeo is his witty self again after falling in love with Juliet, Mercutio comments, "Now art thou Romeo, by art and by nature." Human nature is essentially good—"The inclination to goodness is imprinted deeply in the nature of man"[5]—but it must be cultivated, it must be cared for, it must be attended by the wit, the mind, the *visio intellectus*. Looking into the soul is looking out on the cosmos—"homo, minor mundus, comprehensio est totius universitatis."[6] And to discover the soul is to discover the androgynous nature of the cosmos because the original creation and the incarnation reoccur in each soul, without sex, without division.[7]

The essential discoveries within nature and human nature will be made by the mind in the mind of the mind.[8] God, to speak in sixteenth-century terms, imitated himself when He "made man to His own likeness," to quote Sidney. Both God and man were androgynous. Arnold Williams in *The Common Expositor: An Account of the Commentaries on Genesis, 1527–1633* states unequivocally: "One could gather a sizeable collection of allusions to this notion" (92), and he goes on to record that nine out of ten formal commentaries he is examining mention the point. Since the divine gift of reason, the "erected wit" as Sidney calls it, is the divine characteristic which separates mankind from other animals and joins mankind with the angels, reason itself, as with God and angels, is sexless. Sidney and Spenser, Davies and Donne all refer to the rational soul variously as he or she, and she not just because in the social macrocosm Elizabeth ruled from the throne of England—for that reason, too, but essentially because the soul is androgynous.[9] Ernst Cassirer long ago stated that the central focus of Renaissance philosophy was the individual; using Nicholas Cusanus as his representative thinker, Cassirer, in summary, asserted that because "in man as the microcosm all lines of the macrocosm run together . . . man as a microcosm includes the nature of all things within himself." Hence, to know thyself is to know the world; "between the creative principle and the created, between God and creature, stands the spirit of humanity, *humanitas*, as something at once creator and created."[10] The rational animal stands erect at the center of the deo-, geo- homo-centric world. (See Appendices II and IV.)

Paul Oskar Kristeller has spent a lifetime showing us how *humanitas* means both belonging to the human race and having awareness of that belonging.[11] Human dignity comes from achieving and maintaining respect for humanity, the self and others. The strengthening of innate attributes leads to human fulfillment. To the Renaissance, *virs* mistakenly meant both strength and humanity; hence, the *virtues* were powers of humane dimension, and the greatest of these was love, that which binds the universe and the species, concentrically, laterally, and horizontally[12]—the human body suggesting simultaneously the triangle, the circle, and the square, symbols of perfection.[13]

Sir Thomas Elyot in a single sentence touches on all these issues: "The nature and condition of man, wherein he is lasse than god almightie, and excellinge nat withstanding all other creatures in erthe, is called humanities; which is a generall name to those vertues in whome semeth to be a mutual concorde and love in the nature of man."[14] Elyot's translation of *humanitas* is a bit awkward in context. But we easily excuse Elyot when we recall his effort to strengthen, enlarge, and dignify the vernacular, and when, out of context, his word "humanities" fits so well in modern usage—the humanities as a discipline of learning deal with "the nature and condition of man."

The goal of the humanities, in the sixteenth or the twentieth century, is to show ourselves to ourselves, to help us to know ourselves.[15] The humanities are modes of self-discovery and self-awareness made available through artifacts of self-expression. This emphasis on self is not solipsistic because of the centrality of the circle, and because of the validity of analogy-come-alive, in Renaissance thought.[16] Renaissance thought instinctively realized the holi-istic function of mind in mankind; Una is Truth, the truth of self; Una is therefore integrity, or unity, the true universal unity, unity and harmony sought by the self—that is all we knew on earth and all we needed to know, until the linearism of science broke the circle and rationalism destroyed analogy.[17] But in the sixteenth century, the Ptolemaic commonplaces of medieval thought became dynamic and operated not just up and down some chain of being, but all around (see Appendix IV). When we debate, "Is allegory deductive or inductive?" our assumptions are out of date; allegory is analogy in motion, a moving picture of truth, a mode of perception—a way, therefore, of knowing.[18]

Although the educational goal of the humanities in the sixteenth century was, then, to help us to know ourselves, humanism was at root a bookish movement, a scholarly impulse to set ancient texts completely and correctly. To do so, one needed the basic tools of grammar, logic, and rhetoric. Yet out of this primary inquiry developed the attendant and gradually ascendant interest in the minds of the ancients, their thoughts, which led to the desire to teach contemporaries how the minds of the past could be used as guides for the present purpose of developing human potential.[19] The *trivium* leads to the *quadrivium*: arithmetic, geometry, astronomy, and music. We are indebted to such as Cassirer, Curtius, Kristeller, Panofsky, and their colleagues and disciples for having traced and elaborated this evolution. By the time humanism arrived in England at the close of the fifteenth century,[20] this development of a threefold scholarly, philosophical, pedagogical entity encompassing the seven liberal arts had taken place and, from the early years of the sixteenth century through Milton's years at St Paul's, humanism in

England is synonymous with education, the widespreading of grammar schools and the broadening of access to the universities, from both ends of the social scale. While the opportunity of education was broadened, the curriculum remained narrow—on the surface. The medieval *trivium* and *quadrivium*, the seven liberal arts, still formed the outlines for grammar school and college, and university graduate schools arose around the study of law, medicine, and theology. But the content at all levels was charged with the purpose of developing human potential.[21]

Though formal education, after the elementary,[22] was for men only, the humanistic impulse extended to all of humanity. Erasmus's wisdom figure, earthly sapience, is that traditional figure of earthly folly, a woman, thus suggesting the androgynous union of the wisdom of folly and the folly of wisdom. Sir Thomas More, though exercising some restrictions, educated his daughters (Dame Alice, however, would have none of *that* newfangleness). Sir Thomas Elyot's writings come close to describing an androgynous society of men and women moving in complement toward unity and harmony. And Princess Elizabeth profited from a better education than was available to most men.[23]

From Cicero through Agrippa, rhetoric is the ground plot of education, for the distinguishing characteristic of humankind is the capability of inventing language.[24] Rhetoric may mean the art of persuasion, but only as an extension of its core meaning: word-using-art. Concern with logos leads to the concern with Logos, or the structure of the universe, the unity and harmony of which are discovered through arithmetic, geometry, astronomy, and music (which Kepler traced back to androgynous principles). Logos as both the created and the creating, at the center of theology, received reinforcement through Ficino's work with Plato and the Corpus Hermeticum (which had already incorporated the Cabala and the Gnostic "heresy"). Analogy becomes the major tool of discovery in all philosophy, in all science, and the seemingly stable, static Ptolemaic world suddenly becomes fluid and dynamic. Medicine and theology study natural phenomena for evidence of the spiritual. Alchemy and Hermeticism specifically seek the essence of things. Nature becomes the source of learning and human understanding, and its power is there to be received, to be beneficial. Ficino carefully picks time and place and surrounds himself with sounds, colors, aromas, and numerical and geometric representations of Nature in order to discover and to understand. At what point such modes of discovery became themselves incantory or manipulative of the powers of Nature is the ultimate problematic within Renaissance thought. When does thoroughly "innocent" learning become harmful knowledge and power?[25]

By the sixteenth century this natural inquiry had moved outside of the universities and academies. On many levels and on many fronts, various philosophies of human fulfillment were developing, but were unified by a shared purpose: to replace a neo-Aristotelianism and its seeming reliance on categorical separations with a recharged Neoplatonism which sought the key to unlock the secret door hiding Truth and Beauty. Philosophers of all types sought to discover in the macrocosm the essential, ultimate laws of unity and harmony that lay hidden in nature. Both education and philosophy sought how to nurture nature.[26]

Dame Frances Yates spent a lifetime trying to show us how these sixteenth-century probings of alchemy, Hermeticism, Gnosticism, the Cabala, and other seemingly esoteric -isms were not at the fringes of thought, but stemmed from this centrist desire to discover essential, core truths of life. Thanks to her tenacious efforts (see also Garin, Nauert, Walker), in spite of lingering doubt in some camps,[27] H. C. Erik Midelfort was able to open a 1982 general essay on "Witchcraft, Magic, and the Occult" with this assertion: "It is no exaggeration to say that the biggest surprise of the last generation in studies of early modern European intellectual history has been the rise of the occult sciences to positions of influence and even respectability. No longer scorned or ridiculed, they now appear as essential features of the quest for certitude, power, and coherence in the sixteenth century"(183).[28] Because of the dynamic interactions and transpositions of the microcosm and macrocosm, the pedagogical and metaphysical concerns with being and becoming were not sequential, moving from lesser to greater, but were identical. The study of rhetoric, astronomy, theology, and Hermeticism are all centered on the Logos and logos, Divine Wisdom and human, creative understanding. Cusanus and Alberti, Ficino and Pico, Agrippa and Paracelsus, Leonardo and Michelangelo, Bruno and Dee all worked from this dual assumption toward its elucidation (back in the circle again).[29]

At the center of the circle is the androgyne, that microcosm, that little world, *ille pusillus spiritus mundi*, that subtle knot of body and soul, that creature "belonging to the earth,"[30] *humanus erectus*, Pico's and Hamlet's paragon of animals, the alchemical quintessence of dust. At the center of Renaissance philosophy is the philosophy of humanity which focused on ways of fulfilling human potential, of recovering human strength (virtue), of repairing the damage done by the Fall. The major means was through education, through learning, through (one would like to be able to say with a straight face) self-improvement. Sidney, in the *Defence*, is more eloquent. Learning is the process that purifies wit, enriches memory, enables judgment, and enlarges the power of mind in order "to lead and draw us to as high a perfection as our degenerate souls, made worse by their clayey lodgings, can be capable of." Humankind, like the universe, is a series of concentric circles, but in reverse order with regard to size and worth, for in humanity the greatest is the smallest: our rational soul resides within the circumference of our animal soul which resides within the circumference of our vegetable soul which resides within the body. Because the outer souls and the body fell from their originally generated perfection, all the arts of learning have "this scope: to know, and by knowledge to lift up the mind from the dungeon of the body to the enjoying his own divine essence" (82).

Thus, there are diverse ways to learning, knowledge, and the hoped-for power which the minds of the Renaissance explored: the seven liberal arts; theology, law, medicine; alchemy, Hermeticism, Cabalism, Gnosticism. But, these paths to learning all start out in the same place—the mind—and they all end at the same destination—the mind. Nicholas of Cusa had discovered that to trust the mind was to learn to explicate God; to passively open the mind before the universe was the way to understand the Creator. One of the volumes in Cusanus's library was Raymond Sebond's *Theologia Naturalis*, an early work in what would become a favored genre in the fifteenth and sixteenth centuries: elucidation of a purely natural (*prisca*) theology.[31] Sebond was an early fifteenth-century humanist, a master of arts who practiced both medicine and theology.[32] His claim is that "God has given us two books: the Book of the Universal Order of Things (or, of Nature) and the Book of the Bible. The former was given to us first, from the origin of the world: for each creature is like a letter traced by the hand of God: this Book had to be composed of a great multitude of creatures (which are so many 'letters'); within them is found Man. He is the main, the capital letter." Because Adam was created with reason and the capability of learning, he could read the Book of Nature. After the Fall, God had to provide the second Book, which only clerics can read. In spite of man's fall, "the Book of Nature cannot be corrupted nor effaced nor falsely interpreted. Therefore heretics cannot interpret it falsely: from this Book no one becomes an heretic." The Bible is obscure and difficult; Nature is open and simple. Sebond offers a method of reading Nature aright that prefigures "Trust Nature" and "the proper study of Mankind is Man." Because humanity still has reason (the book was addressed primarily to women), humanity is capable of reformation and enlightenment; even within a month's time, one can learn from nature one's moral duties and obligations. No other "science" is needed (xl-xliv).

Montaigne's father, given a copy of Sebond by a humanist friend, asked his son to translate the work into French so that he (the father) could learn and profit from Sebond's "method." Montaigne did so, but his father died in 1568 just as the son was completing the work for publication the next year. Eleven years later Montaigne published his first two books of essays, one of which was in "defense" of Sebond: the *Apologie de Raimond Sebond* (Chapter 12 of Book II)—an essay infinitely longer than any of Montaigne's other essays, and one which, he tells us toward the end, he could have gone on writing "for ever" (189).

No one has discovered why Montaigne chose to defend Sebond: there is no evidence that Sebond was in disrepute or out of favor; there is no evidence that Montaigne was criticized or in jeopardy for having translated Sebond. He claims, briefly, almost in passing, that Sebond has been accused of putting reason above faith and of putting too much emphasis on what, after Pico, we call "the dignity of Man." Because Sebond *can* be accused of putting faith in reason over faith, and because Sebond certainly *did* subscribe, long before Pico, to "the dignity of Man," my hunch is that Montaigne was writing in his own defense, making an apology for his having translated Sebond, even though at the request of his "beloved" father.

The *Apologie* is not about Sebond's *Theologia Naturalis* at all—contrary to the emphases on the efficacy of reason and the sufficiency of man within Sebond, the *Apologie* is an attack on reason and man, only lightly veiled by a translucent irony. Montaigne sarcastically "praises" while actually damning. Primarily assured of the inadequacy of reason and the insignificance of man among all creatures, Montaigne cannot maintain the breadth and depth of irony that Erasmus employs in praising folly. He was too close to his subject. I think that Montaigne must have been quite uncomfortable translating the *Natural Theology*, for, even though it was nearly two centuries old, it reflected all too clearly to Montaigne the boldness of secular beliefs and inquiries all around him in the second half of the sixteenth century. Indeed, the very length of Montaigne's broadside attack and the very strength of his angry fear and doubt are in themselves strong proof of how widespread and accepted were the liberal-humanist ideas concerning human capability. The enemy was at the inner gate and Sebond was among their number.

Even when publishing the *Natural Theology* itself, Montaigne, as Michael Screech has pointed out, felt compelled to edit Sebond's preface, his statement of assumptions and intentions. Where Sebond boldly asserted that "without difficulty or toil" his method "teaches everyone really *to know . . . every truth* necessary to Man concerning both Man and God; and all things which are necessary to Man for his salvation, *for making him perfect* and for bringing him through to eternal life" (emphasis added), Montaigne writes: "teaches every one *to see clearly . . . truth insofar as is possible for natural reason*, concerning knowledge of God and of himself and of what he has need for his salvation and to reach life eternal" (emphasis added). Sebond writes: "by this science a man learns, without difficulty and in reality, whatever is contained in Holy Scripture," but Montaigne writes: "it [the method] affords him access to understanding what is prescribed and commanded in Holy Scripture," thus reversing Sebond's ordering of the two Books, of Nature and of Scripture (xiv).

In the *Apologie* Montaigne ignores the position of Sebond and initially asserts that man cannot know the natural order of things without the Truth of Holy Writ: "I do not believe, then, that purely human means have the capacity . . . Only faith can embrace, with a lively certainty, the high mysteries of our religion"(3), which is an absolute contradiction of Sebond. Because this position cannot be argued, Montaigne spends only eleven pages (Screech edition) on this assertion, supposedly in defense of Sebond in the face of his critics. He then goes on to spend 179 more pages, again supposedly in Sebond's defense, squashing man because, "Man claims the privilege of being unique in that, within this created frame, he alone is able to recognize its structure and its beauty; he alone is able to render thanks to its Architect or to tot up the profit or loss of the world" (13–14), which is the basis of Sebond's "method"! Montaigne's first attack on an advocate of this humanist position is, fittingly, directed against Cicero, though here anonymously and contemptuously referred to as "that fellow." And so the attack against liberal humanism is launched ("Let us smash down such presumption")—making current attacks against Arnold and Tillyard by academic Marxists look absolutely gentle and genteel in comparison.

All under the names of philosophy and learning, the body of the essay attacks Hermes Trismegistus, Gnosticism, alchemy, magic, the universal soul, the rational soul, micro/macrocosm interactions and relationships, the reemergence of and reliance on geometry, the presence of musical proportion and harmony in the universe, natural law, Seneca, Copernicus, geography and cartology, "some newcomer called Paracelsus," and, everywhere throughout, reason: "this ray of Divinity," "this noble and matchless brightness," "the extreme height of human Nature," "all those goodly prerogatives" of Nature. Through Montaigne's sarcastic enumerations, however, one senses an awe of the variety and extent of secular beliefs and experiences, all of which seem to contain similarities within diversities. Montaigne feels caught up in change, but must deny that in change there is meaning, pattern, or growth "to the perfection of being." In nature's mutability he sees only death: "To conclude: there is no permanent existence either in our being or in that of objects. We ourselves, our faculty of judgement and all mortal things are flowing and rolling ceaselessly: nothing certain can be established about one from the other" (186). The form of his conclusion prefigures uncannily Spenser's final two stanzas in the *Two Cantos of Mutabilitie*, but Montaigne's answer in death is quite opposite to Spenser's optimistic trust in process. His final quotation is from an anonymous pagan, whom Screech identifies as Seneca: "Oh, what a vile and abject thing is Man if he does not rise above humanity"—to which Montaigne sarcastically comments, "A pithy saying; a most useful aspiration, but absurd withal," not bothering to acknowledge that Sebond had used the same quotation with favor. Rather, Montaigne ends his diatribe: "He [man] will rise if God proffers him—extraordinarily—His hand; he will rise by abandoning and disavowing his own means, letting himself be raised up and pulled up by purely heavenly ones. It is for our Christian faith, not that Stoic virtue of his, to aspire to that holy and miraculous metamorphosis" (189–90). No wonder the Roman Catholic Church would not allow Teilhard de Chardin to publish during his lifetime his speculations on humanity as the evolutionary vector of universal process.

In the twentieth century, four generations of scholars—to cite only representatives: Cassirer, Yates, Heninger, and Koenigsberger—have been working to show us the workings of Renaissance thought within the microcosmic, macrocosmic analogy. Montaigne, fearful of these humanizing tendencies of his times, writes a kind of praise of folly in reverse. But, unlike Erasmus, he cannot sustain irony while "praising" human wisdom. The sarcasm and the extreme length of this *essai* in contrast to all of his others indicate the extent of Montaigne's anxiety.[33] In fact, as Jerome Schwartz so delightfully notes, "One cannot perhaps think off-hand of a less androgynously-inclined writer than Montaigne, whose sober reflections, whose skeptical doubt, whose awareness of complexity and diversity, seem to deny the Renaissance obsession with Platonic idealism in all its forms, and whose male chauvinist advice on marriage seems at the opposite pole from the Renaissance cult and vogue of love."[34] Thus by way of a negative proof, Montaigne's violent thrashing out against the currents of sixteenth-century thought shows how strong and in the mainstream they were.

So also, but in a different vein, does Christopher Marlowe's *Dr. Faustus. Dr. Faustus* could be said to mark the beginning of the high Renaissance in England, just as its counterpart, *The Tempest*, marks the apex—and the beginning of the decline. The one sets a goal for human knowledge and power, the other shows the realization—and the limitation. Each suggests that its hero overreaches, and each suggests a corrective for would-be imitators. Prospero was, and Faustus wished to be, a Magus, that learned person who had sufficiently exercised his rational skills to read the Book of Nature in order to uncover her secrets of operation, and who was able through human knowledge and power to replicate those operations.[35] Magic was an art not above, below, or outside of nature, but was an art *of* nature, an art of discovery or invention, which is the same claim Sidney makes for poetry. Magic was a branch of learning, an internalization and utilization of principles of knowledge existing in nature, the uncovering of just enough knowledge to reveal the structures and functions of nature. Magic was the mastering of natural process; sometimes called "natural magic," it was allied to natural theology through Neoplatonism and Hermeticism.[36] Even the practice of alchemy is a practice of magic (see Appendix II).

The chorus to *Dr. Faustus* gives us the biographical, historical, cultural background we need for the play, then ends with five simple lines which give us the plot-line and imply the theme:

And glutted now with learnings golden gifts,
He surffets vpon cursed Negromancy.
Nothing so sweete as magicke is to him
Which he preferres before his chiefest blisse,
And this is the man that in his study sits.[37]

Faustus is prepared to take up the study of magic after having mastered the *trivium*, *quadrivium*, and the "graduate studies" of law, medicine, and theology. In spite of all he has learned, "glutted now with learnings golden gifts," he feels unfulfilled: "Yet art thou still but *Faustus*, and a man." When he turns to the study of magic he is moving with the currents of sixteenth-century thought, swimming along not only with Agrippa, whom he mentions, but also right along with Ficino, Pico, Paracelsus, and John Dee:

These Metaphisics of Magicians
And Negromantike bookes are heauenly:
Lines, circles, sceanes, letters and characters:
I, these are those that *Faustus* most desires.
O what a world of profit and delight,
Of power, of honor, of omnipotence
Is promised to the studious Artizan?
All things that mooue betweene the quiet poles
Shalbe at my commaund. Emperours and Kings
Are but obeyd in their seuerall prouinces:
Nor can they raise the winde, or rend the cloudes:
But his dominion that exceedes in this,
Stretcheth as farre as doth the minde of man.
A sound Magician is a mighty god:
Heere *Faustus* trie thy braines to gaine a deitie.

(77–91)

The language of learning abounds: metaphysics is the reading deeply within the Book of Nature. The student of letters, the professor of learning, is a studious artisan. The dominion of learning "stretcheth as farre as doth the minde of man" because the universe itself can be discovered and explored in the mind. For this reason, a magician has the power of God, but a *sound* magician learns and understands, but does not necessarily *use* the might of that power. Faustus wishes to step beyond knowledge to power, wishes to move from natural magic (*prisca theologia*) to unnatural magic and demonology. But Faustus need not sign his soul away to gain the necessary knowledge which leads to power: he has it already. The Good and Evil Angels enter after Faustus's opening soliloquy (after Wagner has been sent to fetch Valdes and Cornelius) and find him holding one of his necromantic books. The Good Angel tells him to "lay that damned booke aside," but the

Bad Angel reminds him that that same book, because it is about nature, contains "all natures treasury." When Valdes enters he notices the books and says, "These bookes, thy wit and our experience/Shall make all nations to canonize vs," and Cornelius chimes in:

> He that is grounded in Astrologie,
> Inricht with tongues, well seene in minerals,
> Hath all the principles Magike doth require. (167–69)

And Faustus seems to know that he has that within to carry out creative magic: "Heere *Faustus* trie thy braines to gaine a deitie." Nevertheless, he signs a pact to become "*a spirit in forme and substance*."

To become a spirit in form and substance was the paradoxical aim of the Magus, and Faustus thinks he has to sign his soul away to achieve this aim. He expects "new" knowledge, of "new" places, but as Mephostophiles makes clear to everyone but Faustus, everything already exists in our own heads ("Why this is hel, nor am I out of it"). But one irony does not escape Faustus: when he asks for the secrets of nature, Mephostophiles simply points to books Faustus already had in his own library before signing the twenty-four-year agreement. Three times he points to Faustus's own books, at which point Faustus says to himself, of himself, "O thou art deceiued." Mephostophiles mockingly rejoins: "Tut I warrant thee" (with a wonderful pun on the pact). Looking up, Faustus feelingly expresses the deflation of discovery of delusion:

> When I behold the heauens, then I repent,
> And curse thee wicked *Mephastophilus*,
> Because thou has depriu'd me of those joyes. (612–14)

(The evidence survives in the 1604 *Faustus* text.) In fact, one could stage the play as taking place all in Faustus's study, that is, in his mind, and remain true to the spirit of the text and times. (Arthur Miller first titled *The Death of a Salesman*, "Inside His Own Head.") The internal, intellectual nature of Faustus's triumph and torment is what gives lasting poignance to his last line: "Ile burne my bookes, ah, *Mephastophilis*." He is already in hell.

With Montaigne and Marlowe, we have strong evidence of the widespread, public nature of Renaissance thought in the late sixteenth century. The emphasis on learning and the spread and widening of knowledge created a philosophical atmosphere that can best be caught in the term androgyny. Michael Screech, discounting the effectiveness of feminist controversy in and of itself in the fifteenth and sixteenth centuries, makes an interesting observation at the end of his *The Rabelaisian Marriage*: it was not random advocates and martyrs who forced the emergence of a "feminism" in the sixteenth century; rather, it was the general widening of knowledge which, he believes, brought about a forceful and effective feminism (141–42).[38] This certainly was not the case; however, Screech's basic point is accurate: the general growth of knowledge in the sixteenth century contained many strong feminist elements because so much of that knowledge stemmed from or led to equi-sexuality. And in England intellectual, popular, social, and political ideas were sufficiently androgynous to permit a woman to be king for thirty-five years.

4

Sidney's Invention of a New Choice For Hercules: Androgyny

At the end of the film *Tootsie*, Dustin Hoffman, out of disguise, says to Jessica Lange, "I was a better man with you as a woman than I ever was a man with a woman as a man." Unscrambled, this says: "I was a better human being as both a man and a woman than I was before as only a man."[1]

Sir Philip Sidney's young Prince Pyrocles makes much the same discovery as he moves from Book One of the *Old Arcadia*, to Book One of the *New Arcadia*. In comparing that large, three-book fragment to the earlier, smaller, completed five-book version, one finds that only the first books of each retain parallels. In both, Pyrocles disguises himself as an Amazon in order to be admitted to the company of young Princess Philoclea who has been forbidden the company of men. In the *Old Arcadia* the device of this seventeen-year-old is "an eagle covered with the feathers of a dove, and yet lying under another dove, in such sort as it seemed the dove preyed upon the eagle, the eagle casting up such a look as though the state he was in, liked him, though the pain grieved him."[2] Here we notice the polarity of male/female division in the eagle and the dove, the signs of Mars and Venus, and sense an extreme masculine gender-role perplexity and discomfort. In the *New Arcadia* this device is totally altered: "a Hercules made in little form, but set with a distaff in his hand (as he once was by Omphale's commandment), with a word in Greek, but thus to be interpreted: 'Never more valiant'."[3] Pyrocles, who is made a year older by Sidney in this second version, is no longer perplexed and uncomfortable, but is proudly proclaiming that he is as good a man as a woman as he ever was as only a man.[4]

What Pyrocles can be said to have faced could be called a new choice for

Hercules. The traditional choice facing Hercules at the crossroads had been between the active and the passive lives, the heroic and the amorous, the doing and the knowing, the masculine and the feminine. Here our new Hercules has a new choice: to be *both* feminine and masculine, knowing and doing, amorous and heroic, passive and active *at the same time*. By drawing on a fuller potential for human development than merely from the readily available supply of masculine traits and behaviors, Pyrocles is moving toward a fuller realization of his human being.[5]

Sidney's shift of Pyrocles' perception of the feminine from negative to positive is symptomatic of that general shifting perspective on women which one can find in sixteenth-century England, in general movements of thought, in the literature of the woman question, and in the "poetry" of the high Elizabethan Renaissance. Indeed, Sidney's positive, egalitarian attitude toward women is everywhere clear in the *Old Arcadia*, even within the "courtliness" of the letter of dedication "To My Dear Lady and Sister, The Countess of Pembroke," and more especially among the first lines laid down. Early we read that Pamela and Philoclea are "both so excellent in all those gifts which are allotted to reasonable creatures as they seem to be born for a sufficient proof that nature is no stepmother to that sex, how much soever the rugged disposition of some men, sharp-witted only in evil-speaking, hath sought to disgrace them" (4–5). Women are "reasonable creatures" because they are creations of Dame Nature, that androgynous mother of us all.

Sidney repeats this statement some three years later in the *New Arcadia*, where he also changed Pyrocles' emblem and awarded him that one more year toward maturity. In between these two works, Sidney had received, read, and begun translating Philippe du Plessis de Mornay's *De la Verité de la Religion Chrestienne* and had written the *Defence of Poetry*, both of which are bold distillations, intelligent syntheses, and clear articulations of the assumptions and implications of sixteenth-century thought, the subject of the previous chapter. Within *The Truth of the Christian Religion* Sidney found an encyclopedia of classical, Neoplatonic, and Hermetic speculation on theology. In his *Defence of Poetry* Sidney worked out for himself the assumptions and implications of Renaissance androgyny. Reading *De la Verité* and writing the *Defence* were for Sidney acts of discovery.

Duplessis-Mornay's work was published in Antwerp in 1581, the year after the publication of Montaigne's first two books of essays, which concluded with the monograph in supposed defense of Raymond Sebond. Sidney had met Duplessis-Mornay in Paris in 1572 just before the St. Bartholomew's Day massacre, and had entertained him in London in 1578, when Sidney stood as godfather to Duplessis-Mornay's daughter. Duplessis-Mornay had arrived the year before as a Protestant envoy to

Elizabeth from Henry of Navarre, leader of the Huguenots and claimant to the French throne.[6] Given their shared interests in furthering the continental Protestant cause and in writing (Sidney went public in his "unelected vocation" with *The Lady of May* in 1578), the two had much to talk about; when Sidney received his copy of *De la Verité* he found therein a compatible philosophy.[7]

The Truth of the Christian Religion is a work within the genre of natural theology, or, more exactly, the "Ancient Theology," to use the late D. P. Walker's term, for Duplessis-Mornay draws fully on both the evidence within the Book of Nature as well as that to be derived from all of the "western" writers who were available either directly or on report, from the pre-Socratics through Cicero—and almost every list of citations begins with the Thrice-Great Hermes who based all of his theology, linguistics, and mathematics on the Unity of God, the source of all goodness (truth and beauty) and power (creativity)—androgyny and hermaphrodeity united. Such eclecticism is valid for Duplessis-Mornay (as it is for Sidney) because he has the Neoplatonist assumption that all signs of truth, physical and written, are reflections of Truth ("the voice of nature is the voice of truth," 199) and the Thomist assumption that human reason is capable of discovering the truth of God in Nature (God "is the Author of Nature & principle of all principles. The rules therefore & the principles of Nature which he hath made cannot be contrairie unto himselfe. And he is also the verie reason and truth itselfe" [193]). What "is trewe and reasonable in nature" cannot "be false in Divinity" (194) (i.e., theology) because in principle both Nature and theology are above the corruption of second or fallen nature (194); thus, "God and nature are both one" (243). All is connected because the "inward man . . . is the Image of God" (296) and the substance and essence of that image is mind. Duplessis-Mornay quotes Hermes: "God (sayeth he) who is also Mynd, and Life, and Light, & Male-female; begate and bred Logo[s] the Speech or Word, which is another Mynd, and the workmayster of all things; & with that Speech, another which is the fyrie God and the Spirite of the Godhead . . . This Speech, that proceedeth from GOD being altogether perfect, and fruitful, Workmistresse of all things, lighteth upon the water and maketh it fruitful . . . I thy God (sayeth God) am Light and Mynd" (281). Indeed, androgynous-hermaphroditic mind is the source and center of all: "Mynde . . . is the Soule of the Soule" (222).

What Sidney must have found particularly supportive of his own developing thoughts on poetry and the poet was what Duplessis-Mornay had to say on Logos, which he equates with "Word or Speech" and "Reason" (268) and further divides (following Hermes directly, and echoing the Sophists and Cicero) into inward speech or speech of the mind, and utterance or speech of the voice, which "is unable to represent or expresse the inward

Speech perfectly." So also, "the like proportion is between the Speech of the mynd, and the speech of the understanding. The voyce hath need of ayre, and is divided into parts, and requireth leysure: The Mynd in deede is undividable, but yet hath it need of tyme to pass from one conclusion or reason to another. But as for the understanding, it accomplisheth his action or working in lesse than a moment, and with one onely act doth so fill the Reason and mynd, that it is constreyned to make many acts of one" (267). Understanding might be said to be the soul of the soul of the soul, and is the divine within the human, is where Logos, Idea, Conceit are simultaneously logos, idea, conceit:

> Now then, the Conception or Conceyt which Gods understanding hath conceyved everlastingly in himselfe, wee call Speech or Word; which is the perfect image of his understanding, and Gods understanding, is God himself. Also wee call it Reason, because Reason is as ye would say the Daughter, Speech or words of understanding, and we say that by the same Speech or word, God made all things. For, as the Craftsman maketh his worke by the patterne which he had erst conceyved in his mynde, which patterne is his inward word: so God made the World and all that is therein, by that sayd Speech of his as by his inward skill or arte. (267–68)

Montaigne, if he bothered to read *De la Verité de la Religion Chrestienne*, would have been appalled, but he would not have had to read very far into it before he turned it aside, for from the outset, in his preface, Duplessis-Mornay champions human reason (189ff), even the "uninlightened" reason of the pagan past, and he advocates the constant use of human reason to make acceptable and "credible" the mysteries of faith which "were invisible afore" (194ff); reason carries humankind to the point of faith, it supports faith, it understands faith. This thoroughly Aquinian position, shared by Sebond and Cusanus, is offered by a Protestant, but would be rejected by the Catholic who sounds like Calvin—let us be wary of labels.[8]

While Sidney was celebrated, and justly so, in his time and afterwards, as the embodiment of the Renaissance courtier, today we can look through his chivalry and grace into his mind; there we find the traditional aspects of Renaissance thought firmly rooted, but nurtured by some of the newest, most daring and bold, philosophical implications of that thought as discovered and elaborated by writers from Nicholas of Cusa through John Dee. Yet we can be thankful that Sidney's method was that of the Renaissance, for we find in his *Defence of Poetry* the esoteric as well as all of the commonplaces of his day on learning and the humanities, art and the artist. We need not start with the Greeks, the "Egyptians," the Romans, or the Italians and other "moderns" such as Duplessis-Mornay; Sidney has done our reading for us. But he has done more than just read; he has followed his own advice: he has devoured them whole and made them wholly his. As a result, the

Defence is not a report of past knowledge; it is itself an advancement of learning.

Sidney's thesis is that poetry is a living, forceful, multidimensional art which with a "sweet charming force" does both "teach and delight" in order to promote, encourage, and stimulate inner growth and development, which in the humanities we call learning. Poetry moves one to see, think, judge, and act. Poetry shapes. Poets "make to imitate, and imitate both to delight and teach; and delight to move men to take that goodness in hand, which without delight they would fly as from a stranger; and teach, to make them know that goodness whereunto they are moved" (81). The end of poetry may be said to move auditors through delight, to move them to know, and to move them to put learned knowledge into action. "And that moving is of a higher degree than teaching," as Sidney so eloquently states, "it may by this appear, that it is well nigh both the cause and effect of teaching." A poem is more effective than any other kind of instruction because "it moveth one to do that which it doth teach. For as Aristotle saith, it is not *gnosis* but *praxis* must be the fruit. And how *praxis* cannot be, without being moved to practise, it is no hard matter to consider . . . Nay truly, learned men have learnedly thought that where once reason hath so much overmastered passion as that the mind hath a free desire to do well, the inward light each mind hath in itself is as good as a philosopher's book" (91).[9]

The operative words here are *reason*, *mind*, *free desire*, and *inward light*. Because God's gift of the rational soul inhabits the mind, each mind contains seeds of all the information contained in the Book of Nature authored by God. (In terms of Renaissance thought, this circular argument, the kind used by Duplessis-Mornay throughout his *De la Verité*, is both correct and true.) Hence, when Astrophel hyperbolically represents Stella as a symbol of divine perfection ("perfection's heir"), pure mind, perfect reason in Sonnet 71, a quite serious, well-informed Sidney is speaking through him:

> Who will in fairest Book of Nature know
> How virtue may best lodg'd in beauty be
> Let him but learn of love to read in thee,
> Stella, those fair lines which true goodness show.
> There shall he find all vices' overthrow,
> Not by rude force, but sweetest sovereignty
> Of reason, from whose light those night birds fly
> That inward sun in thine eyes shineth so.[10]

The end or function of poetry is, then, that of all the arts: informed persuasion or learning—the process of moving the will to encompass humanistic growth and efficacious development. Poetry highlights the copy of the book that is open in each mind (a book "as good as a philosopher's book"). To use yet another metaphor, poetry brings up, or brings into focus, the lines of information that reside in the book of the mind, untended, unread, not understood—because not yet discovered. Each phrase which Sidney uses to describe the process of learning (hence, as well, the process of poetry) refers to the mind, the seat of the rational soul, the soul of soul, the "anima" soul: "This purifying of wit—this enriching of memory, enabling of judgement, and enlarging of conceit—which commonly we call learning, under what name soever it come forth, or to what immediate end soever it be directed, the final end is to lead and draw us to as high a perfection as our degenerate souls, made worse by their clayey lodgings, can be capable of" (82). All of the arts of learning have "this scope to know, and by knowledge to lift up the mind from the dungeon of the body to the enjoying his own divine essence" (82).

Bodies, as Donne reminds us in "The Extasie," are sex; minds are androgynous because they are of the "divine essence." To learn is the way to participate in one's own divine essence, and in so doing, participate in the Divine Essence because all acts of learning are a study of nature, and God is the Great Maker of all, the Designer of the Universe, the Author of the Book of Nature. Sidney gives examples of the dependency on nature of all the major arts or "serving sciences," of his day—the *trivium*: grammar, rhetoric, logic—the *quadrivium*: astronomy, geometry, arithmetic, music—and "graduate studies": physical and natural science, philosophy, law, medicine, and theology. Hinting at the concept of God as the Master Builder, he concludes that all of these serving sciences "build upon the depth of Nature." But then he moves on to a key humanist passage in the *Defence*:

> Only the poet, disdaining to be tied to any such subjection, lifted up with the vigor of his own invention, doth grow in effect [into] another nature, in making things either better than nature bringeth forth, or, quite anew, forms such as never were in nature, as the Heroes, Demigods, Cyclops, Chimeras, Furies, and such like: so as he goeth hand in hand with nature, not enclosed within the narrow warrant of her gifts, but freely ranging within the zodiac of his own wit. (78)

The human mind is not just *like* the Universal Mind; it *is* the universal mind in small, is a universe unto itself ("the zodiac of his own wit"), within which the poet ranges, observing and gathering truths of life ("lifted up with the vigor of his own invention," his own discoveries, his own flashes of intuitive understanding to be developed by reason). The poet is *born* with the gift of imagination which with God-given right reason forms the energy needed to mold, forge, and *make* imitations and fictions within the crucible of the mind which contains essential truth ("he goeth hand in hand with nature"), but unencumbered by the trivia and distractions of the fallen or brazen world ("not enclosed within narrow warrant of her gifts"). Therefore, when this imitation is delivered, figured forth, led into life, it proves eikastic, efficacious, substantive, effective, and affective. A poem is true gold because it is mined from the realm of pure Truth: "Nature never set forth the earth in so rich tapestry as divers poets have done . . . Her world is brazen, the poets only deliver a golden" (78). Bassanio, upon looking at Portia's picture, her "counterfeit," casually remarks, "what demigod/Hath come so near creation?" (*Merchant of Venice* 3.1.115–16).

When Sidney asks "why and how" the magical, alchemical poet functions, he knows that he is daringly going further than the Italian critics (even Ficino), that he is opening a new frontier in literary theory when he says: "Neither let it be deemed too saucy a comparison to balance the highest point of man's wit with the efficacy of nature; but rather give right honor to the heavenly Maker of the maker, who, having made man to His own likeness [which is androgynous], set him beyond and over all the works of that second nature, which in nothing he ["man"] showeth so much as in poetry, when with the force of a divine breath he [the poet] bringeth things forth surpassing her [second nature's] doings—with no small arguments to the incredulous of that first accursed fall of Adam, since our erected wit maketh us know what perfection [Nature] is, and yet our infected will [fallen, second nature] keepeth us from reaching unto it" (79).

This boldness is rounded off by a sad admission: "But these arguments will by few be understood, and by fewer granted." Sidney's arguments will never be understood or granted so long as the world thinks of poetry as mere riming and versifying. But the calling of the true or "right" poet goes hand in hand with the sixteenth-century ideal of learning: "right poets . . . having no law but wit . . . be they which most properly do imitate to teach and delight, and to imitate borrow nothing of what is, hath been, or shall be; but range, only reined with learned discretion, into the divine consideration of what may be, and should be." The "law of wit" is to be true to yourself, to trust your mind, which is the source of truth and creativity because it is androgynous and hermaphroditic: to know thyself is both to discover truths and to procreate within thyself. Poets range in the zodiacs of their own wits in the universe of the mind, controlled by what they have learned and do learn ("learned discretion") in order to "make to imitate, and imitate both to delight and teach; and delight to move men to take that goodness in hand, which without delight they would fly as from a stranger; and teach, to make them know that goodness whereunto they are moved—which being the noblest scope to which ever any learning was directed, yet want there not idle tongues to bark at them" (80–81).

The poet is a professor of the humanities, and the teacher and poet share the public's scorn and fear ("weave a circle round him thrice"). But the poet is an artist, not a pedagogue. He cometh to you with words set in delightful proportion, either accompanied with, or prepared for, the well enchanting skill of music; and with a tale forsooth he cometh unto you, with a tale which holdeth children from play, and old men from the chimney corner. And, pretending no more, doth intend *the winning of the mind* from wickedness to virtue: even as the child is often brought to take most wholesome things by hiding them in such other as have a pleasant taste: which, if one should begin to tell them the nature of the *aloes* or *rhubarbarum* they should receive, would sooner take their physic at their ears than at their mouth. So it is in men (most of which be childish in the best things, till they be cradled in their graves): glad they will be to hear the tales of Hercules, Achilles, Cyrus, and Aeneas; and, hearing them, must needs hear the right description of wisdom, valour, and justice; which, if they had been barely, that is to say philosophically, set out, they would swear they be brought to school again. (91–92; first emphasis added)

The words, the music, the tale are just the trappings. The heart of the poem lies in the invention. The listener or reader is engaged by a fiction, but a fiction built upon "an imaginative ground plot of a profitable invention." George Gascoigne in his *Certain Notes of Instruction* (1575) concerning poetry stated categorically that "the first and most necessary point that ever I found meet to be considered in making of a delectable poem is this, to ground it upon some fine invention. For it is not inough to roll in pleasant words, nor yet to thunder in *rym*, *ram*, *ruff* by letter (quoth my master Chaucer), nor yet to abound in apt vocables or epithets unless the invention have in it also *aliquid salis*. By this *aliquid salis* I mean some good and fine devise shewing the quick capacity of a writer; and where I say some good and fine invention I mean that I would have it both fine and good" (596). Gascoigne hits on the essentials: invention, capacity, good *and* fine.

Invention is the soul of poetry, just as it is the soul of learning and the soul of living, for invention means the uncovering of the truths of life, the facts, the connections, the relationships, the relative relevances and resonances. Invention functions in the mind, the zodiac of the wit, and what is discovered, uncovered, instantaneously becomes the poet's "idea or fore-conceit," which by assumption and definition is true; it is therefore potentially "profitable." The quick capacity is the range and breadth of the poet's mind, the field of discovery. The significance of the poet's foreconceit depends on the mind's *invent*-iveness, the ability to use inner vision to make the significant discovery or observation. All of this comes under Gascoigne's heading of good. Robert Frost would have agreed emphatically: "The object in writing poetry is to make all poems sound as different as possible from each other, and the resources for that of vowels, consonants, punctuation, syntax, words, sentences, meter are not enough. We need the help of context—meaning—subject matter. That is the greatest help towards variety . . . And we are back in poetry as merely one more art of having something to say, sound or unsound. Probably better if sound, because deeper and from wider experience" ("The Figure a Poem Makes").

But a poem can be good in vain if the reader puts it aside, to paraphrase Samuel Johnson. A poem must be fine or well written to go beyond engaging attention in order to *move* one to make it wholly one's own. The poet must know the craft of poetry, the fine art of effective presentation.

Sidney makes the same point: a good and fine poem can come only from perfectly blended art, imitation, and exercise. The terms are separated but the program is circular: it begins in art as a gifted skill and ends in art as a practiced skill. Both skill and art are involved in imitation, which has its root in invention but is shaped and elaborated through learned forms of expression. What binds all together is exercise, both in school and out. In school, "truly I could wish, if at least I might be so bold to wish in a thing beyond the reach of my capacity, the diligent imitators of Tully and Demosthenes (most worthy to be imitated) did not so much keep Nizolian paper-books of their figures and phrases, as by attentive translation (as it were) devour them whole, and make them wholly theirs" (117). Out of school, "we should exercise to know" so that "our brain [can be] delivered of much matter . . . begotten by knowledge" (112). By the constant interaction of "Art, Imitation, and Exercise" there is developed "that same forcibleness, or *energia* (as the Greeks call it) of the writer" (117). Through this program the poet learns the art of nurturing nature, an art which stems from one's own humankindness. Because art begins and ends within self, for this reason

> undoubtedly (at least to my opinion undoubtedly) I have found in divers smally learned courtiers a more sound style than in some professors of learning; of which I can guess no other cause, but that the courtier, following that which by practice he findeth fittest to nature, therein (though he know it not) doth according to art, though not by art: where the other, using art to show art, and not hide art (as in these cases he should do), flieth from nature, and indeed abuseth art. (118–19)

The essential for Sidney is "idea or fore-conceit"—thought, significant thought. Words are "the outside of" poetry, the trappings of thought, the clay lodging of the erected wit. The Word must precede the word—logos as creating and created, the foreconceit made the conceit, the Idea made idea, Nature creating nature. Words without thought are merely words, empty clothing, even when fancy clothing, if in rime. Of such an empty poem we can say with Kent of Oswald: "Nature disclaims in thee. A tailor made thee." A true poem is filled with nature, but must dis-cover that nature to the onlooking world. While the poet's "idea, or fore-conceit" is potentially efficacious, good, and true, the listener or reader cannot see into the mind of the poet, the poet's field of discovery. The listener must be engaged by the artifact: the words, music, and tale created out of the materials of mind.

The word invention at this point becomes an *apo koinou*, that term in Greek grammar for a word which simultaneously serves two functions. Here, invention means both the moment of creative impulse within discovery (foreconceit) and the act of creation itself (conceit). A poem then is a fiction built upon "an imaginative ground plot of a profitable invention." Whereas a lie is primarily and essentially false because it is simply "made up" (like castles in the air) to look like truth, a fiction is primarily and essentially true because it is grounded in, or traced from, the patterns of and in the mind. Only secondarily does a fiction look "made-up" (artificial, "unreal"). A poem, unlike a lie, is real because it is a fiction of discovery, an invention. Poetry is the fiction of invention. Poetry is invention, invention is the way to knowledge, knowledge is the way to power and control. Poetry is part of the program of Renaissance learning. But invention is a natural process. For Sidney, creativity is the free play of mind.

Because our "erected wit" is without the bodily hindrance of sex, the mind provides the means of secular salvation which is found in the reaching for fulfillment of human potential. Secular salvation is the overcoming of the fruits of the Fall through education, through learning. The growing awareness of the principle of androgyny in the late sixteenth century in England provided an essential part of the milieu within which arose Sidney's invention of a new choice of Hercules—the challenge to be more than just a man, to incorporate both the feminine and the masculine in order to be a whole person. Perhaps this is what Milton meant when he said that one who would be a true poet must first be a true poem.

Sidney, in turn, became a teacher for his age. And what a natural teacher; he loved to talk. Although the technology of movable print was a hundred years old, Elizabethan culture was still primarily oral-aural. Elizabeth *heard* the ambassadors sent to her. All of Sidney's writings sound as if they were to be spoken: *The Lady of May* was presented, *Astrophel and Stella* is an extended monologue, the *Old Arcadia* is told to us by a single voice (Sidney read long patches aloud to his sister and her friends), the *Defence* is an oration, and even the *New Arcadia* retains, for the most part, the controlling voice of a narrator. While Sidney felt that print smacked of commercialism and was literally beneath his dignity (and should have been for Oxford as well!), his works became so well known that they did slowly find their way into print from 1590 on, and the Countess of Pembroke finally oversaw the printing, as close as posthumously possible, of an authorized version of the collected works of Sidney in 1598.

Spenser surely had read the *Defence* before or after going to Ireland in

1580,[11] and manuscripts surely circulated through London until finally published (twice) in 1595. From 1590 on, Spenser too became a teacher for his age, starting with the broadly trumpeted publication of the first three books of *The Faerie Queene*. One doubts that Shakespeare needed many teachers, but he surely found sustenance in the ideas and examples of Sidney and Spenser.

5

"Both male and female, both vnder one name": Spenser, Elizabeth, and The Faerie Queene

The spirit of late Renaissance thought is androgynous, and the embodiment of that spirit in England is Queen Elizabeth. Queen Elizabeth was a living symbol, an emblem in motion—her life was an allegory, one version of which was fully recorded by Edmund Spenser as *The Faerie Queene*. She was John Dee's Monad, she was the alchemical marriage; a virgin mother, Queen and King of England, both male and female in temperament (and rumored to be so in body); Astraea, Venus, Urania, Cynthia, Diana, Gloriana, the Queen of Faerieland; Dame Nature, an androgynous being transcending any sexual identity.

All of this diversity stems from one fact underpinning and overriding all others—she was the Queen of England. As a female monarch, she was unique in every sense: the first, the only, the exception, the unprecedented, the unexpected, the phenomenal. A woman ruler—who had ever heard of such a thing.[1] From the beginning her advisors, male and female, said in effect, "Get married—find yourself a nice king or prince, someone to take care of you, to watch over your country." But she chose not to do as her half-sister Mary had done immediately upon becoming a queen. Elizabeth, instead, married her kingdom, even, like a nun, wearing a wedding ring. Too much cannot be made of the fact of her successful—nay, triumphal—reign.[2] Her constant presence on the throne of England did more for the status of women than all of the theorizing of humanist philosophers, the angry outcries of Jane Anger, and the feminist images and emblems of poets. But there was no separation or contradiction here, for Elizabeth herself received a basic but full humanist education, the fruits of which she demonstrated daily in private and in public. There was substance informing the age's celebration of her as a living myth.[3]

The figuratively embellished, rhetorically colored, contemporary attitude toward Elizabeth typifies the age's essential but unreflecting use of analogy to express concurrent truths in life through art. Elizabeth was simultaneously the actual Elizabeth: irascible yet charming, unpredictable yet reliable, vain yet homely, engaging yet shy. And she was really Astraea and all the rest. Shakespeare needed no sets, scenery, or lights in the Theatre, the Rose, or the Globe to establish time and place—time and place are mental constructs; reality is conceived in the mind; the inventions of fiction are truth. Still, the members of Shakespeare's audience knew where they actually were, just as they knew that what they were watching and hearing was actually happening. Life was merely a play, and it was the only show in town. Venice was Venice, and Venice was London. The cosmic analogy included the stage as a member of the metaphor—the Globe—a living part of the allegory of life.[4] In *The Faerie Queene*, fictive Una is human Una. But Una is Belphoebe is Britomart is Gloriana is Elizabeth. Elizabeth is the Faerie Queene; Elizabeth is *The Faerie Queene*.[5] And she is always androgynous.[6]

I used to end my sixteenth-century course with this question: "*The Faerie Queene* springs from, hence illustrates in full, Elizabethan temperament and taste, prejudices and dreams, ideas and ideals, loves and hates, poetic practice and poetic theory. Write a well-considered essay showing to what extent *The Faerie Queene* is wholly Elizabethan, a true and fitting product of the sixteenth century. Be specific, citing an example from outside *The Faerie Queene* for each illustration taken from within and about *The Faerie Queene*." In 1976, James Nohrnberg published his 896-page answer to the question: *The Analogy of The Faerie Queene*. One small part of an answer could be to point out that Una is Una, that Una is Elizabeth, that both Una and Elizabeth are the True Church, that all—Una, Elizabeth, and the True Church—are the intended Bride of Christ in Revelation, and that the coming together of Christ and His Church, as John Colet pointed out early in the century, is the ultimate reunion or remarriage of the male and female at the end of time—the androgynous circle come full circle.[7]

While androgyny is everywhere in the sixteenth century—in the iconography of Queen Elizabeth, in Reformation symbolism,[8] in the assumptions and aims of humanism (see Appendices II, III, IV)—there is no mythic story of the androgyne—nor has there ever been one, as Marie Delcourt has observed. She explains why: "Androgyny is at the two poles of sacred things. Pure concept, pure vision of the spirit, it appears adorned with the highest qualities. But once made real in a being of flesh and blood, it is a monstrosity, and no more; it is proof of the wrath of the gods."[9] To actualize or physically encapsulate the idea of androgyny is impossible because such an attempt must utilize the two known sexes, which creates a hermaphrodite, which is the "other" of the androgyne. As we have seen, hermaphrodeity is physical, is an attempt to describe genetics; androgyny is psychological, is cultural. The one is fulfilling nature, the other is fulfilled nature fully nurtured.[10]

Although there is no myth of the androgyne, Edmund Spenser in *The Faerie Queene* creates the atmosphere of androgyny and even creates androgynous episodes. In spirit and in theme, the motif of androgyny as process leading to the ideal of human fulfillment runs through and informs *The Faerie Queene* from Book I and Red Crosse through Book VI and Calidore, but especially with regard to the story of Britomart who shows us how inner growth and awareness lead to outward range and calm. Spenser faced the specific problem of effectively symbolizing androgynous wholeness when he composed the original (1590) ending of Book III. Having been freed from Busirane by Britomart, Amoret is reunited with Scudamour. He who had been in doubt, and she who had forced delay, now fall into sexual embrace:

> Lightly he clipt her twixt her armes twaine,
> And streightly did embrace her body bright,
> Her body, late the prison of sad paine,
> Now the sweet lodge of loue and deare delight:
> But she faire Lady ouercommen quight
> Of huge affection, did in pleasure melt,
> And in sweete rauishment pourd out her spright:
> No word they spake, nor earthly thing they felt,
> But like two senceles stocks in long embracement dwelt.[11]

Spenser describes here the moment of mutual sexual climax which John Donne's lover-speaker of "The Extasie" hopes will follow the extended monologue and reported dialogue-of-one. Here, as in Donne's poem, we become, along with Britomart, unseen spectators.

> Had ye theme seene, ye would haue surely thought,
> That they had beene that faire *Hermaphrodite*,
> Which that rich *Romane* of white marble wrought,
> And in his costly Bath causd to bee site:
> So seemd those two, as growne together quite,
> That *Britomart* halfe enuying their blesse,
> Was much empassiond in her gentle sprite,
> And to herselfe oft wisht like happinesse,
> In vaine she wisht, that fate n'ould let her yet possesse.

Thus doe those louers with sweet counteruayle,
Each other of Loues bitter fruit despoile . . .

Spenser wishes to make the point that Britomart will eventually experience spiritual fulfillment through sexual embrace with Artegal, but this scene suggests that that fulfillment will be merely sexual, even if in marriage. Marriage is often presented as a symbol of androgyny—a token of primordial unity and apocalyptic reunion—but marriage itself is only a symbol, just as the hermaphroditic embrace of Amoret and Scudamour is only a symbol. Part of what the onlooking Britomart feels stirring within her are the urges toward attaining personal androgynous fulfillment through marriage. Marriage can be a means toward androgyny because of its powerful offering of sexual and psychic knowledge—"Who knows not that conscience is born of love?" Awareness of androgyny can be shared—*con-science*—but the roots are private, are within. Marriage and sex are only means. (And Plato's Aristophanes reminds us that there are, basically, three kinds of sexual union.)

Camille A. Paglia, in a fine article on "The Apollonian Androgyne and *The Faerie Queene*," suggests why these stanzas do not appear in the 1596 edition: "They dramatize a rich metaphor of heterosexual union, recalling the myth of Plato's Symposium, but they subvert an imagistic pattern universal in the poem. The Hermaphrodite stanzas are an error, thematically apposite but glaringly divergent in aesthetic mode. It is for this same reason that the hermaphroditic Venus of the *Faerie Queene* is veiled. Because of his idealizing artistic style, Spenser parallels the sensibility of classical Greece in his aversion to deformations of the human figure, which are always monstrous." Paglia recognizes that androgyny is "the harmony of subsumed sexual constraints," that "the Dionysian androgyne . . . is pure process," and that in "true Spenserial androgyny . . . the energized form is the ideal."[12]

Even though Spenser rejected this particularized attempt to capture in emblem the notion of androgyny, this at-one-time incorporation of an unveiled hermaphrodite in the epic helps to support my thesis that the spirit of androgyny informs the whole poem. And even though he is never again so specific, Spenser went on to incorporate in Book IV and Book VII two other episodes which confirm this presence of androgyny as an informing principle in *The Faerie Queene*.

Before seeing Venus through Scudamour's eyes in Book IV, and Dame Nature through "Spenser's" in Book VII, perhaps some background is in order.[13] The genealogy of Renaissance gods is just as hazy and confused as is that of the original classical ones—and appropriately so, for in talking of godhead one talks in guesses and hunches and must sort through centuries of overlayed embellishments and repetitions. Overlap and redundancy, though inevitable, are the sources of the truth that is myth. The truth of myth cannot be described but must be experienced, as in dream or ecstasy (or in art), for the human brain, as our development of computers constantly reminds us, calculates in binary reductions and combinations. There is reliable frustration in the fact that binary oppositions are intrinsic to the rational process, to human thought: we can repeat and verify demonstrations of proof, even though we seem not to be able to get behind them. (Oh, to be a Magus!) We can talk about creation (from Genesis to physical astronomy), but we seem to talk around it. We still search for a unified theory of knowledge.[14] Before the beginning, we posit, there had to be a source of all forms and potentials. To begin the beginning, we say, pure light and utter darkness come together—simple, but binary. Out of light and dark, we say, comes life.[15] Because life as observed and lived is full of form and substance, the eternal and the mutable, the changing and the constant, we say that light provides the first member, and darkness the second, of these pairs. And, extrapolating from socialized gender division, we say that the first set of members describes the "male" principle and the second set the "female." Light is Logos; absence of light is Chaos. But that this is so, we must guess from the nature of life. Myth is a collectively taken inductive leap.

FIGURE 5–1: The "Binary Unity" of Creation

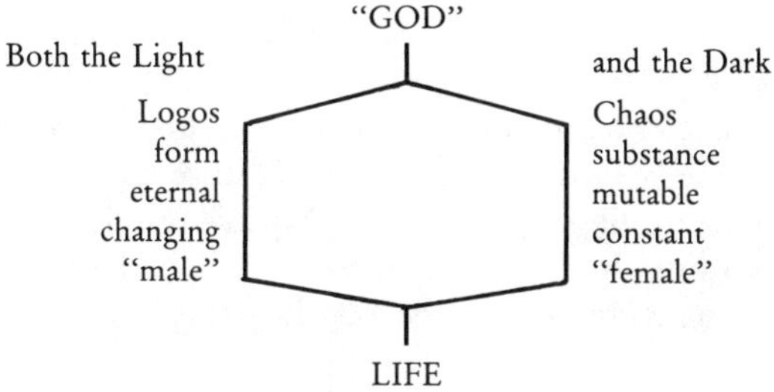

In Greek and Roman cultures, Life is centered in Aphrodite, or Venus, the Roman name used in the Renaissance. Paul Friedrich in his multidisciplinary approach to *The Meaning of Aphrodite* reports that everywhere in the Mediterranean world traces of cults of Venus are to be found among the oldest aspects of ancient culture. He believes that her omnipresence is "liminal"—"she bridges physical reality and metaphysical belief" (134). Venus dissolves the binary appearance of life: Friedrich's list seems endless.

He feels that Venus has been neglected during the recent past because we have become squeamish about her blatant sexual nature; ironically, in averting our eyes, we become blind to the necessary reason for worship of her: "In anthropological terms, sexual love is the ultimate *communitas*, the dyadic union that so often dissolves the grids and paradigms of life" (148). Venus is a bridge, and in every instance of a myth of Venus there is at the far side of the bridge vestiges of her androgynous origins (11, 27–28, 50, 51, 68, 210).

The image of Venus was so diffused in form and function in ancient times that when she came to the Renaissance, Ficino and Pico (with their Aristotelian minds) had to create categories to explain this potent, Platonic ideal. Ficino and Pico both start with a version of the basic creation paradigm outlined above (Figure 5–1) and which we saw in chapter 2: out of the "marriage" of Uranus (sky) and Tellus (earth) comes Nature (called Venus Urania by Ficino, and whom we find embodied in Urania in Sidney's *New Arcadia* and as Sapience in Spenser's "Hymn to Heavenly Beauty").

FIGURE 5–2: First and Second "Generations" of the Gods

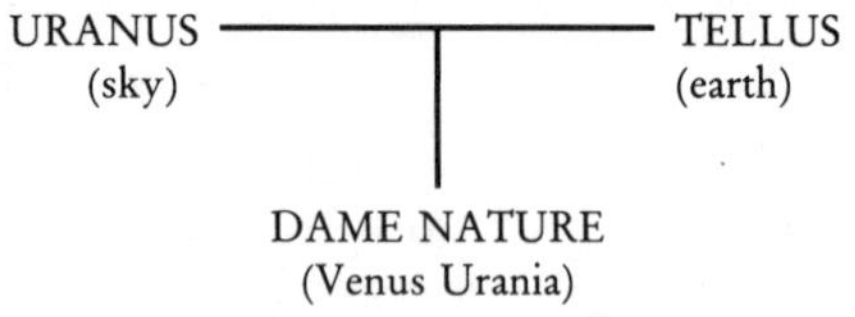

Because of the ancient presence of Venus, Nature in the Renaissance is usually called "Dame" Nature, even though Nature has the total generative forces needed to create life; hence, Dame Nature is said, by deduction, to have both sexes within "her." Thus, Dame Nature is the same as the Venus of "Colin Clout's Come Home" who is both the father and the mother of Eros.

FIGURE 5–3: Third "Generation"

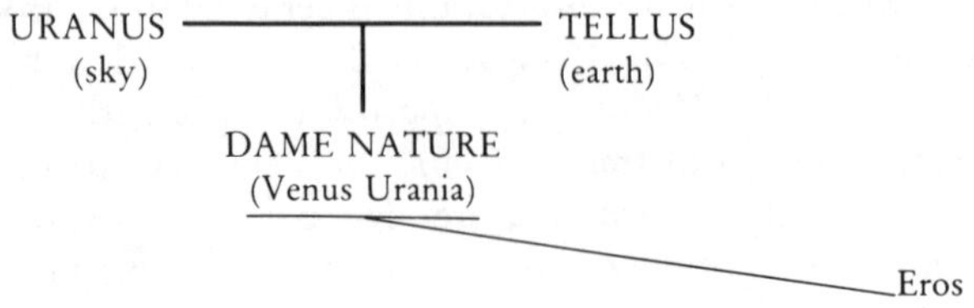

Eros, called "the greatest of the Gods" because of his power not only over humans but also over the gods, was

> Borne without Syre or couples, of one kynd,
> For *Venus* selfe doth soly couples seeme,
> Both male and female, through commixture joynd,
> So pure and spotless Cupid forth she brought
> And in the gardens of Adonis nurst.
>
> ("Colin Clout," 799–804)[16]

As we easily deduce from Spenser's *Four Hymns*, the analogy of Venus and Virgin, Cupid and Christ is consciously created because at this level of myth Eros is the formative force within Nature, as Lucretius describes at the opening of *De Rerum Natura* and Ovid constantly alludes to. This bracketing of, to us, so-called pagan and Christian led, in the Renaissance, to picture after picture of Venus-and-Cupid and Madonna-and-Child, both sets surrounded by little cupids and angels, which are hardly distinguishable one from another (see Appendix V, V–1 and V–2). The two sets, as any humanist could explain, are simply two versions of the same story: one true and the other True; one the guess of pre-Christian human rationality, the other the revelation of Divine Rationality; both are fit subjects for the Renaissance artist.

Venus Urania/Dame Nature/Primordial Virgin is the "Venus" worshipped in the Temple of Love in Book IV of *The Faerie Queene* and described by Scudamour:

> Right in the midst the Goddesse selfe did stand
> Vpon an altar of some costly masse,
> Whose substance was vneath to vnderstand:
> For neither pretious stone, nor durefull brasse,
> Nor shining gold, nor mouldring clay it was;
> But much more rare and pretious to esteeme,
> Pure in aspect, and like to christall glasse,
> Yet glasse was not, if one did rightly deeme,
> But being faire and brickle, likest glasse did seeme.
>
> (IV.x.39)

Because he wants the mythic force of Venus in his poem, not her sculpted presence, Spenser immediately removes her from mimetic actualization to suggest "her" uniqueness (which is achieved in part by suggesting the true uniqueness of the virgin mother):

But it in shape and beautie did excell
All other Idoles, which the heathen adore,
Farre passing that, which by surpassing skill
Phidias did make in *Paphos* Isle of yore,
With which that wretched Greeke, that life forlore
Did fall in loue: yet this much fairer shined,
But couered with a slender veile afore;
And both her feete and legs together twyned
Were with a snake, whose head & tail were fast combyned.

(IV.x.40)

The snake encircled upon itself is a symbol both of eternity[17] and of the idea that the offspring of the virgin will bruise the head of the serpent, all of which is one level of the story of Book I and is symbolized by Charitas's chalice. While this snake looks "forward," the veiling looks back, for her having both bright, heavenly beauty and dark, chaotic ugliness as aspects of her essential, dual-sexual nature suggest her origins: Uranus (Logos) and Tellus (Chaos), the one infinitely radiant, the other eternally repellent. Either or both of these aspects would overwhelm mere mortals, and she has both; therefore, Venus must be veiled:

The cause why she was couered with a vele,
Was hard to know, for that her Priests the same
From peoples knowledge labour'd to concele.
But sooth it was not sure for womanish shame,
Nor any blemish, which the worke mote blame;
But for, they say, she hath both kinds in one,
Both male and female, both vnder one name:
She syre and mother is her selfe alone,
Begets and eke conceiues, ne needeth other none.

(IV.x.41)

The "one name" is, of course, the original androgyne—Shakespeare's "single nature's double name."

In the *Two Cantos of Mutabilitie*, the Venus of Book IV becomes, outright, Dame Nature, and here Spenser moves from Ficino to Pico, who introduced Dame Nature as part of a generation which intervenes between Uranus/Tellus and Ficino's Venus. Thus, Dame Nature becomes the mother of Venus and grandmother of Cupid. (Sidney, too, follows Pico in this regard in "Astrophel and Stella," no. 17, where Nature is the mother of Venus and "grandam" of that rascally, blind Cupid, who randomly and haphazardly shoots off his leaden-headed arrows that inoculate against love and the golden-headed arrows that stimulate desire.)

FIGURE 5–4: Third and Fourth "Generations"

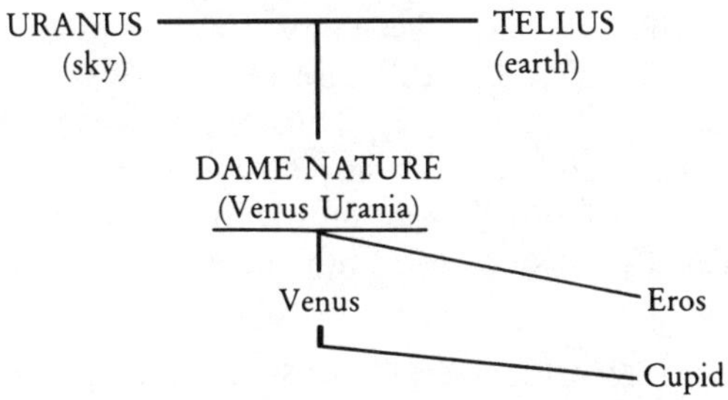

Not only does Dame Nature give birth to "heavenly" Venus and the force of Eros, she also creates Saturn and Titan.

FIGURE 5–5: Additional Third "Generation"

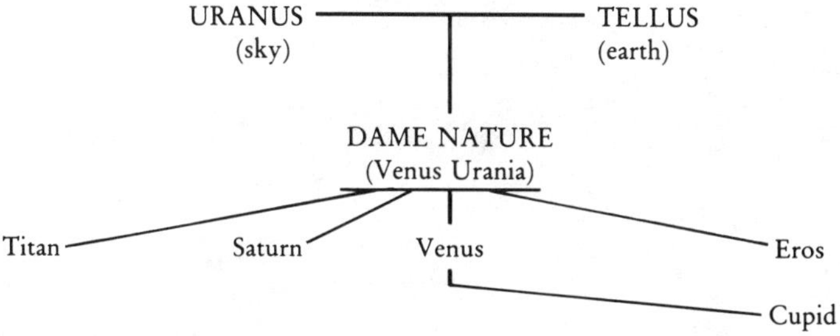

When Saturn is castrated, he "gives birth" to yet another Venus (see Picture V–3), who becomes a member of the third generation of gods along with Saturn's son Jove and Titan's daughter Mutabilitie, all of whom join "brother" Cupid.

FIGURE 5–6: Additional Fourth "Generation"

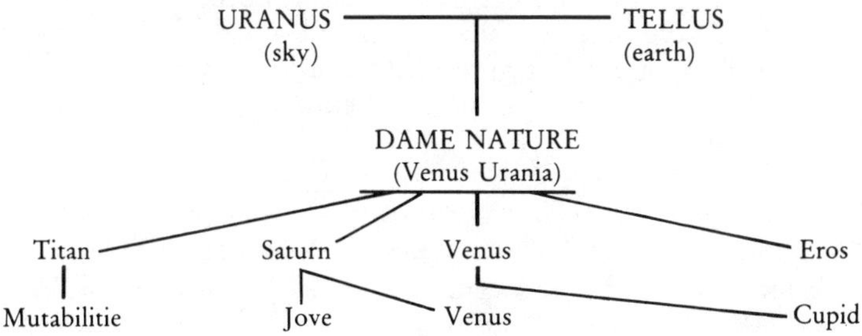

"Brother" Cupid forces "sister" Venus and Mars (a god) to fall in love, which gives rise to yet another Cupid (see Picture V–4), which is a reenactment of the original creation: love plus hate equals harmony. To complicate, but to complete the genesis of Venus, Jove as rebel-ruler in heaven disturbs the harmony of earth which is typified by his siring yet another Venus, who is the earthly Venus of human sexuality, simple but not pure because she both passes on Venus's (venereal) disease and gives birth to yet another Cupid, *cupiditas* (See Picture V–5). Thus, we arrive at a final genealogy of the greater and lesser gods which embraces all aspects of the Venus principle from amorphous, primordial, and androgynous origins to an utterly real, mortal, and sexually divided world inhabited by "Cressid's kind."

FIGURE 5–7: Fifth and Sixth "Generations"

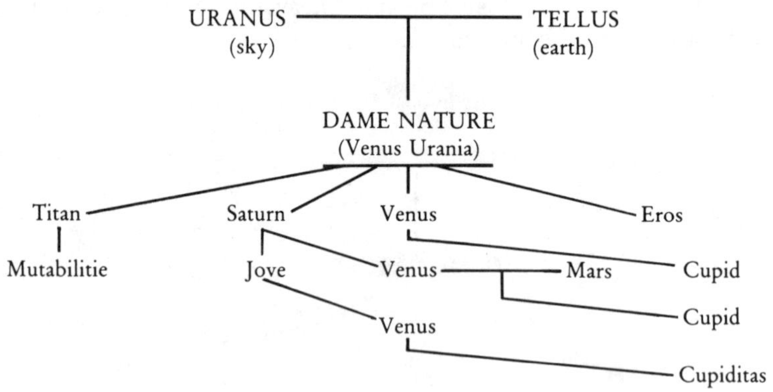

Spenser's genealogy of the gods in the *Two Cantos of Mutabilitie* is based on this composite composition of six "generations," but is somewhat simplified. He has the great grandmother of all of life (the "God" of Figure 5–1) who gives birth to the great god Nature, who gives birth to the gods, who give birth to earthly creatures:

this great Grandmother of all creatures bred
Great *Nature*, euer young yet full of eld,
Still moouing, yet vnmoued from her sted;
Vnseene of any, yet of all beheld.

(VII.vii.13)

Within this scheme Mutabilitie becomes a kind of Venus genetrix governing the fallen (sub-lunary) world, but serving the veiled Venus of Book IV.

FIGURE 5–8: Spenser's Genealogy of the Gods

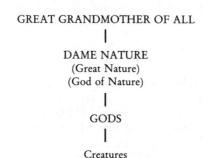

GREAT GRANDMOTHER OF ALL

|

DAME NATURE
(Great Nature)
(God of Nature)

|

GODS

|

Creatures

The notion of Nature as unisexual is reinforced by the fact that, at the end of the first of the *Two Cantos*, Mutabilitie had said that she wished to appeal her case against her cousin Jove before the God of Nature, who would judge whether she or Jove had the proper claim to rule all from the throne of heaven:

> But to the highest him, that is behight
> Father of Gods and men by equally might:
> To weet, the God of Nature, I appeale.
>
> (VII.vi.35)

Nature, at this level, like the human soul is without sex division.

When Nature appears as female in the second canto, Spenser has not dozed off: rather, he is consciously participating in deep myth, and he is also paying his last tribute to Queen Elizabeth, herself a myth, a myth in part created by Spenser. Elizabeth knew that she was the Faerie Queene when she accepted the gift of the first three books of *The Faerie Queene* as belonging to her. In the second of the *Two Cantos of Mutabilitie*, Elizabeth enters the epic once more, now as Dame Nature. In case any reader should need a signal, in the first of the *Two Cantos* we had been told that Cynthia each year (before the "fall" of Ireland) recreated on Arlo Hill—and who knows not Cynthia? Now Dame Nature comes to Arlo Hill; now we know that Cynthia-Elizabeth is Dame Nature-Elizabeth:

> Then forth issewed (great goddesse) greate dame *Nature*,
> With goodly port and gracious Maiesty;
> Being far greater and more tall of stature
> Then any of the gods or Powers on hie:
> Yet certes by her face and physnomy.
> Whether she man or woman inly were,

That could not any creature well descry:
For, with a veile that wimpled euery where,
Her head and face was hid, that mote to none appeare.

Again, Spenser explains the need for the veil:

That some doe say was so by skill deuized,
To hide the terror of her vncouth hew,
From mortall eyes that should be sore agrized;
For that her face did like a Lion shew,
That eye of wight could not indure to view:
But others tell that it so beautious was,
And round about such beames of splendor threw,
That it the Sunne a thousand times did pass,
Ne could be seene, but like an image in a glass.

In the next stanza Spenser takes his discourse in Natural Theology all the way back to the source, to Jehovah, and the traditional three graces of Venus (see Picture V–6) become the three saints on Mount Tabor:

That well may seemen true: for, well I weene
That this same day, when she on *Arlo* sat,
Her garment was so bright and wondrous sheene,
That my fraile wit cannot deuize to what
It to compare, not finde like stuffe, to that,
As those three sacred *Saints*, though else most wise,
Yet on mount *Thabor* quite their wits forgat,
When they their glorious Lord in strange disguise
Transfigur'd same; his garments so did daze their eyes.

(VII.vii.5–7)

From Edgar Wind through Stevie Davies, Botticelli's *Primavera* (Picture V–6) has been a goldmine for the reclaiming of classical, Neoplatonic, Hermetic, Christian icons.[18] Spenser never saw the picture, but he would have understood it at first glance:

In a fayre Plaine vpon an equall Hill,
She placed was in a pauilion;
Not such as Craftes-men by their idle skill
Are wont for Princes states to fashion:
But th'earth her self of her owne motion,
Out of her fruitfull bosome made to growe
Most dainty trees; that, shooting vp anon,

Did seeme to bow their bloosming heads full lowe,
For homage vnto her, and like a throne did shew.

(VII.vii.8)

And Spenser does not leave out her organic function as Flora:[19]

And all the earth far vnderneath her feete
Was dight with flowres, that voluntary grew
Out of the ground, and sent forth odours sweet.

(VII.vii.10)

Here we have depicted the art of nature and the nature of art, as also captured abstractly in Fludd's now-familiar scheme linking within circles God to Nature to Man, that inventive, imitative creature (see Picture II-6).

A great deal of Elizabeth's life was spent settling disputes among her courtiers (Astraea in the Cabala is both Justice and Woman). She loved being the center of attention. She loved staged affairs. Sidney's first "public" piece, *The Lady of May*, not only celebrated her as the actual Lady of May, but allowed her to choose a mate for the fictive Lady of May.[20] G. K. Hunter has showed us how court dramatists incorporated Elizabeth.[21] George Peele, at the arraignment of Paris, has Diana, Venus, and Juno become handmaidens to Elizabeth when Diana awards the ball of gold to the queen herself, and John Lyly gave Elizabeth Paris's task of judging among the three beauties (Helen, Diana, and Venus), who were another version of the three female graces, the same handmaidens of Venus who dance around another figure of Elizabeth in Book VI. Circle within circle within circle, with Elizabeth always in the center.

The scene of the trial of "Mutabilitie vs. Jove for Recovery of Alienated Property"[22] is marvelous to view: Arlo Hill crowded with the presence of all gods and goddesses, great and less, all creatures, all flora, properly arranged and overseen by "*Natures* Sargeant (that is *Order*)." The Elizabethan world is captured here: variety, majesty, show, and talk—always talk. A play within the play, or *The Faerie Queene* as prefiguration of the complete court masque.

The evidence finally has all been heard. The end has come. All eyes, ears, and minds are bent toward the Queen, and,

So hauing ended, silence long ensewed,
Ne *Nature* to or fro spake for a space,
But with firme eyes affixt, the ground still viewed.
Meane while, all creatures, looking in her face

Expecting th'end of this so doubtfull case,
Did hang in long suspence what would ensew,
To whether side should fall the soueraigne place:
At length, she looking up with chearefull view,
The silence brake, and gaue her doome in speeches few.

(VII.vii.57)

Spenser's genius shows in Nature's speech,[23] for, after all of the books, cantos, and stanzas of *The Faerie Queene*, he has the sense and ability to sum up the immediate issue and to pronounce the dominant theme of the whole epic in one stanza:

I well consider all that ye haue sayd,
And find that all things stedfastnes doe hate
And changed be: yet being rightly wayd
They are not changed from their first estate;
But by their change their being doe dilate:
And turning to themselues at length againe,
Doe worke their owne perfection so by fate:
Then ouer them Change doth not rule and raigne;
But they raigne ouer change, and doe their states maintaine.

(VII.vii.58)

From the moment we are born (rather, conceived) to the moment we die (and even after, because we rot and rot) the process of change is the most constant part of our lives. Yet, through all, we remain in kind (in our "first estate"). Change is growth within specific kinds. In humans, growth can be internalized and a process of perfecting undertaken, which can be just as effective as the natural processes of growth (those which transpire "so by fate"). Humankinds can range in the zodiacs of their own wits, reigned only with a learned discretion, to "worke their owne perfection." Humankind is of nature, but has the power to control nature through mind. In fact, the maintenance of human dignity demands the control of mere flux and drift, demands the shaping of natural processes. As Frank Kermode has simply said, art "is man's power over the created world and over himself."[24] Unless centered in the mind, things fall apart. If the center will not hold, entropy, "an universal wolf . . . /Must make perforce an universal prey/And last eat up himself" (*Troilus and Cressida* 1.3.121–24).

Nature tells Mutabilitie this much more simply: "thy decay thou seekest by thy desire":

Cease therefore daughter further to aspire,
And thee content thus to be rul'd by me:
For thy decay thou seekst by thy desire;
But time shall come that all shall changed bee,
And from thenceforth, none more change shall see.

For the moment, Mutabilitie is silent, knows she has lost:

So was the *Titaness* put downe and whist,
And *Ioue* confirm'd in his imperiall see.

What Mutabilitie now knows, we should take with us. The "lesson" of her story is the lesson of *The Faerie Queene*, which shows over and over again how life is the microcosmic attempt to invent and imitate through action the macrocosmic ideal of unity and harmony. The theme is androgynous, pronounced at the end by the most fully realized example of an androgyne in art, Spenser's Dame Nature, who is that androgyne in life, England's Queen Elizabeth. In art and in life, the highly developed androgynous mind speaks from within the body of a woman.

But all of this is only art, only illusion, only a dream:

Then was that whole assembly quite dismist,
And *Natur's* selfe did vanish, whither no man wist.

(VII.vii.59)

Marvelous. Not even "Spenser" knows! He is left alone at this apocalyptic moment, as each of us is, meditating in mind on the natural condition:

All that moueth, doth in *Change* delight:
But thence-forth all shall rest eternally
With Him that is the God of Sabbaoth hight:
O that great Sabbaoth God, graunt me that Sabboaths sight.

Spenser's pronouncements are simultaneously Heraclitian, Platonic, and Aristotelian; cabalistic, gnostic, hermetic; Roman, Italian, and English. His learning comes from Erasmus, More, Colet, and Elyot, is shared with Sidney, Marlowe, Shakespeare, Donne, and Milton, and looks forward to Wordsworth, Coleridge, Keats, Arnold, the Huxleys, T. S. Eliot, and the process philosophy of Teilhard de Chardin. His solution is renaissant, the fully developed expression of "the Renaissance philosophy of man."[25]

While the *Two Cantos of Mutabilitie* provide the fullest English Renaissance record of androgyny in art and in life, in poem and in princess, they were, of course, not published until after Spenser's and Queen Elizabeth's deaths. They provide, nevertheless, compelling evidence of how much androgyny—"Single nature's double name"—was "in the air" in the 1590s. They are, in this sense, good and valid "background." In Part II, "Undertaking the essay," I return to those 1590s to examine some uses of the materials of the myth of androgyny in the early years of the decade, by way of making the transition to Part III: "The Stages and Ages of Androgyny."

PART II

Undertaking the essay

6

Making Myth: Spenser, Marlowe, Shakespeare

Although Shakespeare never uses the single word androgyne, he would recognize its double name, and the text of *King John* implies his awareness of the origins of androgyny as detailed by Plato. In order to avert an English-French storming of Angiers, the Citizen proposes a marriage between Lady Blanch and Lewis the Dauphin. The Citizen starts his speech with praise of Blanch's "beauty, virtue, birth," which are matched by Lewis's. Each is perfect, but not complete:

> He is the half part of a blessed man,
> Left to be finished by such as she,
> And she a fair divided excellence,
> Whose fulness of perfection lies in him.
>
> (2.1.415–45)

In marriage they will be "made one," and in marriage they can become androgynous, if love provides the catalyst, as it did in "The Phoenix and Turtle."

The love of the Phoenix and the Turtle between and for each other was so inner interpenetrating that spiritual possessing ("Either was the other's mine," 36) and physical possession ("Either was the other's mine") were the same because "mine" is both the personal possessive pronoun and the word for a tunnel dug under and into something, as in undermine:

> So they loved as love in twain
> Had the essence but in one;
> Two distincts, division none:

Number there in love was slain.

(25–28)

This is union without seam; thus, sense of self, "Property" (37), is obliterated, and a new identity created, no longer either male or female but the re-joined androgyne:[1]

Single nature's double name
Neither two nor one was called.

(39–40)

Appropriately, only Reason (the rational soul, the androgynous power within humanity)[2] can understand this alchemical marriage ("Simple were so well compounded," 44) because reason is, in and of itself, a compounded/confounded entity ("Reason, in itself confounded," 41). Reason, when it "Saw division grow together" (42), understands the rational role of love in life (just as it had in Sidney's *Astrophel and Stella*, no. 10):

"How true a twain
Seemeth this concordant one!
Love hath reason, reason none,
If what parts can so remain."

(45–48)

Love is above reason, but reason stands under love. And in death this marriage of true minds ("married chastity," 61) becomes the quintessence of dust, as Reason recognized in the "Threnos":

Beauty, truth, and rarity,
Grace in all simplicity,
Here enclos'd in cinders lie.

(53–55)

In the passage from *King John* and in "The Phoenix and Turtle," Shakespeare shows full recognition of the concept of androgyny as a goal of human fulfillment. The journey toward androgyny is arduous and may never be fully attained. As Sidney had said, through reason we can know what perfection is, but our clay lodgings will prevent us from attaining the highest perfection.

As has been emphasized throughout this study, the first steps toward androgyny must be taken through, and move beyond, "role." In chapter 4, we noted how in Sidney's two *Arcadias* his two princes, travelling in order to learn how to be knights and rulers, go into disguise and role-reversal, one as an Amazon (man to woman), one as a shepherd (noble to commoner), and are enabled to look inward, to invent, as Stephen Greenblatt would put it, "self-fashioning." Pyrocles and Musidorus begin to learn that maturity does not come from achievement alone.

Spenser's "Venus and Adonis" (Canto 6 of Book III of *The Faerie Queene*), Marlowe's "Hero and Leander," and Shakespeare's "Venus and Adonis" are all part of the Ovidian vogue of the early 1590s (as are Spenser's *Two Cantos* and the *Epithalamion*, published in 1596). While in these works Spenser, Marlowe, and Shakespeare use cross-sex role-reversal to satirize the restrictiveness of expected gender behaviors, they do so within the larger context of androgynous creation myths. In Spenser, Venus is the keeper/wooer while Adonis is the kept/adored—but the nature of their sexual union becomes a new paradigm for the actual organic process of creation. Marlowe, too, in "Hero and Leander" reveals a similar mythic ingenuity when he parodies the myth of creation not just by reversing male and female descriptions but more importantly by coining a secular myth of heavenly power out of Hero's earthly beauty. And Shakespeare in his "Venus and Adonis," while fully reversing roles in order to question the socially appropriate and customary, does so with an informing awareness of the surging of the forces of creation which are submerged deeply within life as well as deeply within myth. Spenser, Marlowe, and Shakespeare do not transmit the messages of myth; they make myths to transmit their messages.

1
FROM "ANTIQUE BOOKES": SPENSER'S "VENUS AND ADONIS"

Canto 6 of Book III of *The Faerie Queene* has four versions of the same myth, the Venus principle which creates creation: the birth of Chrysogonee, the birth of Belphoebe and Amoret, the Bower of Venus and the Garden of Adonis, and the birth of Cupid and Psyche's Pleasure. A fifth version is implied: the birth of Diana and Venus. And all of this is centered in and reflected from Britomart, a female in sex but both masculine and feminine in "gender."[3] Circles of analogy circling, and circled by, circles of analogy.

Because Chrysogonee means "golden born" we can place her in the Age of Saturn, and because her mother's name, Amphisa, means "double nature," we can call her Dame Nature, the mother of the Titans. But Chrysogonee is herself a kind of Dame Nature; she gives birth to Belphoebe and

Amoret as the result of the conjoined influence of Jove and Venus, and through her operate the basic aspects of creation—light and form, darkness and matter, sky and earth, and, here, the sun and moon of Gnostic creation myth and the key symbols in the incestuous alchemical sacred marriage:

> Great father he of generation
> Is rightly cald, th'author of life and light;
> And his faire sister for creation
> Ministreth matter fit, which tempred right
> With heate and humour, breede the liuing wight.
> So sprong these twinnes in wombe of *Chrysogonee*.
>
> (9)

William Nelson has discussed in detail how the sun is the agency of divine influence, the transmitter of rational seeds/seminal reasons;[4] thus,

> reason teacheth that the fruitfull seades
> Of all things liuing, through impression
> Of the sunbeames in moyst complexion,
> Doe life conceiue and quickned are by kynd:
> So after *Nilus* invndation,
> Infinite shapes of creatures men doe fynd,
> Informed in the mud, on which the Sunne hath shynd.
>
> (8)

This is no simple linear transmission; as Nelson observes, "for Spenser, as for Plotinus, the lesson is that earthly love is a reflection, however pale and distorted, of the generative power of the divine . . . In the schoolroom of the Garden, Amoret is taught that sexual love and the pleasure of sexual intercourse are good because they perpetuate the varied life of this world which reflects or imitates the eternal unity of the Supreme" (222–23), which is androgynous.

Nelson cites and examines Spenser's possible sources, mainly Plotinus, for the constant organic variety figuring forth in the Garden of Adonis; but the sources are everywhere and nowhere—Spenser, as had Chaucer, teases scholars:

> But wondrously they were begot, and bred
> Through influence of th'heauens fruitfull ray,
> *As it in antique bookes is mentioned.*
>
> (6; emphasis added)

This is one way of reminding us that the Garden of Adonis is only one version of one aspect of the multifaceted, variously received phenomenon of creation as recorded in ancient, or natural, theology. Another way of reminding us of the multiple ways of understanding one story is Spenser's having bracketed the actual "garden" stanzas of Canto 6 with, on the one side, the two births generated *from above* nature into nature both of Chrysogonee and of her twin daughters and, on the other side, the birth of Pleasure from a mother and father *within* nature. Being careful not to imply that there is a laddered hierarchy of life, Spenser shows the figure of Venus herself to be fluid, for we see her in all her aspects: she is defined by where she is and by what she is doing. We experience Venus as an earthly presence, as a procreative force, as an informing principle, and as a hidden, heavenly source of all life.

When we first see her searching for Cupid in court, city, country, and unpopulated places, she is the comic Venus of accidental love, that chaotic interplay in life of desire and disdain. But this is the same Venus who comes down from heaven to her bower, "where most she wonnes, *when she on earth does dwel*" (29; emphasis added), becoming the procreative force of all of life, at the same time that she is a shaping force as well as a life-source. Thus, her home is on earth but is not of the earth; it is a "joyous Paradize" and a "blisfull bowre of joy aboue" the earth; it is a

> heauenly hous,
> The house of goodly formes and faire aspects,
> Whence all the world deriues the glorious
> Features of beauties, and all shapes select,
> With which high God his workmanship hath deckt.
>
> (12)

This sort of halfway house between God and the world is the abode of Dame Nature, or Venus Urania, since it has within the creative force of the Divine Essence, the Logos, Venus as Sapience in the bosom of God (see Picture II–6).

After his early earthly death, this became the eternal haven of Adonis:

> There now he liueth in eternall blis,
> Ioying his goddesse, and of her enioyd.
>
> (48)

Adonis, however, is forced to play the captive-maiden role, the kept one who must await visits from the protector:

There wont faire *Venus* often to enioy
Her deare *Adonis* joyous company,
And reape sweet pleasure of the wanton boy;
There yet, some say, in secret he does ly,
Lapped in flowres and pretious spycery,
By her hid from the world, and from the skill
of *Stygian* Gods, which doe her loue enuy;
But she her selfe, when euer that she will,
Possesseth him, and of his sweetnesse takes her fill.

(46)

The gods of the underworld of darkness seek to draw Adonis back into the nothingness of constantly shifting matter, but Venus's immortal juices keep Adonis in shape and in function as the father of all forms:

And sooth it seemes they say: for he may not
For euer die, and euer buried bee
In balefull night, where all things are forgot:
All be he subiect to mortalitie
Yet is eterne in mutabilitie,
And by succession made perpetuall,
Transformed oft, and chaunged diuerslie:
For him the Father of all formes they call;
Therefore needs mote he liue, that liuing giues to all.

(47)

If the gods of darkness had their way, the boar would achieve total not temporary victory over Adonis and life would be reduced to perpetual winter, death, destruction, chaos:

Ne feareth he henceforth that foe of his,
Which with his cruell tuske him deadly cloyed:
For that wilde Bore, the which him once annoyd,
She firmely hath emprisoned for ay,
That her sweet loue his malice mote auoyd,
In a strong rocky Caue, which is they say,
Hewen vnderneath that Mount, that none him losen may.

(48)

Because "that Mount" is a literal Mons Veneris (43, 44, 45), and the bower is her vagina, then the cave is her womb, the material source of life. The paradox of myth is plausible: Venus is a hermaphrodite who must penetrate her own vagina to enjoy her Adonis, who as a sun god becomes the creative force which infuses all matter, converting it to life. The intercourse of Venus and Adonis brings forth life, as symbolized by the Garden of Adonis:

> In that same Gardin all the goodly flowres,
> Wherewith dame Nature doth her beautifie,
> And decks the girlonds of her paramoures,
> Are fetcht: *there is the first seminarie*
> *Of all things*, that are borne to liue and die,
> According to their *kindes*.
>
> (30; emphasis added)

Located "in fruitful soyle of old," the garden is Eden before the Fall; it is the Golden World that Gonzalo dreams about in *The Tempest*:

> Ne needs there Gardiner to set, or sow,
> To plant or prune: for of their owne accord
> All things, as they created were, doe grow.
>
> (34)

> For here all plentie, and all pleasure flowes,
> And sweet loue gentle fits emongst them throwes,
> Without fell rancor, or fond gealosie;
> Franckly each paramour his leman knowes.
>
> (41)

Because Spenser wants to present a vision of life that is process, is growth, is learning and development through change, Time is in the Garden, but not Time the grim reaper. That comes after the Fall, when man's first disobedience brought death into the world and all our woe. But death (the end part of Time, both personal and cosmic) is potentially present in the Garden, underneath the mountain, in the womb of earth—dust thou art, to dust thou shall return. And without death there could be no life, for if the boar had not killed Adonis, Adonis could not live forever. Because Adonis had to be freed from his body in order to be the constructive spirit of life, the suggestion is enforced that the boar is a necessary element in the creation process. Venus through Adonis infuses the earth with the spirit of life, but the earth itself must have its stock of matter:

> Yet is the stocke not lessened, nor spent,
> But still remaines in euerlasting store,

> As it at first created was of yore.
> For in the wide wombe of the world there lyes,
> In hatefull darkenesse and in deepe horrore,
> An huge eternall Chaos, which supplyes
> The substances of natures fruitful progenyes.
>
> (36)

Thus Venus as the shaping force of life is its source both as Idea and as material. She is herself both blind Cupid with the golden arrow and the castrating boar; she is both love and hate:

> All things from thence doe their first being fetch,
> And borrow matter, whereof they are made,
> Which when as forme and feature it does ketch,
> Becomes a bodie, and doth then inuade
> The state of life, out of the griesly shade.
> That substance is eterne, and bideth so,
> Ne when the life decayes, and forme does fade,
> Doth it consume, and into nothing go,
> But chaunged is, and often altred to and fro.
>
> (37)

> The substance is not chaunged, not altered,
> But th'only forme and outward fashion;
> For euery substance is conditioned
> To change her hew, and sundry formes to don,
> Meet for her temper and complexion:
> For formes are variable and decay,
> By course of kind, and by occasion.
>
> (38)

There is no life without death, no light without dark, no form without matter. And that Chaos is the source of Death we are reminded by Marlowe in "Hero and Leander," when the Destinies offer Mercury the "fatall knife/That sheares the slender threads of life" which they had brought up to the "earth from ouglly Chaos."

The controlling spirit of this garden is life, "Old Genius, the which a double nature has" (31)—Dame Nature naturized as male, for we can guess that Genius has a staff; his counterpart, the false Genius of the false garden of that false Venus, Acrasia, has one. Because the Garden of Adonis is Life, our birth into life is a kind of death ("we came crying hither"), but because we return to the Garden, our death in life is a kind of birth, a rebirth.

Belphoebe's conception, like that of the Virgin, was free of sin:

> Her berth was of the wombe of Morning dew,
> And her conception of the ioyous Prime,
> And all her whole creation did her shew
> Pure and vnspotted from all loathly crime,
> That is ingenerate in fleshly slime.

But even a Belphoebe, once living, must be trained and taught, must be nurtured:

> So was this virgin borne, so was she bred,
> So was she trayned vp from time to time,
> In all chast vertue, and true bounti-hed
> *Till to her dew perfection she was ripened.*
>
> (3; emphasis added)

So, too, with Amoret, whom Venus

> farre away conuayd,
> To be vpbrought in goodly womanhed,
> And in her little loues stead, which was strayd,
> Her *Amoretta* cald, to comfort her dismayd.
>
> (28)

A little love takes the place of a little love, and this time Venus seems to want to get it right: instead of a wide-ranging phallic troubler, she wants a nourishing figure of caring. Cupid returns, is reconciled both to his mother and to Psyche; Cupid and Psyche marry and bring forth Pleasure; the body and soul, united as one, create pleasure. To her bower, which Adonis and Cupid and Psyche and Pleasure all inhabit,

> Hither great *Venus* brought this infant faire,
> The younger daughter of Chrysogonee,
> And vnto *Psyche* with great trust and care
> Committed her, yfostered to bee,
> And *trained vp in true feminitee*:
> Who no lesse carefully her tendered,
> Then her owne daughter *Pleasure*, to whom shee
> Made her companion, and her lessoned

In all the lore of loue, and goodly womanhead.

(51; emphasis added)

In which *when she to perfect ripenesse grew*,
Of grace and beautie noble Paragone,
She brought her forth into the worldes vew,
To be th'ensample of true loue alone,
And Lodestarre of all chaste affectione,
To all faire Ladies, that doe liue on ground.

(52; emphasis added)

Belphoebe and Amoret are, of course, the real projections of the abstracted goddesses Diana and Venus, twinned to emphasize that what each stands for, so does the other: together they define womanhood. But we must note that Belphoebe has claim for more respect because she is the elder. Still, "married chastity" is merely an extension of virginal chastity, and Britomart, to be fully a woman, must absorb the behavior traits learned both by Belphoebe and by Amoret. But to be fully human, to grow beyond womanhood toward humanhood, Britomart must also absorb within her being "male" virtues as well. She has undertaken the essay toward androgyny, which is a constant process of learning and growth.

Emblematically informing this need of Britomart to fuse the female and the male virtues is Spenser's special version of the Venus genetrix myth in which Venus is God/father/male and Adonis is matter/mother/female. Through variety and repetition, in Canto 6 of Book III of *The Faerie Queene* the vast range of the myth of androgyny is uniquely suggested.

2
CONFOUNDING "NATURES SWEET HARMONY": MARLOWE'S "HERO AND LEANDER"

The Garden of Adonis and the House of Busirane are living emblems to show us indirectly what Britomart must and will discover within herself about the complementary forces in life of love and hate, sexual desire and sexual lust, pleasure and pain. Marlowe in "Hero and Leander" concentrates directly on the experience of these forces in life. The poem is a delightfully comic story of two young lovers ignorantly, innocently struggling to express and experience their feelings for one another, totally unaware of how typical and how ancient are their conscious and unconscious behaviors. 'Tis new to them.

Early on, Hero is identified as Venus, literally taken for her by Cupid, "so like was one the other,/As he imagyn'd *Hero* was his mother" (40). In fact, Hero is so radiant that, "some say," Cupid, "looking in her face, was strooken blind" (138). This radiance allies Hero with Venus Urania, the Sun, and God, for her sheer beauty rules and controls all who see her at Sestos at the annual spring rite of "Rose-cheekt Adonis" (93), collectively so radiant themselves that their coming together is like a new meeting of sky and earth:

> For euerie street like to a Firmament
> Glistered with breathing stars, who where they went,
> Frighted the melancholie earth, which deem'd
> Eternall heauen to burne, for so it seem'd,
> As if another *Phaeton* had got
> The guidance of the sunnes rich chariot.
>
> (97–102).

Within this tension between light and dark, Hero represents the creative urge of the universe to move toward unity and harmony:

> But far aboue the loueliest *Hero* shin'd,
> And stole away th'inchaunted gazers mind,
> For like Sea-nimphs inueigling harmony,
> So was her beautie to the standers by.
>
> (103–106)

When Marlowe goes on to compare Hero to the moon as well as the sun (the brother and sister of Gnostic and alchemical marriage), he suggests that she has within her beauty the two contrasting but necessary ingredients of creation, the two-sexes-in-one of Venus as Dame Nature. Indeed, this alliance to creation and to the creative force of Dame Nature is made specific. "Since Heroes time, hath halfe the world beene blacke" (50).

This suggestion is further strengthened by Marlowe's three times calling Hero "*Venus* Nun," a vestal virgin who honors the source of life by carrying out sacred rituals and mysteries in Venus's temple. Indeed, she even surpasses Dame Nature: "So louely faire was *Hero*, *Venus* Nun,/As nature wept, thinking she was undone" (45–46). But when we recall that "nun" was an Elizabethan cant word for whore, and when we pay attention to the scenes portrayed within the Temple in "*Venus* glass" (142) (a kind of MTV survey of the gods in action), we are reminded of the range of the Venus principle from the rational seeds of Sapience to Venus's disease and *cupiditas*. Hero has within the potential to be any and all.

Role-reversal in "Hero and Leander" is on the surface, but serves the purpose of breaking down gender separation to push for sexual bonding. Marlowe describes Hero's attire as if she were a knight on his way to a court tournament, and has as much fun in satirizing the extravagance of the kind of accoutrement so dear to a Sidney as did Nashe in describing Surrey in *The Unfortunate Traveller*. Leander is described, of course, as having the pure beauty of a simple maid, and Marlowe summarizes the effect he wished to achieve: "Some swore he was a maid in mans attire" (83). Leander could play "the woman's part." But when we hear that the moon longs for him, Endymion-like, and when we listen to him being typically male, Jack Tanner-like, talking, talking, talking, we catch him in the male role as the formative force in life (Logos, name-giving, rhetoric—Prospero teaching Caliban the names of the lesser light and the greater).

Marlowe brings Hero and Leander together literally and figuratively through the story of the coming together of Salamacis and Hermaphroditus (son of Hermes/Mercury and Aphrodite/Venus), whose coupling created Hermaphrodite, whose two-sexes-in-one brings us back to creation myth yet again: "And like light *Salamacis*, her body throes/Vpon his bosome" (46–47). At this first encounter, both blindly grope, but Marlowe is careful to put their lovemaking in the context of that old dance of the Wife of Bath:

> But know you not that creatures wanting sence
> By nature haue a mutuall appetence,
> And wanting organs to aduaunce a step,
> Mou'd by Loues force, vnto ech other lep?
> Much more in subiects hauing intellect,
> Some hidden influence breeds like effect.
> Albeit *Leander* rude in loue, and raw,
> Long dallying with *Hero*, nothing saw
> That might delight him more, yet he suspected
> Some amorous rites or other were neglected.
> Therefore vnto his bodie hirs he clung,
> She, fearing on the rushes to be flung,
> Striu'd with redoubled strength: the more she striued,
> The more a gentle pleasing heat reuiued,
> Which taught him all that elder louers know.
>
> (II, 55–69)

Their parting this first time is within the course of a natural dawn, but not without foreshadowing the a-natural dawn of their second parting:

> Now had the morne espy'de her louers steeds,

Whereat she starts, puts on her purple weeds,
And *red for anger* that he stayd so long,
All headlong throwes her selfe the clouds among.

(87–90; emphasis added)

The sexual consummation of their next and last encounter is prefigured in Hero's taking off and Leander's putting on of Venus's ring at the end of this first encounter:

The sacred ring wherewith she was endow'd,
When first religious chastitie she vow'd.

(109–10)

When Leander returns naked the next night, Hero rushes to open the door even before covering her own near-naked self,

Where seeing a naked man, she scriecht for feare,
Such sights as this to tender maids are rare,
And ran into the darke herselfe to hide.

(237–39)

But Hero cannot hide her beauty; it shines: "Rich iewels in the darke are soonest spide" (240). When she takes her "siluer body" back to bed, Leander can easily follow her and climbs in:

Herewith afrighted *Hero* shrunke away,
And in her luke-warme place *Leander* lay,
Whose liuely heat like fire from heauen fet,
Would animate grosse clay, and higher set
The drooping thoughts of base declining soules,
Then drerie *Mars* carowsing *Nectar* boules.

(235–58)

And we are back in the mythic world of Venus Urania, Sidney's Urania of the *New Arcadia* (and Milton's muse in *Paradise Lost*), the creation of Adam, and the Titan Prometheus. When Hero "dyu'd downe to hide her" (262) under the covers Marlowe adds an ominous reminder of the omnipresence of "dim and darksome" Chaos:

And as her siluer body downeward went,

With both her hands she made the bed a tent,
And in her owne mind thought her selfe secure,
O'recast with dim and darksome couerture.

(263–66)

Within this context of radiance and no light, Hero and Leander go through the movements of the first dance, the cosmic dance of creation, combining the anguish of the House of Busirane with the pleasure of the Bower of Venus:

Loue is not ful of pittie (as men say)
But deaffe and cruell, where he meanes to pray.
Euen as a bird, which in our hands we wring,
Foorth plungeth, and oft flutters with her wing,
She trembling stroue, this strife of hers (like that
Which made the world) another world began
Of vnknowne joy.

(287–93)

Their intercourse is a reenactment of creation as sketched by Heraclitus, Lucretius, and the Gnostic Gospels. Marlowe extends the description in an heroic vein:

Leander now like Theban *Hercules*,
Entred the orchard of *Th'esperides*,
Whose fruit none rightly can describe but hee
That puls or shakes it from the golden tree:
And now she wisht this night were neuer done,
And sigh'd to thinke vpon th'approching sunne,
For much it greeu'd her that the bright day-light
Should know the pleasure of this blessed night,
And them like *Mars* and *Ericine* display,
Both in each others armes chaind as they lay.

(297–305)

Adam and Eve, Mars and Venus, Cupid and Psyche, Jove and Themis, Uranus and Tellus, Sun and Moon, Day and Night, Light and Dark, Form and Matter, Logos and Chaos—eros creating, creating life, the world, content, pleasure.

At this point Marlowe, anticipating John Donne in "The Sunne Rising," reverses the usual direction of myth, for Hero's naked, earthly, human beauty here is so powerful that it not only figuratively lights up the room, it literally brings "foorth the day before the day" should be born. Hero slips out of bed, her embarrassment compounded as Leander embraces her:

> Thus neere the bed she blushing stood vpright,
> And from her countenance behold ye might
> A kind of twilight breake, which through the heare,
> As from an orient cloud, glymse here and there.
> And round about the chamber this false morne
> Brought foorth the day before the day was borne.
>
> (317–22)

In "Hero and Leander," as in *Dr. Faustus*, Marlowe welcomes the high Renaissance to England. Humankind takes stage-center. Human beauty has the power to control the world:

> By this *Apollos* golden harpe began
> To sound foorth musicke to the *Ocean*,
> Which watchful *Hesperus* no sooner heard,
> But he the day bright-bearing Car prepar'd,
> And ran before, as Harbenger of light,
> And with his flaring beames mockt ougly night,
> Till she o'recome with anguish, shame, and rage,
> Dang'd downe to hell her loathsome carriage.
>
> (327–34)

Understanding Marlowe's secular myth allows us to experience the end of the poem as triumph. The powers of darkness are vanquished, not darkness simply as evil, but darkness as formlessness, mere motion, absence of purpose, un-informed matter, the absence of light—nothingness. The emphasis is on the energies of human sexuality, which have the power to conquer chaos, to mock ugly night with human fire.

In spite of Chapman's, or the printer's, "Desunt nonnulla," Marlowe's poem lacks nothing; he has made his point: humanity is not just at the center of creation; creation is centered in humanity. Once again the gods are jealous of and angry at the fun-loving androgyne.

3
"THE TEXT IS OLD, THE ORATOR TOO GREEN": SHAKESPEARE'S "VENUS AND ADONIS"

Shakespeare begins where Marlowe ends:

> Even as the sun with purple-colored face
> Had ta'en his last leave of the weeping morn,
> Rose-cheeked Adonis hied him to the chase.
>
> (1–3)

Role reversal begins immediately, with Venus the suitor, the talker:

> Hunting he loved, but love he laughed to scorn.
> Sick-thoughted Venus makes amain unto him
> And like a bold-faced suitor 'gins to woo him.
>
> (4–6)

But Venus is a goddess and need not plead at all, a fact which provides a continuously running irony underneath the text of the poem as well as the texts of what she has to say. Adonis is described in womanly terms similar to those used to describe Leander, but the hyperbole of Dame Nature's jealousy that was applied to Hero is here applied to Adonis, when Venus says that hermaphroditic Nature naturizing outdid herself:

> "Thrice fairer than myself," thus she began,
> "*The field's chief flower*, sweet above compare,
> Stain to all nymphs, more lovely than a man,
> More white and red than doves or roses are,
> Nature that made thee, with herself at strife,
> Saith that the world hath ending with thy life."
>
> (7–12; emphasis added)

Although this points to what some would say is the "serious" ending of the poem in a double death, of man and flower, basically, as Norman Rabkin has observed, the poem is comic.[5] The comedy of Amazonian Venus's assault on the boy Adonis by prowess of word and body, the irony of Venus's appeals to the "law of nature" from which she is exempt and to the example of the behavior of animals from which Adonis is excluded, and the variety of tones and attitudes which permeate the poem are all worthy of extended comment. But what is shared in all aspects of the poem is the essential element of comedy, detachment, and that detachment serves to make a point similar to that of "Hero and Leander": the worlds of gods and men are separate. The mythic elements in the poem, as in "Nature that made thee, with herself at strife," refer to humanity as the focal point. Throughout the poem, Adonis is associated with the sun:

> "O thou clear god, and patron of all light,
> From whom each lamp and shining star doth borrow
> The beauteous influence that makes him bright,
> There lives a son *that sucked an earthly mother*
> May lend thee light, as thou doest lend to other."
>
> (860–64; emphasis added)

But as this stanza implies, Adonis is human; he is an "earthly sun" (198): he is both the father of all forms and himself the chief living example of human beauty, male and/or female. One could cite Shakespeare's stanza describing Adonis's horse as the kind of description which could be appropriated to describe Adonis:

> Look when a painter would surpass the life
> In limning out a well-proportioned steed,
> His art with nature's workmanship at strife,
> As if the dead the living should exceed—
>   So did this horse excel a common one
>   In shape, in courage, color, pace, and bone.
>
> (289–94)

Because of Adonis's extreme beauty, even the chaste Diana, according to Venus, wants Adonis; the night is totally dark because

> "'thy lips
> Make modest Dian cloudy and forlorn,
> Lest she should steal a kiss and die forsworn.
>
> "Now of this dark night I perceive the reason:
> Cynthia for shame obscures her silver shine,
> Till forging Nature be condemned of treason
> For stealing moulds from heaven that were divine;
> Wherein she framed thee, in high heaven's despite,
> To shame the sun by day, and her by night."

Diana's reported desire for revenge on the world of great creating nature foreshadows Venus's closing prophecy:

> "And therefore hath she bribed the Destinies
> To cross the curious workmanship of Nature,
> To mingle beauty with infirmities
> And pure perfection with impure defeature,
> Making it subject to the tyranny
> Of mad mischances and much misery;
>
> "As burning fevers, agues pale and faint,
> Life-poisoning pestilence, and frenzies wood,
> The marrow-eating sickness whose attaint
> Disorder breeds by heating of the blood,
> Surfeits, imposthumes, grief, and damned despair
> Swear Nature's death for framing thee so fair."
>
> (724–44)

Venus states that Cynthia has already put "forging Nature" into disarray because Adonis is so fair, and Venus will increase this disorder upon his death: thanks both to Cynthia and Venus the course of true love never will run smooth. But the goddesses do not kill Adonis; the boar does. Death and the boar are synonymous, and both are associated with "ugly night," ugly being the code word for chaos:

> "Hard-favored tyrant, ugly, meagre, lean,
> Hateful divorce of love!"—thus chides she Death—
> "Grim-grinning ghost, earth's worm, what dost thou mean
> To stifle beauty and to steal his breath
> Who, when he lived, his breath and beauty set
> Gloss on the rose, smell to the violet?
>
> "If he be dead—O no, it cannot be,
> Seeing his beauty, thou shoudst strike at it!
> O yes, it may! Thou hast no eyes to see,
> But hatefully at random dost thou hit . . .
>
> "Love's golden arrow at him should have fled,
> And not Death's ebon dart to strike him dead.
> . . . .
> Now Nature cares not for thy mortal vigor,
> Since her best work is ruined with thy rigor."
>
> (931–54)

Venus states that Adonis must live until doom's day:

> must not die
> "Till mutual overthrow of mortal kind!
> For he being dead, with him is beauty slain,
> And, beauty dead, black chaos comes again." (1017–20)

When he is dead, beauty's pattern is broken:

> "Alas, poor world, what treasure hast thou lost!
> What face remains alive that's worth the viewing?
> Whose tongue is music now? What canst thou boast
> Of things long since, or any thing ensuing?
> The flowers are sweet, their colors fresh and trim;
> But true-sweet beauty lived and died with him."
>
> (1075–80)

Thus, Adonis is Adam before Eve, or is perfect androgyne-beauty. And that beauty is so great that even the boar sought to make love with Adonis:

> "Witness the entertainment that he gave.
> If he did see his face, why then I know
> He thought to kiss him, and hath killed him so . . .
>
> "But by a kiss thought to persuade him there;
> And nuzzling in his flank, the loving swine
> Sheathed unaware the tusk in his soft groin."
>
> (1105–16)

On a deep level of myth the poem is completed: form and matter, sun and earth have met and kissed, have interpenetrated each other. Each spring blood must be shed on the land. Just as high Venus must penetrate her own vagina in order to reach enwombed matter, so the hunter Adonis must pierce and be pierced by the boar. The king must die.

But Venus continues:

> "Had I been toothed like him, I must confess,
> With kissing him I should have killed him first."
>
> (1117–18)

Now that the courtship is over, the truth can be told—no one is around to hear. And her basic indifference to life and her goddess-sanctioned indifference to what humans call truth are revealed:

> "But he is dead, and never did he bless
> My youth with his—the more am I accurst."
>
> (1119–20)

Her "prophesy" is no prophesy at all, as Richard Lanham has argued,[6] but a report of Venus's curse on the world, her spread of the venereal and of random *cupiditas* within an already fallen, subluminary world. Her ego can claim that human discord arose because "in his prime death doth my love destroy" (1163), but the actions of this Venus from the beginning show how far from concord is her conception of love, *here*.

The metamorphosis takes place, Adonis becoming an anemone. But Shakespeare is mocking metamorphosis because from the beginning Adonis was in Venus's eyes merely a flower, a pretty natural thing. Venus, continuing to intercede within nature's processes, plucks Adonis as flower (an act of death, see line 946) as easily as she had plucked Adonis alive from his horse:

> She crops the stalk, and in the breach appears
> Green-dropping sap, which she compares to tears.
>
> (1175–76)

Her indifference to the green world of the biosphere (the vegetable soul) is shown when she admits that the flower really would prefer to grow to natural maturity, as would have Adonis:

> "To grow unto himself was his desire,
> And so 'tis thine."
>
> (1180–81)

And, with equal disregard for boy and flower, she arrogantly sets her own goddess-centered values up over those of life:

> "but know, it is as good
> To wither in my breast as in his blood."
>
> (1181–82)

Which is as much as to say that Adonis would be better off dead, having been killed by me, than having been allowed to follow his desire:

"Fair queen," quoth he, "if any love you owe me,
Measure my strangeness with my unripe years.
Before I know myself, seek not to know me."

(534–35)

The intertwined questions of knowledge (self-knowledge and sexual knowledge) and of generation are poignantly caught here, and even at the outset Venus had recognized that Adonis was "unripe" (128). But goddesses are goddesses and cannot be convicted for child molestation or attempt to rape.

The next to last stanza of the poem continues in prevarication and self-serving impossibility:[7]

"Here was thy father's bed, here in my breast;
Thou art the next of blood, and 'tis thy right.
Lo, in the hollow cradle take thy rest;
My throbbing heart shall rock thee day and night.
  There shall not be one minute in an hour
  Wherein I will not kiss my sweet love's flow'r."

(1183–88)

At least until the next target of opportunity should appear. Then she departs:

  Thus weary of the world, away she hies
And yokes her silver doves, by whose swift aid
Their mistress, mounted, through the empty skies
In her light chariot quickly is conveyed,
  Holding their course to Paphos, where their queen
  Means to immure herself and not be seen.

(1189–94)

At least, not until . . . tomorrow, at least.

The poem shows a comic mismatch from beginning to end. (Some might say mish-mash.) Venus is a goddess, is immortal; she can appear as any kind she may wish because she is free of the limitations of time and space. Adonis is human and mortal and can only change by determined exercise of will within the defining strictures of space-time, within kind. Yes, "to grow unto himself was his desire."

The text is old, the orator too green.

Richard N. Ringler has suggested that one of the "reasons" for the Faunus episode of the *Two Cantos* which separates Mutabilitie's complaint against Jove from the actual trial or hearing is to deny the claims of metamorphosis in life.[8] The age of miracles is past. Our fates lie not in our stars but in ourselves. By denying metamorphosis, Spenser emphasizes the significance of Nature's ultimate judgment. In Canto 6 of Book III the emphasis is on the organic and the earthly. The Destinies and Mercury episode which divides "Hero and Leander" has the same kind of reinforcement of a basic theme of the whole poem: the Fates and gods no longer affect our lives (unless we are scholars). The madly mating horses in "Venus and Adonis" likewise serve to emphasize the point of separation which must be accepted: gods are gods, humans are humans, and animals are animals. Humankind finds itself partaking of higher and lower, but can never be higher and should never be lower.

Spenser, Marlowe, and Shakespeare are playing with myth, playing around as in experimenting, and they end up transmuting myth, they secularize myth, they de-classic-fy myth. They show that the ancient stories of creation are our stories. They are fictions which we ourselves invent. The essay toward androgyny is essentially making myth.

7

"Half sleep, half waking": A Midsummer Night's Dream

Shakespeare's earlier young lovers are not quite so self-aware as was young Adonis, but they surely are self-conscious, seeking to know who they are by wondering what they are. Indeed, in his first comedies (those played before "Venus and Adonis" was published in 1593: *The Comedy of Errors*, *The Taming of the Shrew*, *Two Gentlemen of Verona*, and *Love's Labor's Lost*) Shakespeare makes "role" and "identity" central to plot, character, and theme.[1] The concentration of this concern comes after "Venus and Adonis" in *A Midsummer Night's Dream*, where these motifs are developed in comparison and contrast at four levels: the heroic, the psychological, the personal, and the social. The theater world, the dream world, and the green world are all places where one can step out of "role" because the immediate context of social pressure is removed. Stepping into a theater, we leave reality outside, and the re-creation of a new reality does not take place onstage but in the theater of our mind. In sleep we are at the mercy of ourselves; external reality is translated, transmuted, transfigured into things rich and strange: reifications uniquely ours, private possessions, our own property. Our dreams are more real than reality, which is what Prospero tells us when he says that our little life is rounded with a sleep, which makes life a dream. And getting away from the new news of the new court, getting out of society, being closer to nature, our own and the world's, we can more easily discover, and be, ourselves. In all three worlds, one can learn to grow and to develop and to become, properly, one's self. Shakespeare's comic world (theatrical, dream, green) ultimately refers us back to the social world, where we must dwell, but taking with us on return discoveries experienced in the theater world,[2] the dream world,[3] the green world:[4] the inner world.

The questions "Who am I?" and "What am I?" ring throughout *The*

Comedy of Errors. Proteus and Valentine in *Two Gentlemen of Verona* seem as trapped within the meanings of their names as they are by the standard schoolboy *topos*, "love vs. friendship." The young lords of *Love's Labor's Lost* seek to know themselves through learning, but are woefully unprepared to undertake the journey. And Kate the shrew in *The Taming of the Shrew* must be tamed to Katherina the wife before she is socially acknowledged—her identity is forced upon her. In all four plays, the young are prisoners of role, both personal and social. Andriana in *The Comedy of Errors* struggles in and against her roles as woman and wife; Antipholus of Syracuse does not know whether he is a single stranger or a coupled citizen of Ephesus; and the Dromios are confused of a sudden because each seems no longer to be a proficient servant to his master. In *Two Gentlemen of Verona* no apparent resolution seems possible to the apparent conflict between male love for a man and male love for a woman. In *Love's Labor's Lost*, the lords cannot become scholars, cannot play Russians, and are not permitted simply to assume the role of lover until some testing, some assurances of change, some maturing takes place—but *after* the play is over. And in *The Taming of the Shrew*, Kate seems to give up her struggle with role and identity when no one in her world will allow her to be the kind of woman she is by nature and by nurture.

In all of these first plays, comedy is generated by the conflict between self and society's expectations of self, but in none is there any sense of a self-aware, self-generated resolution to this age-old human dichotomy and staple of comedy. *A Midsummer Night's Dream* may not present resolute answers, but the love-plot of the play searches and suggests solutions. Although all of the earliest comedies had more than one plot-line, the context of the love plot in *A Midsummer Night's Dream* is much richer and much more dense. Both the overplot and the underplot (to borrow one word from Harry Levin and to coin a new one based on his innovation in order to identify the heroic plot of Theseus and Hippolyta and the psychic plot of Oberon and Titania: the antique fable and the fairy toy) provide resonance for and reflection of the central, personal plot: the sounds and actions of the young lovers. The overplot and the underplot are both myths, one epic and one folk, one elevated above the ordinary and public, one submerged in the ordinary and private; and they are similar, as the stage tradition of doubling of Theseus and Oberon and of Hippolyta and Titania shows. Both couples, like the sky and earth, have power over humans and are types of Mars and Venus (with Puck the Cupid of Oberon and Titania—or is it the changeling boy, whom Oberon may have fathered?). Theseus, all reason, is a god on earth, commanding certain public behavior. Oberon, all magic, is a god within, disturbing psychic patterns of private behavior. Hippolyta, Queen of the Amazons, an archetype of female assertiveness and independence (now sadly curbed), is so softly sympathetic that she is moved by "the story of the night." And Titania is a goddess of the moon richly associated with change and fertility.[5] Each of the four, in different ways, controls the personal lives of the four young people.

The escape from the populated world to the deserted, from the public to the psychic, from the daylight world of ordered action to the night-time world of chaotic accident, from the bright marble world of Athens to the dark green world outside the palace walls, frees each of the young from conventional demands to discover and test inner needs and desires. At the beginning of the play Hermia and Lysander are types of young lovers right out of Greek and Roman literature, who plot to trick a stern father by escaping to a dowager aunt who will solve their problems for them. Helena, Echo-like, would be anyone, anything rather than be herself. And Demetrius, still a Narcissus, has been so frightened by the mystery of what he feels for Helena that he willingly accedes to Egeus's plan to arrange a marriage for him. All four, in self confusion, follow the way of adolescence: flight. Keep moving before your self catches up with you.

Once in the circle of the forest they are caught up in confrontation with self and with the other(s). Only when each is able to reach far and deep enough into self to discover and to admit that she or he hates, in part, the other(s), can each begin to build a respect for another that is based on a new discovery: a new, major acceptance of self. Metamorphoses begin to take place before our eyes, not where expected, in the play of "Pyramus and Thisby," but in the play of the young lovers performed on a "green plot" marked by "the Duke's Oak" (1.2.98), the perfect vaginal/phallic setting for celebration of the initiations within the "rite of May" (4.1.132).

Theseus, referring to the four lovers as wood nymphs and invoking the ceremonies both of May Day and of Saint Valentine's Day, acts as a chorus, speaking as if he, as well as we, had been witness to the dark night of anguish, jealousy, and hate:

> How comes this gentle concord in the world
> That hatred is so far from jealousy
> To sleep by hate and fear no enmity?
>
> (4.1.142–44)

Theseus's words suggest an awakening in a new world, and the responses of Lysander and Demetrius confirm that the young lovers have been wandering in an ancient maze and fell asleep at the center where the realization of love is permitted. Or, like the lover in the *Romance of the Rose*, Lysander has been admitted into the Garden by Genius:

My lord, I shall reply *amazedly*,
Half sleep, half waking; but as yet, I swear,
I cannot truly say how I came here.
But, as I think (for truly would I speak),
And now I do bethink me, so it is—
I came with Hermia hither.

(145–50; emphasis added)

Demetrius had followed "in fury," and Helena "in fancy": both irrational emotions. But Demetrius has grown into man's estate, and put away his childish behavior:

But my good lord, I wot not by what power
(But by some power it is) my love to Hermia,
Melted as the snow, seems to be now
As the remembrance of an idle gaud
Which in my childhood I did dote upon.

(163–67)

Now he feels rational emotions and has reached a healthy, balanced state:

And all the faith, the virtue of my heart,
The object and the pleasure of mine eye,
Is only Helena. To her, my lord,
Was I betrothed ere I saw Hermia,
But, like a sickness, did I loathe this food;
But, as in health, *come to my natural taste*,
Now I do wish it, love it, long for it,
And will for evermore be true to it.

(168–75; emphasis added)

Within this show of concord the harsh rules of Athens are waived and the young couples are invited to augment the public ceremony of marriage between the mythic heroes, and they will be strengthened within because of the reunion of Oberon and Titania, who will no longer "square" (which had forced all their followers to "creep into acorn cups and hide them there"). At the beginning of the play, in the absence of controlling, ordering love, chaos surged up from the bowels of the earth. Discord became rampant in the world when Oberon and Titania were at odds:

The spring, the summer
The childing autumn, angry winter change

Their wonted liveries; and the mazed world,
By their, increase, now knows not which is which.
And this same progeny of evils comes
From our debate, from our dissension;
We are their parents and original.

(111–17)

But now that they are even, the penalty of Adam—at least for now—will also be waived, permitting immaculate conceptions:

Now, until the break of day,
Through this house each fairy stray.
To the best bride-bed will we,
Which by us shall blessed be;
And the issue there create
Ever shall be fortunate.
So shall all the couples three
Ever true in loving be;
And the blots of Nature's hand
Shall not in their issue stand.
Never mole, harelip, no scar,
Nor mark prodigious, such as are
Despised in nativity,
Shall upon their children be.
With this field-dew consecrate,
Every fairy take his gait,
And each several chamber bless,
Through this palace, with sweet peace.

(5.1.390–407)

But this comes later.

After Theseus and Hippolyta and their hunting party leave (this time, Diana has disturbed Venus), the remarks of the four young people are complementary: each one speaks for all in a quadralogue of one. And the reconciliations here, unlike those of the early comedies, are not only one with another, but are also reconciliations with self. Each of the four has learned the lesson of "The Phoenix and Turtle," where "either was the other's mine," signifying that one can possess without possessing and can be possessed without being possessed, if one is self-possessed without being selfish. Such awarenesses are a waking up, simultaneously so and not so:

DEMETRIUS
These things seem small and undistinguishable,

Like far-off mountains turnèd into clouds.
HERMIA
Methinks I see these things with parted eye,
When everything seems double.
HELENA
So methinks;
And I have found Demetrius like a jewel,
Mine own, and not mine own.
DEMETRIUS
Are you sure
That we are awake? It seems to me
That yet we sleep, we dream. Do not you think
The Duke was here, and bid us follow him?
HERMIA
Yea, and my father.
HELENA
And Hippolyta.
LYSANDER
And he did bid us follow to the temple.
DEMETRIUS
Why then, we are awake. Let's follow him,
And by the way let us recount our dreams.

(4.1.186–99)

This clearly is a liminal moment, a moment of growth, of maturing.[6] Something has happened, something strange and admirable, as Hippolyta is persuaded when the story of the night is told. But what has happened can only be experienced as a dream, not a dream triggered by an internal physical disorder which provokes images of mere fancy, but a dream such as Adam experienced, as in Keats' account of the truth of the imagination: "He awoke and found it true."

Bottom, too, awakes, he thinks, from a dream. How else can one explain his "most rare vision"? Prologue to both of these dream sequences is Oberon's casual remark added after he had instructed Puck to remove Bottom's ass-head:

He awaking when the other do,
May all to Athens back again repair,
And think no more of this night's accidents
But as the fierce vexation of a dream.

(4.1.65–68)

Jung would have leapt with joy at this remark, for vexation is the alchemist's term for that agitation of the Philosopher's egg, or vessel of Hermes, needed to achieve the alchemical, or sacred, marriage, an act of love taking place within the mind both on the part of the alchemist and within the *vas*, a bringing together of opposites in conception, an ecstatic moment most often anticipated in a dream-vision.[7] The lovers have indeed been "transfigured" and Bottom has indeed been "translated" within the fierce vexation of a midsummer night's dream. And just as the lovers are compelled to recount their dreams, so must Bottom (so must we all).

But first Bottom has to establish that he is alone—that none of the cast is lingering about. Then, in the rich tradition of the stage-clown, which evolved into the more sophisticated soliloquy ("Now, I am alone . . ."), Bottom is free to turn to the audience to share with us the privacy of his experience:

> I have had a most rare vision. I have had a
> dream, past the wit of man to say what dream it
> was. Man is but an ass if he go about to expound
> this dream. Methought I was—there is no man can
> tell what. Methought I was, and methought I had
> —But man is but a patched fool if he will offer
> to say what methought I had. The eye of man hath
> not heard, the ear of man hath not seen, man's
> hand is not able to taste, his tongue to
> conceive, nor his heart to report what my dream
> was. I will get Peter Quince to write a ballet
> of this dream. It shall be called "Bottom's
> Dream," because it hath no bottom.
>
> (203–15)

Bottom's story (his connection with Titania *and* Peter Quince's play) is the fourth major plot element in *A Midsummer Night's Dream*, the social element—the established, the expected, the normal, the insistently conservative. Bottom, like Adam, establishes reality by giving names to things, by putting things in their place. This is the way to make things real. To Bottom all things are real, and he can be all things: man or woman, beast or stone. He is the totally accepting fool-in-Christ who is capable of piercing to the bottom of God's secrets, which have no bottom.[8] Bottom may be an ass, the lowest of creatures, but he is also a fool, the highest of creatures. As Christ was an androgyne, so also is Bottom.

Hippolyta would understand; Theseus would not. To him, Bottom's Dream would be only the babbling of a lunatic. Theseus does not believe the story of the lovers, as does Hippolyta; why then should he believe a madman?

I never may believe
These antic fables nor these fairy toys.
Lovers and madmen have such seething brains,
Such shaping fantasies, that apprehend
More than cool reason ever comprehends.

(5.1.2–6)

In creating these words, Shakespeare delightfully has Theseus deny his own being through his restricted vision, his reliance on "cool reason." Shakespeare's own alliance to the right reason of the lovers and of Bottom is definitive:

The lunatic, the lover, and the poet
Are of imagination all compact.
One sees more devils than vast hell can hold: •
That is the madman. The lover, all as frantic,
Sees Helen's beauty in a brow of Egypt.
The poet's eye, in a fine frenzy rolling,
Both glance from heaven to earth, from earth to heaven;
And as imagination bodies forth
The forms of things unknown, the poet's pen
Turns them to shapes, and gives to airy nothing
A local habitation and a name.

(7–17)

Theseus, tied to "cool reason," could never range freely in the zodiac of his own wit; he can only scoff at all of this nonsense. But we have seen Bottom see the invisible fairies, we have seen Demetrius worship Helena's beauty in dark-complected Hermia, and we have seen Shakespeare give form to no-things, place them in space-time, and give them reality by giving them names: Theseus, Titania, Egeus, Robin Starveling, Moth. We have been witness to creation of something out of nothing.[9]

Partly in this sense, Shakespeare calls the fairies "shadows" (Oberon is "King of Shadows"), not only because they are supposedly invisible (no things) but also to suggest their illusory nature, that *we* must make them up, must imagine them—as he had. For this reason, Shakespeare also calls actors "shadows"; they really are not what they pretend to be, for what they pretend to be can be realized only in the minds of the audience. Theseus, humanly inconsistent or as changeable as a god, explains this to Hippolyta, who has laughed at the play of "Pyramus and Thisby" as performed: "The best in this kind are but shadows; and the worst are no worse, if imagination amend them . . . If we imagine no worse of them than they of themselves, they may pass for excellent men" (5.1.209–14). To his earlier list of lunatic, lover, and poet, Theseus now adds actors and audience.

Because the "best in this kind" are the Chamberlain's men, the very performers of both plays, the audience is being set up for Puck's epilogue, spoken by Puck the fairy-shadow and Puck the actor-shadow:

> If we shadows have offended,
> Think but this, and all is mended:
> That you have but slumb'red here
> While these visions did appear,
> And this weak and idle theme
> No more yielding but a dream.
>
> (412–17; punctuation altered)

So—a play is, after all, only a dream—that ultimate reality—that totally private experience—our inviolable "property"—our proper selves—our androgynous selves.

Puck's "epilogue" may end the play, but Hippolyta's "prologue" to the long, final scene, her response to Theseus's attack on lunatics, lovers, and poets, still resonates:

> But all the story of the night told over,
> And all their minds transfigured so together,
> More witnesseth than fancy's images
> And grows to something of great constancy,
> But, howsoever, strange and admirable.
>
> (23–27)

I have repunctuated these last two lines, for I am sure that the meaning of Hippolyta's speech is: Each of the lover's account of, and contribution to the report of, the collective and separate experiences in the forest is so consistent and complementary, and the observable new love bonds between the couples and among the foursome, taken together, constitute proof that events transpired which transformed them; no false dreams triggered by the fumes of indigestion can account for their account; what they have reported and what we have received must be taken for real, even though at the same time, what they have reported is above the realm of nature ("strange") and calls for faith as well as rational assent ("wonder"); indeed, perhaps even more natural and real because beneficently supernatural. This idea of strangeness and wonder looks forward to the end of *The Tempest*, where the vexation within Prospero's "old brain," his vessel of Hermes, also effects transfigurations: "all of us [found] ourselves/When no man was his own" (5.1.212–13).[10]

Returning from the green world, the lovers think they have dreamed, awaking Bottom thinks he has dreamed, and now we are free to think that we have dreamed. And it may be that, like fairies and actors, "a dream itself is but a shadow" (*Hamlet* 2.2.257). But we know that the lovers and Bottom did not dream—nor have we. The lovers are transfigured, Bottom has been translated, and we have been transformed. We may leave the theater just as snotty on the surface as the young aristocrats are back at court, and just as cocksure on the surface as Bottom is during the play, but we are just as haunted as they all are by their midsummer night's dreams—yes, we did dream these not very weak and not very idle themes of love overcoming hate, concord overcoming discord, and union overcoming division. We have dreamed the alchemical dream of achieving androgyny.

The experience of theater is like the experience of dream because in entering them we leave behind, to a degree, the immediate, direct influence of our most intimate, direct, social environment: our roles. Our focused awareness of our own roles is relaxed as we watch the performance of other roles unfold before us, and as we drop our surface roles we move into those other roles. Yet, we can participate in those other roles only with a degree of intensity that is inversely proportionate to our forgetting who, and where, and what we are. It is both a psychological and a religious truth—and, hence, an aesthetic truth—you must lose yourself in order to find yourself. And *that* truth yields *this* truth: as does the theater world, so also do the dream world and the green world offer models of growth toward androgyny.

PART III

The Stages and Ages of Androgyny

8

Explorations in Disguise: As You Like It *and* Twelfth Night

In 1941, Theodore Spencer, who taught Shakespeare at Harvard, gave a lecture series in Boston which was published in book form the next year as *Shakespeare and the Nature of Man*. Spencer's work is a brilliant example of how a "New Critic" could use the essential revelations of the "old" historical scholarship (the Lovejoy-Craig-Tillyard axis) to elucidate Shakespeare (mainly the tragedies). Spencer's book was for at least two decades a standard work for graduate students in North America who were "doing" the English Renaissance, and so also in England, I would assume from the title of Juliet Dusinberre's *Shakespeare and the Nature of Women*, published in 1975. Dusinberre's title cleverly drew attention to a nearly new approach to a grossly neglected area of that vast territory called "Shakespeare." The feminist movement had been launched some twelve to fifteen years earlier, and interdisciplinary programs in women's studies were in various stages of formation in the North Atlantic community, but not much had yet been published on "Shakespeare" from a feminist perspective. In those heady days, we thought we pretty much knew what "feminism" was all about, and many of us, only loosely connected, were at work on "feminist Shakespeare" projects when Dusinberre's work came out (a good bit of that early work was collected in *The Women's Part: Feminist Criticism of Shakespeare* [1980]; I had begun research which led to essays published in 1981, 1982, and 1983).

Shakespeare and the Nature of Women was instantly recognized as a landmark work, one which conducted us into an area that needed exploration, clearing, and cultivation. Not everyone agreed with the details and contours of Dusinberre's charting, but everyone learned from her pioneering efforts and achievements. There has been no feminist approach to Shakespeare and the English literary Renaissance that does not in some way lead back to Dusinberre.

Given my own interests and findings, I was relieved to be supported by Dusinberre's discovery and depiction of an emergent feminism within Renaissance thought (Chapter 4: "Femininity and Masculinity"), but I was particularly pleased by her remarks in the section called "Disguise and the Boy Actor," where she first describes the range and talents of the girl-actors—that is to say, the boys who were apprenticed and trained to play the young female roles—and I was especially encouraged by her further description of how the disguising of those girl-actors as boys allowed Shakespeare to explore themes which led beyond masculinity and femininity toward androgyny.

Two of the many works which were triggered, or were at least encouraged, by *Shakespeare and the Nature of Women* were *Women and Drama in the Age of Shakespeare*, the subtitle of Lisa Jardine's *Still Harping on Daughters* (1983), and *Literature and the Nature of Womankind, 1540–1660*, the subtitle of Linda Woodbridge's *Women and the English Renaissance* (1984). Both are concerned, as is Dusinberre, with the status of women in sixteenth-century England, but the one is an angry rebuttal of Dusinberre and the other is a patient re-exploration of the area opened by Dusinberre.

Jardine claimed that all those "Christian" and "humanist" gestures toward feminism discussed by Dusinberre were really clever devices to control and to suppress women in order to prevent subversion of the patriarchy. For example, in her opening chapter on the boy actors, she said in effect that boys as girls in disguise as boys really amounted to no more than homosexuals stereotypically, flamboyantly acting like homosexuals, thus so mocking women that any potentially feminist aspects of the script were muted. Women were not just marginalized; they were wiped off the pages of the text.

Linda Woodbridge did not have to deal with Jardine's claim that the actual sex of the girl-actors and their backstage reputations blocked feminism because both of their books were in press at the same time; nevertheless, Woodbridge substantially agreed with Jardine that Dusinberre was wrong about the disguise device: "Transvestite disguise in Shakespeare does not blur the distinctions between the sexes but heightens it" (154). Her reasoning is curious: no woman disguised as a man is actually able to act fully like a man, to enter the male-world of power, to undergo total metamorphosis: "When Shakespeare's romantic heroines play at being men, Shakespeare invites us to smile at their trepidations and their posturings, with the affection of a parent watching his child play at being grown-up" (155).[1]

By the middle years of the 1980s, breathtakingly imaginative, feminist criticism of Shakespeare dominated research and publication, and with this growth came awareness of the complex of meanings of, and contradictions within, the term "feminism." Discord soon followed and erupted in open warfare at the Berlin meeting in 1986 of the International Shakespeare Association, and skirmishes continued at the 1987 meeting of the Shakespeare Association of America. But the need for peace and good will was made apparent by the publication in *PMLA* (January 1988) of Richard Levin's broadside attack on feminist criticism. In essence, Levin played the patriarch and said to all of the multiplying number of little Hic-Muliers and Haec-Virs: There, there—you've had your little fun—don't you think it is time you rejoined "us" in the practice of serious scholarship and criticism. Levin wanted to put feminist criticism in its place, yet the effect of his remarks had the opposite of his intention. The responses to his attack proved that feminist scholarship and criticism had indeed already found its place, a place of strength and respect.

The year before, *PMLA* had published Phyllis Rackin's "Androgyny, Mimesis, and the Marriage of the Boy Heroine on the English Stage" (1987), an harmonious synthesis of diverse feminist approaches to the particular issue at hand: the effect on an audience of a girl-actor in disguise as a boy. Rackin wisely and informedly broadened the question beyond the effect on an audience to effects on audiences because she agreed with Woodbridge that the woman question had experienced remarkable rephrasings and new answers during the last decade of the sixteenth century and the first decade of the seventeenth. Because of tremendous economic, political, aesthetic, and demographic shifts, there were vastly different audiences for plays by John Lyly, Shakespeare, and Ben Jonson: a court audience watched Lyly's *Gallathia* being performed in closed session by his semi-professional choir boys in the late 1580s; a "popular" cross-class audience watched *The Merchant of Venice*, *As You Like It*, and *Twelfth Night* being performed publicly by professional adult and apprentice-aged males in the 1590s; and a "mixed" city-court audience watched Jonson's *Epicoene* being performed "privately" by a fully professional boy company in 1609. The actual sex of the actors in the first play and the last play has less significance, fewer extra-dramatic implications, than it does in the plays performed in public by an adult/adolescent group. With regard to Shakespeare's three plays, Rackin agrees with Dusinberre that the disguise device works to promote feminism through the use of the theme of androgyny, but she feels that this is so *not* in spite of the actual sex of the actor but *because* of it: "For a Renaissance audience, the sexual ambiguity of the boy heroine in masculine attire was likely to invoke a widespread and ambivalent mythological tradition centering on the figure of the androgyne" (29); thus she agrees with both Jardine and Woodbridge while at the same time disagreeing with them. Yet, Rackin quotes my published assertion of a point of view which denies the immediate, dramatic pertinence of the actual sex of the actors, man or boy: "Human actors have sexual bodies, but the characters they play are 'whatever sex . . . the playwright asserts' (Kimbrough, 'Androgyny' 17)" (36).

The full statement in my article is based on a generic fact of drama which was "casually remarked upon by Sidney and Johnson: people going to the theater check their literal-mindedness at the door and willingly believe anything they are asked to believe; the theater is where illusion becomes reality. An actor in role is whatever sex, age, and cultural origin the playwright asserts." Drama cannot work any other way.

This does not mean that upon entering a theater we cease being multiple, variably stimulated human beings: we read the "bios" in the program to satisfy our curiosity concerning who the actors really are; we respond with our bodies to the movements and shapes of human bodies (both male and/or female) displayed before us; we admire (or detest) the author's phrasing for its own sake; we judge the skill of performance in and of itself as separate from text; later, we say we saw "so and so" do "such and such." Yet, while we are watching and listening, we are primarily (and unconsciously so) attuned to the through-line, the plot, the story being told. We are not prevented from appreciating the curve of a bum—how *can* we prevent it?—but that is not why we (or, well, most of us) go to a play. "The *play* is the thing"—wherein a stool is a throne, a pillow is a crown, and a dagger is a scepter—and because a lion is a lion, let half the actor's face be seen so as not to afright the gentle. Anyone who has done any theater at any level knows that you do not know what kind of a play you have until you have an audience—indeed, you cannot have a play until you have an audience. Johnson talked about an audience's willing suspension of disbelief, but perhaps a more accurate formulation might be: one's unreflecting surrender to belief. The reality of a play is discovered within the zodiac of our own wits.

Thus, having taken a long way around Robin Hood's barn, we can continue our journey into androgyny because we all now agree that a speech assigned by Shakespeare to a woman in disguise as a boy works in the theater because the audience knows and accepts that the speaker is really a woman—even in Elizabeth's day when, in an entirely different and dramatically extraneous mode of consciousness, the audience simultaneously knew and unconsciously accepted that the speaker was actually a male and not a female.[2] We do Shakespeare a disservice not to accept his women as women, for we risk missing the full significance of the lines which he wrote for them.[3]

Pertinent illustration of these assertions can be found in *Two Gentlemen of Verona*, when Shakespeare presents his Julia-as-Sebastian talking with Silvia in 4.4. For the benefit of Silvia as audience, "Sebastian" says: Once when giving a play, my friends (male) cast me (one of the boys) in "the woman's part," for which I wore Julia's dress that fitted perfectly and which part "I so lively acted with my tears" that Julia, watching, also cried; I (man) felt woman's sorrow, both Ariadne's and Julia's:

> at Pentecost,
> When all our pageants of delight were play'd,
> Our youth got me to play the woman's part,
> And I was trimm'd in Madam Julia's gown,
> Which served me as fit, by all men's judgments,
> As if the garment had been made for me;
> Therefore I know she is about my height.
> And at that time I made her weep agood,
> For I did play a lamentable part.
> Madam, 'twas Ariadne passioning
> For Theseus' perjury and unjust flight;
> Which I so lively acted with my tears
> That my poor mistress, moved therewithal,
> Wept bitterly; and would I might be dead
> If I *in thought* felt not her very sorrow.
>
> (4.4.156–70; emphasis added)

For us as audience, understanding the situation does not rest in the fact that Julia is played by a boy who is now playing a boy's part; rather, because Julia's fiction involves the playing of herself, her invention is grounded upon our knowing that the person playing "Sebastian" *is* a woman: indeed, the very woman named Julia. And only in this immediate, primary context can we fully open ourselves to the implications of Julia's remark that, in essence, as a man "he" experienced in "his" head what women can feel: here, because compassion is an emotion which reaches beyond gender labeling, Shakespeare makes a gesture toward androgyny.

Androgyny, as we have seen, in its simplest form appears in Shakespeare when a character of one sex experiences thoughts and emotions beyond those traditionally associated with the gender values of that sex, as reported by Julia. Because a woman disguised as a man has both sexes in one, the theatrical device of girl-into-boy disguise allowed Shakespeare to isolate moments of heightened awareness of androgyny. After a discussion of the general nature of transsexual disguise in Shakespeare, the major focus will be on definitions of socio-sexual androgyny which come from the reversed sex roles, first in *As You Like It* and then in *Twelfth Night*.

1
Girl-actor as Boy

There are seven examples of girl-into-boy disguise in Shakespeare: Julia, Portia, Nerissa, Jessica, Rosalind, Viola, and Imogen. The last is (ironically, but befitting the world of romance) the most typical of Elizabethan stage-practice: Imogen's disguise in *Cymbeline* is used to allow her to escape and to protect her from attack while on the road. Unlike Julia in *Two Gentlemen of Verona*, Portia in *The Merchant of Venice*, Rosalind in *As You Like It*, and Viola in *Twelfth Night*, Imogen makes no significant reference to the sex of her new sex. Other than to remark casually (and certainly ambiguously) upon entering dressed as a man that "I see a man's life is a tedious one" (3.6.1), her words and behavior are what Elizabethans would call fearfully effeminate, and she, like Jessica in *The Merchant of Venice*, is uncomfortable dressed as a boy.[4] Jessica's embarrassed disguise in "a page's suit" is merely a means of escape from her stern father's house—typical of romantic literature and plays—while Nerissa's disguise is merely a necessary complement to Portia's, the most significant disguise of the three in *The Merchant of Venice*.

Shakespeare has Julia, Portia, Rosalind, and Viola (both before entering disguise and once within disguise) all refer vividly and amusedly to male characteristics, organic as well as behavioral, sex as well as gender, in order to reinforce the dramatic illusion that they are so much women that they must make conscious efforts to "turn to men," a phrase Shakespeare seems to have taken, most appropriately, from what Woodbridge has now defined as the genre of "the formal controversy about women" (13). On a literal level, Julia, Portia, Rosalind, and Viola are able to display a broader range of human character traits in disguise than they could as women only; they are, in a sense, liberated from the confines of the appropriate. But in the case of Julia and Portia there is no psychic exploration beyond the realms of their hidden, contained female selves. While she is in disguise, Julia's asides all refer to her hidden self; they contain no reference to the irony of her surface self. Portia (and Nerissa) uses surface identity for *double entendres* and for situational comedy; they do not use it as the basis for turning inward psychologically. Through the disguises of Rosalind and Viola, however, Shakespeare begins to explore androgynous potentials beyond the surface and the situational.[5]

Still, a closer look at Portia in disguise reveals techniques and issues that become more fully developed by the time Shakespeare is writing *As You Like It* and *Twelfth Night*. First of all, Shakespeare emphasizes the sexual differences between men and women by the manner in which he has Portia announce that she and Nerissa will see their husbands

in such a habit
That they shall think we are accomplished
With that we lack.

He continues this teasing vein by having Portia mock stereotypical male gender behavior:

When we are both accoutered like young men,
I'll prove the prettier fellow of the two,
And wear my dagger with the braver grace,
And speak between the change of man and boy
With a reed voice, and turn two mincing steps
Into a manly stride, and speak of frays
Like a fine bragging youth, and tell quaint lies,
How honorable ladies sought my love,
Which I denying, they fell sick and died—.

(3.4.60–71)

As Portia is well aware, the social posturing of men is different from that of women. So different in *The Merchant of Venice*, in fact, that critics label the world of Venice "masculine" and the world of Belmont "feminine." Venice is a busy, daytime, harsh, scheduled world; Belmont is calm, nighttime, soft, and relaxed. The separation of these worlds is so great that Portia must literally and figuratively become a man in order to invade Venice. She has to become a man because, as Rackin observes, the practice of law was forbidden women, and in order to save Antonio she must hide her sense of "feminine" mercy behind the cloak of "masculine" law.

Barbara Everett believes that "Portia is the salvation of the play; her wealth, her wits, and her pleading of a feminine quality of mercy—deeply Christian in its language and connotation, but allied too to that quality of compassion that is reserved for the women in the comedies—defeat the harshly logical and loveless intellectualism of Shylock. But they do so in masculine disguise, in a masculine court of law, and at the service of a chivalric friendship between men."[6] This is perceptive, but an overstatement of the actual case. Portia is not merciful, and Shylock is not the only representative of Venice. What troubles us about the play is that compassion does not triumph. The potential for an androgynous resolution is inherent in the play, but in the end the two worlds stand still at loggerheads, refusing the nurture of "the milk of human kindness."

Yet, accidentally or on purpose, Shakespeare does present through Portia in disguise a possible exploration of androgyny on a symbolic level. Plato's playfully serious Aristophanes' seriously playful account of the divisive origin of the three sexes in the *Symposium* bothered the morally earnest Marsilio Ficino. Ficino's "allegorizing" in his Fourth Speech of the *Commentaries on Plato's Symposium* is worthy of an ancient father, for in his hands the original, comically well-rounded Androgyne becomes a symbol of justice: "Courage in man because of their strength and bravery is called Masculine. Temperance is called Feminine because of a certain relaxed and cooler nature of Woman's passion and her gentle disposition. Justice is called Bi-Sexual; feminine inasmuch as because of its inherent innocence it does no one any wrong, but masculine inasmuch as it allows no harm to be brought to others, and with more severe censure frowns upon unjust men."[7] (Poor Shylock.) Whether or not the audience sees Portia as an androgynous justice-figure depends ultimately on whether or not they have come fresh from reading Ficino, for the point is not highlighted within the play.

2
As You Like It

In *As You Like It*, in order to suggest the androgynous dimensions of the characterization of Rosalind, Shakespeare provides within the play three special audiences for her playing: Celia, Orlando, and Phebe. Alone with Celia, Rosalind can show her intellect and wit, which must be hidden in part from the male world, and she can be relaxed, giddy, and giggly, which in public would be very un-ladylike. With Orlando, she can be one of the boys: wisecracking, shoulder-thumping, slightly salacious, and pragmatically knowing, in an eye-winking way. And with Phebe, with her sex hidden, Rosalind is able to reveal the maturing range of her attractive human person. In disguise, Rosalind grows into a fuller human self.

At the outset of the play Rosalind reveals a kind of restlessness with her situation in life. From her first conversation with Celia in 1.2, she shows the witty, educated side of her nature along with this restlessness. It is she who suggests the game "of falling in love" and it is she who, in agreeing with Celia that there is not equity in the world, feels that Fortune "doth most mistake in her gifts to women." Celia responds with an anti-female commonplace much older than "The Wife of Bath's Tale": "'Tis true, for those that she makes fair she scarce makes honest, and those that she makes honest she makes very ill favoredly." But Rosalind keeps the attention on her first remark: on inequities and the unfortunate lot of women. Celia's response concerns "Nature," which causes one's birth as male or female, whereas "Fortune reigns in gifts of the world," which come after birth thus allying Fortune to gender. When Rosalind is banished, it is almost with relief that she decides to put on an unnecessary-but-wished-for male disguise behind which she can escape not just the court, but in part what has been so far her Fortune-dealt, restricted feminine role.

Three points support this bald assertion. When Celia suggests that to be less provocative during their journey to the Forest of Arden they put on "poor and mean attire," Rosalind, sounding like Portia, goes one step further:

> Were it not better,
> Because that I am more than common tall,
> That I did suit me all points like a man?
> A gallant curtle-axe upon my thigh,
> A boar-spear in my hand; and, in my heart
> Lie there what hidden woman's fear there will,
> We'll have a swashing and a martial outside,
> As many other mannish cowards have
> That do out face it with their semblances.
>
> (1.3.111–18)

Although there might be some hope of male protection in Rosalind's proposed disguise, when she suggests that they take Touchstone along, she negates the actual need for any protective male appearance. The second point is more persuasive: once in the forest Rosalind stays in male dress and makes no attempt to seek her father; she must, perforce, like the part she has created and cast. The third is conclusive: when Rosalind discovers from Celia in 3.2 that Orlando is in the forest, she consciously elects to stay in disguise. Her first reaction to Celia's news is doubt and dismay: "Alas the day! what shall I do with my doublet and hose?" In her next speech, she asks, "Doth he know that I am in this forest, and in man's apparel?" But after she sees him and after Jaques leaves, she comes to a clear decision; she tells Celia, "I will speak to him like a saucy lackey, and *under that habit* play the knave with him" (3.2.283; emphasis added).

Up to this point, Shakespeare has given Rosalind lines emphasizing the woman within the knave's clothes in order to maintain a sense of contrary doubleness; for example:

> I could find in my heart to disgrace my man's apparel
> and to cry like a woman
>
> (2.4.4)

> Dost thou think, though I am caparisoned like a man,
> I have a doublet and hose in my disposition?
>
> (3.2.185)

Do you not know I am a woman?

(3.2.237)

Once she has spoken to Orlando, she is committed to her self-selected part. She mocks herself and mocks men by using her wit in the manner of men who belittle women's wit: "Make the doors upon a woman's wit, and it will out at the casement; shut that, and 'twill out at the keyhold; stop that, 'twill fly with the smoke out at the chimney" (4.1.149). So well does Rosalind swagger along in male assuredness of supremacy that she completely ignores Celia's touchstone comment on the contradiction between Rosalind's masculine, misogynous wit and her actual sex: "You have simply misused our sex in your love-prate. We must have your doublet and hose plucked over your head and show the world what the bird hath done to her own nest" (4.1.185). But alone with Celia, Rosalind can still be delightfully open and emotional: "O coz, coz, coz, my pretty little coz, that thou didst know how many fathom deep I am in love! But it cannot be sounded. My affection hath an unknown bottom, like the Bay of Portugal" (4.1.189).

When Rosalind met Orlando at court, she entered into a real game "of falling in love." When she discovers that he is in the forest, she decides to continue playing the game by forsaking father and clinging unto Orlando, as we can see after the one time Rosalind came upon her father: "I met the Duke yesterday and had much question with him. He asked me of what parentage I was. I told him, of as good as he; so he laughed and let me go. But what talk we of fathers when there is such a man as Orlando?" (3.4.30). In this speech both the giddy girl that she is and the saucy boy that she is able to play emerge. To this duality, because she is not sure that either she or Orlando is ready for an open, mutual commitment, she adds the role of "Rosalind," which is a hidden way of being openly herself.

On the surface, then, Rosalind is now both male and female. As a man, she is freed from societal convention and can speak her *mind*. Also, because of her being a man, Orlando, relaxed in the presence of male company, can reveal his *emotions*. If Orlando knew he was in the presence of a woman, let alone Rosalind, he would once again become as tongue-tied as he had been at court. With Adam, and with Jaques, we see him to be a bluntly articulate, plain-spoken young man. Love is new to him, and with a stranger in a strange place he can show his befuddlement openly and honestly, with no need to be "manly": he has no past social or psychological investment regarding Ganymede to impede or embarrass him (as indeed that poetry should).

That Rosalind carries off her double-t role with ease and accomplishment is attested by her confrontation with Phebe. Rosalind's gently chiding speech to Phebe regarding her treatment of Silvius is so full of good, common sense that Phebe would not tolerate it from another woman. And, because Rosalind is a woman, the speech is delivered without a subtext of sexual threat: there is more safety for Phebe in Rosalind's aggressive passiveness than in Silvius' passive aggressiveness. Yet more than a defense mechanism is at work; Phebe could not fall into love at first sight were not the object of her love an attractive human being.

Thus, Rosalind's male behavior simply emphasizes the wit which governs that behavior, a wit which by strict definition is a "woman's wit." But her wit is in essence and exercise indivisibly both masculine and feminine because it emanates from the androgynous mind; it is, therefore, more fully human than a gender designation can indicate; it is epicene. When Rosalind receives Phebe's letter, she is strategically and personally able to test Silvius by toying with society's definitions of masculine and feminine because her own experience has taken her beyond the bounds of those definitions:

> I say she never did invent this letter;
> This is a man's invention and his hand.
> . . . .
> Why, 'tis a boisterous and a cruel style,
> A style for challengers. Why, she defies me
> Like Turk to Christian. Women's gentle brain
> Could not drop forth such giant-rude invention.
>
> (4.3.29–35)

She has achieved a position as woman and man from which she can understand and mock the absurdity of the social restrictions caused by gender stereotyping.

Rosalind's "male" wisdom and common sense—"Men have died from time to time, and worms have eaten them, but not for love"—have often been noted, but her seemingly anti-female jibes have not been understood as ways of wrestling with attributes created for women by society. In consciously using her disguise to act in a way that society will not allow a woman to act, she is more her real, essential self—or can move more easily to discovery and revelation of that essential self. As a saucy knave she can mock the very passions that she, Phebe, and Orlando are all subjected to; in testing and purging those two, she is testing and purging herself. Thus, by a directness allowed by an indirectness, Rosalind and Orlando find each other out and in their own way they (as do Celia and Oliver) by degrees make "a pair of stairs" to marriage.

At the end, Rosalind claims that she will resolve all of the conflicts among the lovers through magic. As Albert R. Cirillo has pointed out, "she assumes an important role which is central to the entire play and which makes her something of a *magus* or magician who controls nature and sets all things aright through her influence on the amorous relationships in the circle of the forest."[8] Her magic is one of the world's oldest forces bringing harmony out of conflict—love. Not only is Rosalind the magician she claims to be, she is herself the product of her magic. More accurately, she is that special magician, the alchemist, who seeks to achieve the Sacred Marriage in order to compound higher substances out of lesser, contrary elements, all of which are carefully divided under male and female headings. As a magician/alchemist, Rosalind will take the male-Rosalind and the female-Rosalind and merge them into a human Rosalind:

> Believe then, if you please, that I can do strange [supernatural] things. I have, since I was three years old, conversed with a magician, most profound in his art and yet not damnable. If you do love Rosalind so near the heart as your gesture cries it out, when your brother marries Aliena shall you marry her. I know into what *straits of fortune* she is driven; and it is not impossible to me, if it appear not inconvenient to you, to set her before your eyes to-morrow, *human as she is*, and *without any danger*.
> (5.2.56–65; emphasis added)

"Straits of fortune" takes us back to the beginning of the play. There Rosalind had lamented over the constraints Fortune had placed over women. Then (to use Sir Toby's metaphor) she confines herself in men's clothes, which she now finds confining. Figuratively, Rosalind has outgrown her clothing. She needs to be seen "human as she is." When she adds, "without any danger," the primary implication is that her magic is *prisca*, innocent, natural, and "white"; yet, a secondary suggestion is planted: disguise is evil, harmful, unnatural, and "black"—but this is a point Viola will elaborate.

Rosalind has been growing all during the play.[9] She started as a wise and witty young woman, became a wise and witty young man, and through her interactions with both a man, Orlando, and a woman, Phebe, reached toward a fuller realization of her humanhood, or potential for androgyny. The catalyst in the process toward wholeness is love. Once Rosalind knows herself and what she wants, she can remove what has been her self-protective disguise to come before lover and father, leaving her earlier restlessness behind.

Rosalind has "promised to make all this matter even" (5.4.18) through marriage, both favored terms of alchemists signifying unity and concord.[10] Hymen, not Cupid, is the harmonious agent of love she invokes "to make these doubts all even" (5.4.25); Hymen, not Cupid, because here, as in "The Phoenix and Turtle" and in *The Tempest*, we are talking about love as a *rational* principle:

Then is there mirth in heaven
When earthly things made even
   Atone together . . .
Peace ho! I bar confusion:
'Tis I must make conclusion
   Of these most strange events.
Here's eight that must take hands
To join in Hymen's bands,
   If truth holds true contents . . .
Whiles a wedlock hymn we sing,
Feed yourselves with questioning,
That *reason* wonder may diminish
How thus we met, and these things finish.

(5.4.102–34; emphasis added)

The power of sex in human intercourse is represented in the play through the manner in which Shakespeare shaped his through-line,[11] as well as through Audrey and Touchstone and, by report, Celia and Oliver, but the emphasis within the central love plot has been on gender differentiations. In the epilogue Shakespeare brings sex and gender together in order to give a final plea in behalf of androgynous behavior. Just as he had used Puck's epilogue to emphasize the handy-dandy of his illusion/reality motif within *A Midsummer Night's Dream*, Shakespeare now uses Rosalind's address to the audience to emphasize the androgynous element of *As You Like It*.[12]

The plea in behalf of the play opens with a reference to a "lady" and a "lord" and goes on to address both the "women" and "men" in the audience: "I charge you, O women, for the love you bear to men, to like as much of this play as please you; and I charge you, O men, for the love you bear to women (as I perceive by your simp'ring none of you hates them), that between you and the women the play may please." This is most appropriate, for the play has celebrated the play between men and women. Now, the dramatic illusions of that play within the play must be made real, for Shakespeare's art celebrates life as the ultimate pleasure. In the end, the individuals in the audience are asked to enter into the sport "of falling in love." Rosalind before, during, and after disguise has shown them how. Just as an actor's role is a disguise, so also is gender a disguise, and all disguises must be removed for people to be themselves. Because this androgynous "message" is also a "Puritan/Protestant" message, it is no accidental irony that Shakespeare now has Rosalind as male actor subtly establish the fact that indeed, ultimately (as Viola will say): "Disguise, I see thou art a wickedness."

When Shakespeare has the actor say, "What a case am I in," Rosalind's gown becomes a costume for a male actor.[13] His "case" is both his costume and the problem it presents as a female costume on a man presenting the epilogue: "If I were a woman, I would kiss as many of you as had beards that pleased me, complexions that liked me, and breaths that I defied not; and I am sure, as many as have good beards, or good faces, or sweet breaths, will, for my kind offer, when I make curtsey, bid me farewell."[14]

His words are intended to startle us: "If I were a woman . . . when I make curtsy." Indeed, such is the enchanting power of acting that William Carroll voices a dramatic truth: "We had forgotten she was not a woman" (137). When the man strides off the stage after executing a female gesture, the men and women in the audience should be able in some small way to understand that while the differences in being men and women are important and powerful, we are all most human under the surfaces. The play has shown us that if we can accept our sex instead of hiding it behind the disguise of gender, we will have established a base upon which to build human fulfillment. The boy Rosalind has brought us out of the circle of the forest into the circle of the theater; now we must go back out into the encircling London, that island encircled by England, encircled by the sea.

3
Twelfth Night

In *Twelfth Night*, Shakespeare displays much of Viola's person through soliloquies and asides that consider inner as well as surface facts and ironies. Like Rosalind, Viola experiences human freedom and growth in male disguise, but unlike Rosalind, Viola feels self-constricted and self-conscious throughout the play. She is especially conscious of her sexual identity, far more sex-aware, far more troubled by the sex of her sex than was Rosalind.

As a result, the girl-as-boy motif is presented as somewhat, though innocently, unnatural, and the effect of Viola's disguise on the play is different from the effect created by Rosalind's. Here Shakespeare openly plays off sexual identity against gender identity in order to suggest with more impact than in *As You Like It* that one must accept one's genetic sex before one can reach toward psychic androgyny. He touches on homosexuality as well as heterosexuality in order to bring home to the audience that androgyny has no necessary connections with any particular kind of sexual orientation. As must Viola, the audience must learn that androgyny is not a physical state, but a state of mind.

Shakespeare summarizes his plot, character, and themes in Viola's soliloquy in the short 2.2: "I left no ring with her. What means this lady?/Fortune forbid my outside have not charmed her" (16–17). When Viola says, "Disguise, I see thou art a wickedness," Shakespeare, beyond talking about the rising complication in the play, is mocking the Puritans whose mounting attack on the impious mummery of satanic players has always been based in part on the abomination of men dressing unnaturally as women—monstrous, indeed. As Juliet Dusinberre, Linda Woodbridge, and others have pointed out, at the turn of the century some few women were beginning to roam the streets of London dressed as men to taunt protesting Christendom. Surely Shakespeare must have enjoyed for himself the joke of having a girl mockingly apologize for playing a boy. Shakespeare is saying, if that is all small-minded people can think about, so be it. But Viola's self-consciousness about her "unnatural" transformation leads to a more serious moment as she characterizes herself as an hermaphrodite and a homosexual:

> How will this fadge? My master loves her dearly;
> And I (poor monster) fond as much on him;
> And she (mistaken) seems to dote on me.
> What will become of this? As I am man,
> My state is desperate for my master's love.
> As I am woman (now alas the day!),
> What thriftless sighs shall poor Olivia breathe?
> O Time, thou must untangle this, not I;
> It is too hard a knot for me t'untie.
>
> (2.2.32–40)

When Viola parenthetically calls herself a "poor monster" (Elizabethan for unnatural) and Olivia "mistaken" (both deceived and morally wrong), Shakespeare introduces the concepts of hermaphroditism and homosexuality—to be sure, only fleetingly. A hermaphrodite was unnatural because of the seeming presence of both male and female sex organs, supposedly the result of a kind of monstrous birth like that of Richard, Duke of Gloucester, out of the natural order of things. And, leaving aside any question of actual practice, homosexuality was, of course, automatically stamped unnatural by religious and secular officialdoms.

In spite of her recognition of natural and social aberration, Viola decides to stay in disguise. She could "come out" at this crucial moment, but for the time being what she seeks is freedom within the restrictions of disguise. Liberated from her role as young lady, she moves into realms of self-discovery. And having been raised with a twin brother she knows how to adapt to her adopted sex. The result is Shakespeare's furthest venture into androgyny in disguise.

At the outset, after shipwreck, Viola's normal, sensible course of action upon finding out where she is and whose domain it is would have been to have the captain take her to the friend of her father for protection, to identify herself, and to arrange her return home as, she thinks, an heiress. But hearing the name "Orsino" leads her to make a statement which carries all the weight of a rhetorical question: "He was a bachelor then." Her instantly formulated plan, seen even in the talk about Olivia, is obviously to woo him (or to see if she wishes to), which course of action, paradoxically, she would not be able to carry out if she presented herself as a hapless aristocratic lady because it would be Orsino's duty to send her, protected, right home. So she bribes the captain:

I prithee (and I'll pay thee bounteously)
Conceal me what I am, and by my aid
For such disguise as haply shall become
The form of my intent. I'll serve this duke.
Thou shall present me as an eunuch to him;
It may be worth thy pains. For I can sing,
And speak to him in many sorts of music
That will allow me very worth his service.
What else may hap, to time I will commit;
Only shape thou thy silence to my wit.

(1.2.50–61)

In disguise, she can exercise that wit which women are not supposed to reveal, and the role and costume which she chooses are ones for which she is fitted:

I my brother know
Yet living in my glass. Even such and so
In favor was my brother, and he went
Still in this fashion, color, ornament,
For him I imitate.

(3.4.359–63)

In acting like her twin brother, she becomes, so to speak, a walking example of Ascham on Imitation: similar treatment of dissimilar matter. Even though one twin is female and one is male, they share a common humanity. Extending the rhetorical metaphor, she need not search for the basis of her *tractatio*; she is herself the basis of her own invention. Brother and sister have spent their young lives discovering each other.[15]

The effect of her disguise on Orsino is like that of Rosalind's on Orlando: men can be relaxedly, if only superficially, confessional with others of the same sex—the sort of just-between-us collusion that men easily fall into.

Within her first three days of service, Orsino shows more of his essential self (though young and in flux) to Cesario than he has so far been able to show to his neighbor, the distant Olivia, or would ever reveal to Viola as a newcomer of the opposite sex.

Because he is a bit older than Cesario, Orsino shares his experience in order to teach his younger companion (he literally and figuratively lords it over him). But the lessons learned are not the ones being taught, as Cesario's responses reveal. When Orsino, out of the presence of women, confesses that,

> boy, however we do praise ourselves,
> Our fancies are more giddy and unfirm,
> More longing, wavering, sooner lost and worn,
> Than women's are,

Viola wisely nods, "I think it well, my lord." And then delightfully not much later in the same scene, Orsino all so humanly contradicts himself:

> There is no woman's sides
> Can bide the beating of so strong a passion
> As love doth give my heart; no woman's heart
> So big to hold so much; they lack retention.
> Alas, their love may be called appetite,
> No motion of the liver but the palate,
> That suffers surfeit, cloyment, and revolt;
> But mine is all as hungry as the sea
> And can digest as much. Make no compare
> Between that love a woman can bear me
> And that I owe Olivia.
>
> (2.4.31–34, 92–102)

To which nonsense Viola can quietly respond, "Ay, but I know." While indeed she does, she also is coming to know, as Olivia and Orsino will learn, that many apparent differences between men and women are dissolvable. When Orsino asks her what she knows and she answers that women are as "true of heart as we," "we" becomes truly androgynous because Viola means both we women and we men: "we" here means we human kinds. And from her strategic advantage she in her turn can school Orsino, while hiding behind a disguise that cancels out her sexuality, making her a "blank" (like blank verse, neither feminine nor masculine). From her position and experience, she knows

Too well what love women to men may owe,
In faith, they are as true of heart as we.
My father had a daughter loved a man
As it might be perhaps, were I a woman,
I should your lordship.

(2.4.104–08)

In response to Orsino's "And what's her history?" Viola says:

A blank, my lord. She never told her love,
But let concealment, like a worm i'th'bud,
Feed on her damask cheek. She pined in thought;
And, with a green and yellow melancholy,
She sat like Patience on a monument,
Smiling at grief. Was not this love indeed?
We men may say more, swear more; but indeed
Our shows are more than will; for still we prove
Much in our vows but little in our love.

(2.4.109–17)

Because she is a man, Viola can turn women's complaint of masculine infidelity tellingly against that gender which in point of fact is really the loquacious one. The lesson she is learning and teaching is one her birth into life as the twin of a male has already prepared her for: once sexual differentiation is acknowledged, men and women are essentially very much alike. She has no trouble playing a boy, for her childhood has readied her for the role she is now successful in, even though Orsino remarks that Cesario has all the physical characteristics which would promote the successful portrayal of "a woman's part" (1.4.33); Cesario would make a convincing girl-actor.

Thus Shakespeare allows us to see androgyny through disguise. Viola is first of all a woman, but society, being so conscious of sex identity, assumes that Viola is a man when she appears in male clothing (which is enough to trigger Olivia's interest and to start Sir Andrew quaking). As a result she can be Viola and Sebastian, woman and man, at the same time. Since this is only metaphorically true, she is freed to act out the full range of her human personality in her acting out. When Shakespeare has Orsino say that Viola could play "a woman's part," he is doing more than calling the audience's attention to her girl-as-boy disguise; he is calling attention to a two-in-one nature through the part-acting metaphor.

By giving Viola this metaphor of acting in her dialogue with Olivia—"my speech," "my part," "I am not that I play"—Shakespeare develops the idea that Viola is Viola at the same time that she is Sebastian. Stated plainly, she does not *become* Sebastian; she is Sebastian—but without a penis ("a little thing would make me tell them how much I lack of a man"). Such is the nature of successful acting. As an actor, Viola is herself "a natural perspective that is and is not." As Viola-Cesario she can charm Orsino; as Sebastian-Cesario she can charm Olivia. And the audience is just as charmed as are Orsino and Olivia; we are delighted to share with Viola her recognition of her emotional self—"I am almost sick for [a beard]," "I am no fighter," "I am one that had rather go with sir priest than sir knight." Because of disguise, the usual social barriers of custom are removed, allowing Orsino and Olivia to get to know the essential Viola-Sebastian. Thus, with the arrival of Viola's literal surrogate, her self's other self—"One face, one voice, one habit, and two persons"—the apparent problems afforded by sexual delusion are solved. A happy ending is a natural ending. The marriages are founded on surer ground than if they had been initiated through more artificial means than artifice.[16]

In this sense, Viola's disguise did not turn out to be a total "wickedness." It merely covered those parts of her that too often prevent society from accepting women as human beings. Over the three-month span of the play Orsino develops his instinctive liking of Cesario without having a wrestle with Viola's sex. Olivia's decision to marry Sebastian is only seemingly sudden. She, too, has had three months to get to know the dominant human aspect of Viola-Sebastian. Not until Sebastian enters does sex, in the form of marriage, enter Olivia's mind. Here, in following her sexual instinct, as Sebastian observes, "nature to her bias drew in that."[17] But, sex is only part of the attraction. Because Viola and Sebastian are twins, Olivia has not really been deceived; Shakespeare has Sebastian say in full:

> So comes it, lady, you have been mistook.
> But nature to her bias drew in that.
> You would have been contracted to a maid;
> Nor are you therin, by my life, deceived:
> You are betrothed both to a maid and a man.
>
> (5.1.251–55)

Orsino, too, is betrothed to "a maid and a man." There has been no ultimate deception. Viola has shown us through her disguise that one can overcome gender differentiation regardless of sex. Olivia and Orsino, who started the play each trapped within stereotypically appropriate patterns of gender behavior, are as blessed by disguise as is Viola. They were stimulated by her to draw on their androgynous potential for human growth to develop toward full, whole, integrated selves. Herein lies the lesson for the audience.

Phyllis Rackin summarized movingly the nature and function of Rosalind and Viola:

> Shakespeare marries his unlike lovers, joining male and female characters on his stage just as he joins masculine and feminine qualities in the androgynous figures of his boy heroines. Refusing to collapse the artistic representation into a simple replica of the world outside the theatre or to abandon that world for a flight into escapist fantasy, he insists on the necessary ambivalence of his play as a kind of marriage, a mediation of opposites, which can be brought together only by the power of love and imagination. (37)

As late twentieth-century readers and spectators observing Rosalind and Viola, we do sometimes have to wonder about Shakespeare's all-male casts, and how he could write such full parts for women when the parts were played by men—nay, by boys. The answer is on stage in front of us. He would not have written the parts if the boys could not act them. The respect Shakespeare felt for humanity is experienced in his plays; his respect for all of his actors is reflected in the complexities of his characters; and his trust in the ability of a boy to draw on his own capacity for androgyny is proved by the range of demand Shakespeare created for one taking the woman's part. Imagine the burden on a boy actor to stay in character when during the intense climax of *Antony and Cleopatra* he as Cleopatra is given these bold, proud lines signifying Cleopatra's refusal to be taken captive to Rome:[18]

> Saucy lictors
> Will catch at us like strumpets, and scald rhymers
> Ballad us out o'tune. The quick comedians
> Extemporally will stage us, and present
> Our Alexandrian revels: Antony
> Shall be brought drunken forth, and I shall see
> Some squeaking Cleopatra boy my greatness
> I'th' posture of a whore.
>
> (5.2.214–21)

On a literal level, this is what we experience in *Antony and Cleopatra* for five acts, which is what makes Cleopatra's verb "boy" so marvelous, meaning: How could any mere boy come close to suggesting my completeness; in his actions he would seem to be only a rambunctious child at a play. But no mere boy played Cleopatra,[19] any more than any mere boy played Lady Macbeth—or Imogen, Julia, Jessica, Nerissa, Portia, Rosalind, or Viola. Much of the androgyny in Shakespeare can be attributed to the playwright's recognition of the androgyny of his company of players. In fact, one of the healthiest facts of drama is that the experience of theater permits us in the audience a freer (licensed) play of our own androgynous potential than do the appropriate "rules" of behavior within mere everyday life.

9

Myth and Counter-Myth In Macbeth

Sex is to nature as gender is to nurture—gender could not exist without society, for gender receives its formative messages not from the genetic code but from society's signals. From birth through adolescence the development of gender is the most powerful formative force we experience. Our gender label is subsumed within all of our other early labels: offspring, child, student, athlete. Gender is a social role which leads to and is reinforced by other social roles. For example, Elizabeth I of England was born a girl, and her identity as a girl was immediately reinforced by such things as dress and over-the-crib counsel that she would one day be a wife and then a mother. Being born into the role of princess also meant that she would one day be that special kind of wife, a queen, and that special kind of mother, a queen-mother, the mother of royalty. The roles she was cast to play were readied for her. But Elizabeth chose another role: she chose to be both mother and father, queen and king. She chose neither a sex role nor a gender role. She chose the role of androgyny through which to exercise power tempered by goodness. How successful she was as an androgynous monarch and what hindrances were placed in her way are not the issues here. Her example shows that one can essay androgyny, and shows how the movement toward androgyny involves more than just overcoming gender-restriction; it involves the not becoming restricted by the roles that sex and gender lead to. As we "mature," any role that restricts our inner growth restricts our essay toward androgyny.

Rosalind's wedding masque centered on the ancient concept that in marriage the odd will be made even. Marriage, in which two are made one, and in which one and one are two, the basic multiplier, the replicator. Marriage re-enacts the deep myth of creation, of the coming together of opposites to form the world as reported in eastern Mediterranean stories for some 4,000 years (that same time-span designating the history of the world, accurate after all, insofar as it designates the history of western history): the Greek gods and goddesses; the Bible and attendant Cabalistic mysteries and Gnostic teachings; the lore of Hermes Trismegistus, whose depiction of the Sacred Marriage inspired alchemists and reinforced the promise of Revelation that Christ would one day marry his Church, the ultimate marriage, the reclamation of unity and harmony.

And on the terrestrial, secular level such is the hope implied by Duke Senior's couplet which closes *As You Like It* and fittingly introduces the "Rosalind" epilogue:

> Proceed, proceed. We'll begin these rites,
> As we do trust they'll end, in true delights.

And indeed, such is the trust, generation after generation—mythically, religiously, theoretically, romantically, we trust that marriage will bring true delight through our fulfillment with and through another.

Shakespeare celebrates the promise but never shows us courtship *and* marriage. In fact, out of thirty-eight plays, he focuses on marriage in only five: *The Merry Wives of Windsor*, *The Winter's Tale*, *Julius Caesar*, *Othello*, and *Macbeth*. And it is in *Macbeth* that the focus is most intense and is most intensely held, from beginning to end.

In *The Merry Wives of Windsor*, "happy" marriage is necessary to the plot, but the nature of the actual relationships of each of the two married couples is hardly examined—I mean, after all, Ford! In *The Winter's Tale*, once again the fact of marriage is central to the plot and the issue of marriage is discussed, but we see little of the actual marriage and we never see Hermione and Leontes by themselves.[1]

In *Julius Caesar* (or "The Tragedy of Marcus Brutus") we have an intense focus on marriage in part of one scene and fuzzy focus on marriage in part of another. On a deep, personal level, Portia tries to break away from prescribed roles in order to share with and participate in the brutal world of Brutus. But Brutus is so private a person that it is difficult for him to share with anyone else, female or male—so much so that it is impossible to assess the nature of the impact of Portia's suicide on him. Nevertheless, we know that his love is strong, for he agrees to share with Portia (off stage) "the secrets of my heart" (2.1.305). (Caesar is also swayed by his wife, but only momentarily; he is so totally caught up in himself that he easily spurns Calpurnia's warnings, putting the obligations of public role as Caesar before those within his private role as Julius.)

Portia's appeal to Brutus is based upon the ideal of marriage: that it makes two people one through the bond of love:

You have some sick offense within your mind
Which by the right and virtue of my place
I ought to know of . . .
By all your vows of love, and that great vow
Which did incorporate us and make us one,
That you unfold to me, your self, your half,
Why you are heavy . . .
Within the bond of marriage, tell me, Brutus
Is it excepted I should know no secrets
That appertain to you? Am I your self
But, as it were, in sort or limitation?
To keep with you at meals, comfort your bed,
And talk to you sometimes? Dwell I but in the suburbs
Of your good pleasure? If it be no more,
Portia is Brutus' harlot, not his wife.

(2.1.268–87)

Marriage should be centered in the mind, where man and woman can meet as one because the mind has no barriers of sexual division. The contemporary denotations, connotations, and reverberations of Shakespeare's employment of the word "suburbs"—the location of the place of performance of the play, the area of unlicensed behavior, and the potential source of subversions of many sorts—beckons seductively, asking to be pursued, but here, in immediate context only, "suburbs" is a powerful capping of Portia's appeal not to be portioned out, split into multiple "appropriate" roles, marginalized, decentered, denied the full title of wife. Brutus is won:

You are my true and honorable wife
. . . .
And by and by thy bosom shall partake
The secrets of my heart.
All my engagements I will construe to thee,
All the characters of my sad brows.

(2.1.288–307)

Even so recognizing the "right and virtue" of her place as wife, he adds, "leave me with haste," for he has a visitor and a woman still had no equal right of access to a man's world.[2]

Desdemona was aware of this fact long before Othello was invited to her father's house; she attended the telling of the warrior's tales as a chaste, silent, obedient daughter. *Othello* is a play from beginning to end about marriage, but we not only do not witness any courtship, we do not feel that we have even witnessed any marriage. Desdemona and Othello each entered marriage so conditioned by their respective feminine and masculine worlds that their gestures to bridge separation are childlike and futile even before Iago separates them absolutely. We do not see them alone until after Othello has allowed his mind to be moved from innocent goodness to militant evil: what is innocent, good, beautiful, and true, he already had decided is harmful, evil, ugly, and false. Desdemona's innocence, goodness, beauty, and truth failed to convert Iago in the Virtue-tempts-the-devil scene, and, although we are frightened for her, we do not feel her person, her presence, can re-convert Othello. He and Iago come from the military world, which is bonded by degrees of sublimated and actual homosexuality and from which women—be they Desdemonas, Emilias, or Biancas—will always be excluded (I once heard a commissioned Marine say, "There are thousands of officers' wives but there is no such thing as a married officer"). In *Othello*, the focus on marriage never narrows, never comes together, but remains bifocal, giving us a divided field of vision; we see male in one eye and female in the other. Androgyny is impossible because Othello is all Narcissus and Desdemona is all Echo.[3]

Marjorie Garber has recently claimed in a brilliant chapter in a wonderfully mysterious book that "gender undecidability and anxiety about gender identification and gender roles are at the center of *Macbeth*."[4] This is appropriately so, for marriage is at the center of this play more so than in any other that Shakespeare wrote. Marriage is an appropriate place to study sex and gender roles, not just because of the necessary presence of a woman and a man but mainly because of the psychic, social, theoretical (philosophical and theological), and mythic assumptions and speculations about the act (secular or sacramental) of marriage.

At the beginning of *Macbeth*, Lord and Lady Macbeth are "happily" married; they exist within an earthly state of unity and harmony. It is clear that their fellow aristocrats believe the Macbeth marriage to be what we call "a good marriage." Macbeth, at the outset, seems to have handled fairly well and healthfully his awareness of his manhood.[5] But impatience with his role as thane leads him to assume two inappropriate roles, one which runs against his nurture and one which runs against his nature: he would be king, which he has been taught is not his to be by social right, and to become king, he must kill, which is against nature. That he is aided and abetted by his wife does not excuse his errors of choice; her guilt only highlights his guilt. But that other role of husband is significant, for the entire story of ambition, regicide, and tyranny takes place within the context of marriage. And the center of that marriage will not hold because Macbeth and Lady Macbeth fail to inhabit a full range of character traits because of cultural attempts to render some exclusively feminine and some exclusively masculine. Macbeth's death, first psychic then physical, stems from his failure to allow the tender aspects of his character to check those tough characteristics which are celebrated by the chauvinistic war-ethnic of his culture,[6] championed by his wife, and defined in the extreme by the nature of the first two murderers. In his attempt to "better" himself by becoming king, he is "helped" by Lady Macbeth, a medieval woman who more resembles an early seventeenth-century one, for her role as woman and wife has been reduced to mere "helpmate"; therefore, her tragic career parallels and counterpoints her husband's. Although they fail miserably on the stage of this life, Shakespeare constantly keeps before us the Macbeths's potential for androgynous fulfillment. In spite of their isolating, alienating behavior in the play, through their love a bond with the audience is established. At the end, we are not left merely repulsed; we are moved through pity to understand and fear the personal and social destructiveness of polarized "masculinity" and "femininity."[7]

In *Macbeth*, and elsewhere in Shakespeare, as in Elizabethan literature in general, to be "manly" is to be aggressive, daring, bold, resolute, and strong, especially in the face of death, whether giving or receiving. To be "womanly" is to be gentle, fearful, pitying, wavering, and soft, a condition often signified by tears. What we call machismo, a positive cultural virtue in Shakespeare's day, lies behind and gives point and meaning to Lady Macbeth's strikes against her husband. Indeed, the play opens and closes with ceremonial and chivalric emphasis on brave manhood. In the beginning, such is the theme of the description given of "brave Macbeth" by that "good and hardy soldier" whose "words become thee as thy wounds./They smack of honor both" (1.2.4, 16, 43–44). Even the traitor Cawdor comes in for praise for his stoic bravery: "Nothing in his life/Became him like the leaving it" (1.4.7–8). At the end of the play, Malcolm gives young Siward the honor of leading the first charge against Macbeth's castle; Ross tells old Siward about his son's ensuing death:

> Your son, my lord, has paid a soldier's debt.
> He only lived but till he was a man,
> The which no sooner had his prowess confirmed
> In the unshrinking station where he fought
> But like a man he died.
>
> (5.8.39–43)

No tears for the father; to Malcolm's "He's worth more sorrow,/And that I'll spend for him," old Siward responds:

> He's worth no more.
> They say he parted well and paid his score,
> And so, God be with him.
>
> (5.8.50–53)

This refusal to show sorrow—rather, this complete rejection of sorrow—is so extreme that it makes most in a modern audience uncomfortable, and such a reaction may have been intended by Shakespeare, for his fullest definition of humanity involves the show of both "manly" courage and "womanly" sorrow.

When Ross announces to Macduff that his family has been exterminated, Malcolm is taken back by Macduff's complete silence. Yet, when Macduff's emotions do break out, Malcolm counsels in embarrassment, "Dispute it like a man." There follows one of those great Shakespearean moments; Macduff quietly responds:

> I shall do so;
> But I must also feel it as a man.
>
> (4.3.220–21)

Here Macduff declines to be merely manly, as that gender term has so far been defined and as is meant by Malcolm. But Macduff is not for this moment becoming merely womanly. Here he expresses a fuller range of his being: his humanity. For this moment in the play, Macduff becomes an androgyne, both strong and sensitive. In order to emphasize this short, quiet, significant moment, Shakespeare has Macduff reject both simplistic, stereotypical "feminine" behavior ("O, I could play the woman with my eyes") and simplistic, stereotypical "masculine" behavior ("And braggart with my tongue") (230–31). When Macduff goes on to say, in effect, "bring on Macbeth," Malcolm responds, "this tune goes manly" (235). I would like to think that Malcolm has understood the full significance of what he has seen and heard and intends "manly" to mean more than bravely—but I doubt it; Shakespeare is too aware of the moral obtuseness of everyday human behavior to allow actuality to defer to ideality. Nevertheless, the point Shakespeare makes through Macduff, even though lost on Malcolm, is clear: bravery and compassion are not incompatible; they are both natural, human attributes. When Macduff says, "I must also feel it as a *man*," had he said *woman*, the speech would be just as powerful because Macduff's response is an androgynous response.[8]

Richard Levin in "Feminist Thematics and Shakespearean Tragedy" makes the observation that "Macduff's decapitation of Macbeth . . . is not very androgynous" (136, n8).[9] "Decapitation" is a loaded term, but the question raised is a valid one: Is Macduff's killing of Macbeth and then cutting off of his head for display an androgynous act? The answer is, yes it is. As can be seen in the portrait of François le Premier in Appendix III, and as discussed by Marina Warner in her book on Joan of Arc, the concept of the androgyne incorporates the full range of *balanced* character traits.[10] The wasted Scots' land needs a champion to free her from the terrors of the dragon. Malcolm takes up the challenge and Macduff becomes his agent. First Macduff offers Macbeth his life (to be a living example of tyranny curbed), then he kills Macbeth in single combat, and last he cuts off his head for display as warning to would-be traitors, the customary procedure with traitors, in Macbeth's world as well as in the worlds of Elizabeth and James: witness London Bridge. Macduff acts bravely and justly, both in offering Macbeth his life and in taking his life. The manner of Macduff's birth also suggests that he was specially delivered to carry out a destined function to be the redeemer of the land.[11] Indeed, Marjorie Garber suggests that Macduff is a type of Perseus, the "hero" who successfully beheaded Medusa, turning a figure of death into a figure of life preservation.[12] Her chapter on the play is called "Macbeth: The Male Medusa." In this regard what could be more fitting than having Macduff proclaim that "the time is free" while holding high the dead traitor-tyrant's head? Decapitation of a dead body is not in and of itself a "good" thing any more than is the ritualized killing of a king, but the death of Macbeth is good in that it allowed Scotland to be renewed, to become fertile again. The king must die, long live the king. Here, the death of Macbeth is ritualized by Macduff's act as part of the natural cycle of life.

There is no need at this point in the late twentieth century to rehearse the significances of the Shakespearean terms natural and unnatural.[13] What is natural is good, balanced, positive, normal, generative, and healing. Such a definition is the assumption behind Macduff's rebuff to Malcolm in England: "Boundless intemperance/In nature is a tyranny" (4.3.66–67). And such a definition informs Banquo's remark upon seeing the witches: "You should be women,/And yet your beards forbid me to interpret/That you are so" (1.3.45–47). The witches are out of nature; they are unnatural. They are hermaphroditic, not androgynous.[14] The point is important because Banquo's description is usually taken as a misogynous jibe. What Shakespeare reminds us of is that witches have no normative sexual identity. In fact, one of a witch's most pronounced and commonly invoked powers was to destroy normal sexuality, be it in a man or in a woman. Furthermore, witches have the ability to turn a woman into a man (although not a man into a woman). And it is in this doubled context that Lady Macbeth's famous "unsex me" speech (1.5.39) can be labeled unnatural. The "spirits" she invokes might just as well be Macbeth's witches.[15]

Within the intracontained and mutually reinforcing microcosms of Elizabethan thought, killing a human, a king, a guest, and a kinsman are, of course, all unnatural acts, and Lady Macbeth is afraid that her husband's nature is too good—or, too natural—to allow him to commit murder:

> Yet I do fear thy nature.
> It is too full o' th' milk of human kindness.
>
> (1.5.14–15)

The phrase makes us pause, rings in our ears: "the milk of human kindness." No other expression better reveals Shakespeare's basically optimistic vision of the nature of humankind (except possibly Miranda's speeches). Kindness is humanness; mankind is humankind.

And "the *milk* of human kindness"—how perfect. Basic nourishment, passed from mother to child—generation after generation. Madonna and child, symbol of goodness and love—humankindness (see Appendix V, Pictures V–1 and V–2). No wonder the language of Lady Macbeth's command to her own witches always startles us:

> Come to my woman's breasts
> And take my milk for gall, you murd'ring ministers,
> Wherever in your sightless substances
> You wait on nature's mischief.
>
> (1.5.45–48)

Yes, nature's first mischief was the unnatural act of fratricide. Yes, we live in a fallen world, where "fair is foul, and foul is fair." We live in Macbeth's world. The Thane of Fife had a wife:

> Whither should I fly?
> I have done no harm. But I remember now
> I am in this earthly world, where to do harm
> Is often laudable, to do good sometime
> Accounted dangerous folly. Why then, alas,
> Do I put up that womanly defense
> To say I have done no harm?
>
> (4.2.72–78)

Evil is a natural phenomenon, even though we call it unnatural. We do so, for confronting evil reality is the countervailing power of "the milk of human kindness," a redemptive force in nature.[16]

Shakespeare keeps the contrast of natural and unnatural before us when he again uses the metaphor of nourishment in Lady Macbeth's later direct challenge to her husband:

I have given suck, and know
How tender 'tis to love the babe that milks me:
I would, while it was smiling in my face,
Have plucked my nipple from his boneless gums
And dashed the brains out, had I so sworn as you
Have done to this.

(1.7.54–59)

Lady Macbeth knows that love, compassion, pity, remorse are all emotions which Macbeth has in his nature and which she must repress in him in order for Macbeth to carry on with the "bloody" business.

And she states before he arrives that she must repress in herself these same emotions, which she clearly thinks of as feminine (Buckingham ironically praises Richard's "tenderness of heart/And gentle, kind effeminate remorse" [*Richard III* 3.7.201–02]). Here, now in full, is the "unsex me" speech which Lady Macbeth addresses to her own witches:

Come, you spirits
That tend on mortal thoughts, unsex me here,
And fill me from the crown to the toe top-full
Of direst *cruelty. Make thick my blood*;
Stop up th' access and passage to *remorse*,
That no *compunctious visitings of nature*
Shake my fell purpose nor keep peace between
Th' effect and it. Come to my woman's breasts
And take my milk for gall, you murd'ring ministers,
Wherever in your sightless substances
You wait on nature's mischief.

(1.5.38–48; emphasis added)

Lady Macbeth wants to become cruel, which is a so-called masculine trait. But in order to become cruel, she must prevent the flow of blood from having "access and passage" to the heart, which is the seat of love, the source of "remorse," pity, compassion, and contrition—all of which are "compunctious" (Shakespeare coined the word) attributes of our human nature.[17] Human nature, in turn, takes its shape and being from the vital spirits that are carried in the atomies of the bloodstream, a major function of which, according to Aristotle and the Elizabethans, was to keep the heart alive. When the blood stops flowing into the heart, the heart loses its source of vitality and hardens—which leads to despair and suicide, the ultimate murder, the sin against life itself (hence the unpardonable sin).[18] Shakespeare is saying that compunction (the ayenbyte of inwyt) is natural and therefore human. But Lady Macbeth and her society confuse womanhood and humanhood.[19] In rejecting that which she has been made to think is weak and womanly within her in order to become cruel and manly, she moves away from her humanity toward the demonic, toward becoming a life-denying witch instead of toward that sixteenth-century secular ideal, Dame Nature, the androgynous force that created the world and keeps it in motion toward fulfillment.

We are told before we meet him that Macbeth is "noble," and he shows us when he is first in the presence of the witches that he is "compunctious" because the confrontation with the "supernatural soliciting" "doth unfix my hair/And make my seated heart knock at my ribs/*Against the use of nature*" (1.3.130, 135–137 emphasis added). The "If it were done when 'tis done" soliloquy (1.7.1ff) is all about conscience, and by the time his wife appears on stage he has concluded that "we will proceed no further in this business" (31). When his wife calls him afraid, casts doubt on his "act and valor," and taunts him with "letting 'I dare not' wait upon 'I would'," still he can wisely, humanly answer,

> Prithee peace!
> I dare do all that may become a man;
> Who dare do more is none.
>
> (1.7.40, 44, 45–47)

Here Macbeth has an androgynous view of humanity: "I *dare* do all that may *become* a man"—I am sufficiently courageous to do whatever is fitting to humanity, what is appropriate in the fullest sense. This is the climax of the opening action of the play: "We will proceed no further . . . I dare do all that may become a man." Macbeth has so far shown strength and dignity and seems activated by "the milk of human kindness," by compunctious visitings of nature.

In a sense, the play at this point becomes Lady Macbeth's, although Macbeth remains the main actor,[20] for he cannot resist and counter her next speech. Lady Macbeth responds immediately to the philosophical nature of his reply concerning what is right action in terms of manhood/humanhood by retorting boldly:

What *beast* was't then
That made you break this enterprise to me?

(47–48; emphasis added)

She is on target; we have seen Macbeth tempted by the witches and have just heard him admit his ambition. She insists on her definition of manhood as cruel, fearless, active, consistent, and brave in behalf of which she has sought to "unsex" herself (rather, uncultivate her cultivated "feminine" self): "When you durst do it, then you were a man" (49). Not valor or courage, but guts and balls. To this she adds the appeal of bettering one's self, using "man" in a very modern, colloquial way (by way of Nietzsche):

And to be more than what you were, you would
Be so much more the man.

(50–51)

She then cleverly ties these two meanings together when she sarcastically adds that now, having the time and place fit for murder "does unmake you" (54)—unmans you and uncrowns you. The ultimate challenge to his machismo—"I have given suck . . ." (54–59)—has been quoted above. Now it is she who here takes charge to present the plan for murder, and Macbeth's reluctant agreement is presented through the metaphor of the manly woman:

Bring forth men-children only;
For thy undaunted mettle should compose
Nothing but males.

(72–74)

Macbeth has succumbed to the limited definitions of male and female of his society as they have been expressed by Lady Macbeth—divided, separated definitions which reject the bonding nurture of the milk of human kindness—as can be seen in his reductive, simplistic syllogism: all men are tough; you are tough; therefore, all children coming from you will be, should be, had better be men if they are to survive in this cruel world. Even though his response is strained and sarcastic, it shows his conversion to her point of view. The two are in league against androgyny.

While Macbeth has acquiesced to a definition of masculinity which comes from dominant societal norms that equate machismo with manhood, Shakespeare does not allow us to forget that once Macbeth had a fuller vision, nor does he try to shift the blame for Macbeth's fall to Lady Macbeth. The "dagger" speech (2.1.33ff) arises from Macbeth's conscience (a sign of "compunctious visitings of nature"), but this soliloquy does not end with any "we will proceed no further." This time, before Lady Macbeth enters, the bell rings and Macbeth concludes, "I go, and it is done" (62), echoing Dr. Faustus when he signed the pact: Christ's *consummatum est*. In going to kill the king—Christ on earth—he is on his way literally and figuratively to becoming the kind of man his wife has urged.[21] When he pretends to discover the murder of Duncan, his words carry piercing ironic truth:

from this instant
There's nothing serious in mortality:
All is but toys.

(2.3.88–90)

For him, this is the precise truth; once he has destroyed the order of nature, all is reduced to triviality. Hence, his rhetorical question is devastatingly ironic:

Who can be wise, amazed, temp'rate and furious,
Loyal and neutral, in a moment? No man.

(104–05)

No, not the kind of man he is becoming, but the ideal answer is any man—or all humanity should strive for this androgynous fulfillment. Still, he presents his thoughts within a philosophical framework, one now perverted:

The expedition of my violent love
Outrun the pauser, reason.
. . . .
Who could refrain
That had a heart to love, and in that heart
Courage to make 's love known?

(106–14)

Shakespeare was well aware that true love is reasonable and that courage means heart-stuff: we still say "take heart," meaning be calmly resolute, be patient—a meaning opposite to Macbeth's counsel, "Let's briefly put on manly readiness" (129).[22]

"Manly readiness" is what the two murderers have when they respond to Macbeth's challenge to carry out revenge against Banquo: "We are men, my liege" (3.1.91). The self-reflective irony within Macbeth's long diatribe, "Ay, in the catalogue ye go for men" (92), takes its force from our recognition that Macbeth recognizes that he is like these men even while some vestige of his former view of life—"I dare do all that may become a man"—informs the speech.[23]

This counterplay between two views of manhood is expanded in the banquet scene (which I am tempted to call the further milking of Macbeth). When Banquo's ghost first appears, Lady Macbeth tries to calm her husband by a near-Pavlovian technique; she says in an aside to him, "Are you a man?" Shakespeare's repetition of the verb "dare" in Macbeth's answer signals the degree that Macbeth has slipped from true manhood ("I dare do all that may become a man"):

> Ay, and a bold one, that *dare* to look on that
> Which might appal the devil.
>
> (3.4.5–60; emphasis added)

Still, compunctious visitings of nature continue to shake him, bringing Lady Macbeth to direct irony, but embracing ironies only fully apparent to us and Shakespeare:

> O proper stuff!
> This is the very painting of your fear.
> This is the air-drawn dagger which you said
> Led you to Duncan. O, these flaws and starts
> (Imposters to true fear) would well become
> A woman's story at a winter's fire,
> Authorized by her grandam.
> . . . .
> What, quite unmanned in folly?
>
> (60–73)

The conscience-invoked dagger *was* a sign of true (reason-able) fear; thus, Shakespeare indicates that Lady Macbeth's mockingly feminine "flaws and stares" are *not* "imposters to true fear" as she claims, but are final visitings of nature which could redeem, restore, or remake Macbeth.

With the second entry of Banquo, Macbeth is even more distracted, and Shakespeare has Macbeth return a third time to the concept of daring in a way that calls attention to how far Macbeth has drifted away from his earliest vision. There is frenzy now in his rejection of conscience:

> What man *dare*, I *dare*.
> Approach thou like the rugged Russian bear,
> The armed rhinoceros, or th'Hyrcan tiger;
> Take any shape but that, and my firm nerves
> Shall never tremble. Or be alive again
> And *dare* me to the desert with thy sword.
> If trembling I inhabit then, protest me
> The baby of a girl.[24]
>
> (99–106; emphasis added)

Macbeth here makes the final division of humanhood into manhood and womanhood, and reduces them to mere derring-do and cowardice. Thus his words when Banquo leaves for the last time have a fulfilled ironic thematic significance: "Why, so, being gone,/I am a man again" (107–108). He is not a weak girl-baby, but one of Lady Macbeth's "men-children."

Shakespeare returns to this motif of manhood at the very end of the play. On finding out about Macduff's Caesarean delivery (at that time considered to be an unnatural manner of birth), Macbeth gasps:

> Accursed by that tongue that tells me so,
> For it hath cowed my better part of man.
>
> (5.8.17–18)

Johnson defined "cowed" as depressed with fear, dispirited, overawed, intimidated. Indeed, the tragedy of Macbeth lies in the fact that during the play his "better part of man" has increasingly been repressed by his worse part, his merely tough part. The androgynous understanding of humanity—as illustrated through Macduff's reaction to the slaughter of his family, and seemingly at the outset felt and acknowledged by Macbeth—has been completely perverted. After the murder of Duncan, Macbeth's heart receives fewer and fewer visits from compunctious nature. Because his heart is gradually hardening, Macbeth can no longer feel, or rather, has just enough memory of feeling to highlight his isolation and pathos:

> I have almost forgot the taste of fears.
> The time has been my senses would have cooled
> To hear a night-shriek, and my fell of hair
> Would at a dismal treatise rouse and stir
> As life were in't. I have supped full with horrors.
> Direness, familiar to my slaughterous thoughts,

Cannot once start me.

(5.5.9–15)

At the beginning of the play, the sight and unnatural temptings of the witches did rouse and stir his hair (1.3.135); now, at this point, he admits his state of degeneration. The androgynous promptings of Dame Nature have become so sluggish, so deadened, his heart so hardened, that nothing can startle him.

Why is it, then, that we do not detest Lord and Lady Macbeth? Both are clearly evil. She is early determined to play the serpent (1.5.24–25), and from the outset we are given the disturbing suspicion that even before encountering the witches Macbeth has entertained the unnatural act of regicide:

My thought, whose murder yet is but fantastical,
Shakes so my single state of man that function
Is smothered in surmise and nothing is
But what is not.

(1.3.139–42)

So why cannot we simply dismiss them? Why do we not join the chorus of Thanes who cheer Macduff's announcement that "the time is free"? We cannot because Macbeth and Lady Macbeth have been all too human throughout—through them Shakespeare appeals to our shared humanity, our common capability and desire for human fulfillment.[25]

In Lady Macbeth's derangement and death we experience her humanity, for they show that she was not as tough as she thought she was. Ironically, to Elizabethans, insanity and suicide were considered signs of weakness, signs of cowardice, therefore partaking of the "feminine." (Ophelia's suicide is handled more tolerantly than it would have been had she been a man, of course, who was of equal social status.) Lady Macbeth's culture, however, does not allow her to truly develop her full self. She operates from the increasingly restrictive culturally defined assumptions of a seventeenth-century feminine self. Furthermore, when she says "unsex me," she really means ungender me, which serves to point up the cultural confusion and misunderstanding of sex and gender in the early seventeenth century (as well as in the present twentieth). And the irony of this attempt to masculate herself is highlighted by the fact that she was trying to be the "good and dutiful" wife of the newly emerging middle-class, mercantile, Protestant, work-ethic culture: helping her husband to better himself. In the words of Marilyn French, she "seems to be . . . an exemplary wife," who "encourages and supports her husband in good wifely fashion."[26] Through a literal self-effacement, she attempts to back and support her spouse in his worldly ambition and to force him to compete in the male hierarchy. But in trying to act a socially appropriate role, she acts unnaturally, she moves counter to the pulls of kindness. She cannot deny her humanity; insanity is the only path out of the position she has fashioned. Yet, even in resolution and in madness there is moving recognition of the bond of nature: "Had he not resembled/My father as he slept, I had done't (2.2.12–13); "Yet who would have thought the old man to have had so much blood in him?" (5.1.35).

So too with Macbeth. No matter how steeped in blood, he never loses sight of a different life, a truly better life:

> My way of life
> Is fall'n into the sear, the yellow leaf,
> And that which should accompany old age,
> As honor, love, obedience, troops of friends,
> I must not look to have; but, in their stead,
> Curses not loud but deep, mouth-honor, breath,
> Which the poor heart would fain deny, and *dare* not.
>
> (5.3.22–28; emphasis added)

This last and final use of "dare" embraces both senses of manhood—I should not and I cannot—and tends to bring Macbeth back into the pale of humanity. The speech allows us to pity Macbeth because it shows he retains a vision of a fuller, healthier, "wholier" life, even though he has narrowed his life, repressed his nature, choked his humankindness.

And together they are humanized through their love for each other. From the outset we can observe their love from the way they address, treat, and respect each other and from the way, in most productions, they lovingly handle each other. This love observed is what gives power to Macbeth's melancholy response to the announcement, "The Queen, my lord, is dead":

> She should have died hereafter:
> There would have been a time for such a word.
>
> (5.5.16–18)

Macbeth realizes that in the natural course of events, Lady Macbeth would have lived her life through to its natural end. On some tomorrow there would have been occasion for such a word.[27] But, he, she, they have prevented all that. Time now for Macbeth merely "creeps in this petty pace from day to day." Their ambitions have merely led to death. Now that the brief candle of her life has been extinguished, his own life is merely

a tale
Told by an idiot, full of sound and fury,
Signifying nothing.

(5.5.19–28)

Lord and Lady Macbeth may end in despair, but we do not share that state with them. While Shakespeare in *Macbeth* criticizes the destructive polarity of masculine versus feminine, counterpointing that destructive polarity is the suggestive presence of creative mutuality, both the merging of masculine and feminine in a person and the merging of male and female in marriage, that age-old symbol of primordial unity and apocalyptic harmony. However, marriage itself is not androgyny. Marriage is a symbol of androgyny because in the experience of marriage—same-sex or across-sex—one can lose one's self to find one's self: I was half, now I am whole. The experience of androgyny is in the self; marriage does not save us from solitude. Marriage can be a *means* toward androgyny because of its powerful offering of sexual and psychic knowledge—"who knows not that conscience is born of love?" Awareness of androgyny can be shared—*con-science*—but the roots and realization are private, are within.

10

Lear and Cordelia: "Cosmic Man" and "Heavenly Queen"

King Lear is Shakespeare's most deeply searching, disturbing, and provocative tragedy: his greatest play. As such—in short and most dogmatically—*King Lear* is one of the world's great works of art. Like the works of Michelangelo, its value to humanity is unceasing and unending.[1]

The play moves through the classic sequence of opening in order, moving through disorder, and achieving final order. But the movement is much more subtle and sophisticated, for the opening order is superficial and the final order is won at too great a sacrifice for us to attend to it. We need no deconstructionist newly come from France to tell us this. Indeed, the central disorder contains more clarity, meaning, and reliable truth in its revelations than do the opening and closing orders, cloaked as they are in the structures of ceremony.

King Lear is the story of a man, we are told, who hath ever but slenderly known himself, but which of us can say any more about ourselves? This is the story of a man who mistakes appearance for reality, but which of us does not? Unlike us, this man is a king—a man of command, of mastered achievement—one who is "everything." But such a person is not really so, for such a one is, as we all are, absolutely dependent on others. When such a man finds that he is not totally just, wise, and generous, that all is not well, that the world for most is full of care—a kind of care totally different from the cares of being a king—the recognition is overpowering, disordering, deranging, chaotic. He loses his primary modes of identity when he consciously removes himself from the role of king and unconsciously removes himself from the role of parent; there is little left except his folly to guide him. Unwittingly, he was preparing himself for a journey toward androgyny.[2]

We early recognize our humanity in the king (*genus humanus*),[3] and when he recognizes his in ours, a bond is formed which allows us mutually to confront and oppose the evil of the world, an evil largely defined and understood through the multiple meanings of that favored word of the Renaissance, Nature.[4] The meanings rung upon this word in *Lear* are totally inclusive. Framing the play is the assumption that Nature in the abstract is ideal, is perfect, but filling the play is evidence of fallen Nature. Behind Lear's curses of his daughters stands Dame Nature ("Hear, Nature, Hear; dear goddess, hear"), just as mere nature, the "raw matter" of chaos, is invoked by Edmund ("Thou, Nature, art my goddess"). Dame Nature, nourishing, bountiful, renewing, gives rise to and preserves the bonds of nature; mere nature is wild, random, violent, destroying all but the strong, thus denying the bonds of nature. The interplay of the two, supernature and subnature, gives definition to the natural condition ("Let me wipe it first; it smells of mortality"). Gloucester has an essentially medieval mind; blind to the world, he sees nature as fixed, ordained, destined—and those of like mind take his "As flies to wanton boys" speech as the statement of the theme of the play.

To so read the play is to miss the emphasis on inner nature. As is made exceedingly dramatic by the storm within the storm of Lear, the microcosm, humankind, is where the action takes place and where the theme is found. Emerson said, "We come into this world not to find out how good it is, but how good we are." Not "good" in any superficially moral sense, but essentially good—what is our make-up, our temperament, our worth, our inner emotional balance and strength—wherein, if in anything, are we good? Such is the burden of *King Lear*, and the burden of proof is the play.

When Albany in 4.2 says to Goneril upon her return from the shutting-out of Lear at Gloucester's castle, "You are not worth the dust which the rude wind/Blows in your face," we are given by Shakespeare one of those lines which is fittingly spoken in the heat of the moment, fully appropriate for that moment in the action, but which reverberates well beyond context to suggest broadly implied and broadly applied meanings. Albany's sentence is emblematic, picture and words. The "rude wind," the storm of life, the tempest, is the natural condition, spreading the seeds of life but also bringing discomfort to the living; the "dust" is us, nothing and everything, Hamlet's belief in the alchemical marriage, the potent and potential "quintessence of dust." Shakespeare through Albany implies that life is a test ("the trial by existence" of Robert Frost), a proving ground, where the readiness, the ripeness is all. "Maturity" was the word Sir Thomas Elyot brought into English to suggest the concept of growth to fully realized development, and it is the word modern critics use to describe the theme of this old play.[5]

Paraphrasing a play in order to reveal its theme runs the danger of parodying both play and theme, but criticism is rarely shy. Having been buffeted by the rude wind in Act 3, Lear, by scene 4, recognizes in his own "unfed sides," "houseless" head, and "looped and windowed raggedness" the lack of adequate food, shelter, and clothing experienced by most "poor naked wretches." The metaphor of the storm is simultaneously threefold: internal, external, and extended. Earlier in 2.4, he had sarcastically asked Regan if he must disgrace himself by humbling himself to ask Goneril's "forgiveness" and to "beg . . . raiment, bed, and food"; and he had arrogantly, aphoristically asserted, after Goneril's arrival, that if we "allow not nature more than nature needs,/Man's life is cheap as beast's." But having experienced what others experience, Lear realizes that he has "ta'en/Too little care of this." Now he can ask, seeing Edgar-as-Tom stripped to the skin, "Is man no more than this?" He realizes that mankind without food, shelter, and clothing ("unaccommodated man") is undefended, needs help, and his instinct is to share that clothing he has: "Off, off, you lendings! Come, unbutton here." Lear, king, has become Lear, man, and the second subsumes the first, a truth he had not realized until now.

This moment and this truth he recalls later at the height of his sanity when on the heath near Cordelia's camp he enters, "*mad, bedecked with weeds*" (4.6.80):

> They flattered me like a dog, and told me I had the white hairs in my beard ere the black ones were there. To say "ay" and "no" to everything I said! "Ay" and "no" too was no good divinity. When the rain came to wet me once, and the wind to make me chatter; when the thunder would not peace at my bidding; there I found'em, there I smelt'em out. Go to, they are not men o'their words. They told me I was everything. 'Tis a lie—I am not ague-proof.

"I am not ague-proof"—a clause well beyond need of paraphrase, certainly capturing the essence of the human condition. When Gloucester asks if this is the King, Lear's response underscores his recognition of his humankindness—"Ay, every inch a King"—*Rex humanitas* has become *humanitas*; in both cases a proud and yet a wretched thing.

Up to this point in the play, the Fool has been present to remind Lear of his common humanity.[6] Now his presence is not needed, for Lear has become the wise fool: "O matter and impertinency mixed; Reason in madness," Edgar observes. Edgar is our chorus, but all dramatic function and any thought of metadrama dissolve when he says, "I would not take this from report—it is,/And my heart breaks at it." Lest the lesson be lost, Shakespeare has a Gentleman comment, "A sight most pitiful in the meanest wretch,/Past speaking of in a King." Shakespeare goes on to give him these emblematic lines:

> Thou hast one daughter
> Who redeems Nature from the general curse
> Which twain have brought her to.

The "twain" are simultaneously Goneril and Regan, Adam and Eve; therefore, Cordelia is Lear's daughter and is Christ.[7] Over the years, many have alluded to an undocumented stage tradition that the actor who had played the Fool also played Cordelia. Whether or not historically true, the idea is fitting because of the similarity of one function shared by the two characters: to remind Lear of his humankindness, to help him step beyond the barriers which imprison him in the roles of king and father. Differences abound between the two, but in this function the role of the fool is to bring Lear into the pale of humanity, and the role of Cordelia is to redeem and reform that humanity once it has reached this solid, shared ground. In this sense, Cordelia ("dear heart") is a type of Christ, who was the first among fools (according to St. Paul and Erasmus) for caring so much for humankind that he actually, willingly clothed his free spirit within flesh. Fool, Cordelia, Christ—all androgynes.[8]

There is no need to argue whether or not Cordelia is or is not a Christ-figure; of course she is, of course she is not. According to Christians, all humans should become fools in Christ, living in love and charity with their fellow creatures, as does Cordelia; but Cordelia dies, and Lear dies—there is no redemption from death, no miracles occur.[9] All of the action takes place on the secular level; nevertheless, on this level, Cordelia "redeems Nature," for Cordelia here acts like a humanist-educator, as well as a Protestant-reformer, even an alchemist-philosopher, to raise Lear from the realm of fallen nature toward the ideal, and she does so by her example of herself. The King of France had paid her the highest of compliments within a mercantile, materialistic culture (at the same time highly insulting Lear) when he had said of Cordelia in 1.1 that "she is herself a dowry." The King of France had recognized Cordelia's inner worth, her integrity. In this sense, she, like Una, stands for Truth, the truth of unity of mind.

Although Shakespeare three times uses allusions to Christ in describing Cordelia,[10] the reunion scene in the French camp (4.7), filled with the rituals of rebirth, love, and forgiveness, is alone sufficient to suggest the comparison. The scene is a form of Revelation with Lear, in the role of bride, dressed in white, and Cordelia as the redeemer, bringing with her even the heavenly music of the spheres, that ultimate expression of unity and harmony that Kepler in his theory of musical composition labeled androgynous.

When Lear awakes, he is not just restored to his senses; he awakes with a peace of mind which surpasses understanding. He now operates on a higher plane of awareness than others do. He has the patience and calm of sweetened reasonableness. His words are intended to have a level of communication with us that is lost on the characters surrounding him in the play—his life has become a parable. He is correct when he calls Cordelia "a spirit," just as she is incorrect when she comments, "Still, still, far wide!" All of his life, Lear has judged and been judged on a literal scale. Things and people are what they are called. But people and things are better understood by being likened to other things and people. (Robert Frost was fond of repeating, "What she is, is what she's like.") Lear has been "king" and "father"; Cordelia has been "daughter," "princess," "sister." Roles are dress which seem to reveal identity, but hide what is within. Lear has learned that roles can be prisons, even for those who live in palaces. He is able now to see Cordelia not as daughter who has a duty to love a father, but as a spirit of love.

Lear's instinctive action of kneeling marks how far he has grown in feeling and sensitive awareness since the beginning of the play. Then, for a king, father, and man to kneel to a subject, daughter, and woman was beneath all dignity—social dignity. Here, such an act fully shows the true dignity of the man. When he says, "I am a very foolish fond old man," we know he has gained wisdom, and when he says, "I fear I am not in my perfect mind," we know he is more sane than most of us. Restored, reposed, and reintegrated, he casually lets slip what amounts to the strongest of oaths: "*As I am a man*, I think this lady to be my child Cordelia." Her quiet verification is beyond comment, "And so I am! I am!" And Lear leaves the scene in androgynous fulfillment: "Pray you now, forget and forgive. I am old and foolish." Most wise, because most human.[11]

During the first twenty-five lines of what turns out to be the long and complicated last scene of the play (5.3), when Lear and Cordelia are seen briefly, both alive, the values of the world they have entered together are made quite clear. No need to "see these daughters and these sisters." Lear and Cordelia will not indulge in social role-playing with daughters and sisters and courtiers; they will enact and reenact the rituals of mutual love, blessing and forgiving. Where they are and the status assigned them do not matter, for they have discovered within themselves the strength to live and love and truly endure:

> No, no, no, no! Come, let's away to prison.
> We two alone will sing like birds i' th' cage.
> When thou dost ask me blessing, I'll kneel down
> And ask of thee forgiveness. So we'll live,
> And pray, and sing, and tell old tales, and laugh
> At gilded butterflies, and hear poor rogues
> Talk of court news; and we'll talk with them too—
> Who loses and who wins; who's in, who's out—
> And take upon's the mystery of things

> As if we were God's spies; and we'll wear out,
> In a walled prison, packs and sects of great ones
> That ebb and flow by th' moon.

To pray, to sing, to tell old tales, and to laugh at the new news of the new court is to live in the golden world and to fleet the time carelessly. As we saw with Sidney's help in chapter 4, old tales and a golden world are the realms of poetry, of myth and dream. And that is the realm—the realm of Caliban's dream—where Lear and Cordelia will dwell, even if in prison. (Hamlet would envy them.) They may weep, but the cause will be from within, not from the "real world." They may be tortured and separated, but they will not be parted. United, each is able to live in the other; each is now able to experience androgynous fulfillment:

> Upon such sacrifices, my Cordelia,
> The gods themselves throw incense. Have I caught thee?
> He that parts us shall bring a brand from heaven
> And fire us hence like foxes. Wipe thine eyes.
> The good years shall devour them, flesh and fell,
> Ere they shall make us weep! We'll see'em starved first.
> Come.

When Lear reenters, "*with Cordelia in his arms*" (257), he continues his existence on this special plane of awareness, alert to, but beyond, the merely mundane and social. ("I'll see that straight"; "Ay, so I think.") "Howl, howl, howl" is a self-parody of his macho braving of the storm in Act 3. Here he patiently accepts what life has to offer: "She's dead as earth." He does not heed or need "the chorus" of Kent, Edgar, and Albany proclaiming a secular apocalypse:

> Is this the promised end?
> Or image of that horror?
> Fall and cease.

This is *an* end, and it is final. Cordelia is no Christ. If she lives, "It is a chance which does redeem all sorrows/That I have ever felt." No miracle—but no rage: acceptance. Acceptance of the world, bad and good together, fallen and ideal.

Fallen nature isolates, but ideal nature bonds, and together they define life: all life is cellular, constantly breaking and bonding. When in conjunction with the first, the second fact is denied, we have existence defined in a tragic mode. As Maynard Mack has observed: "Existence is tragic in *King Lear* because existence is inseparable from relation; we are born from and to it; it envelops us in our loves and lives as parents, children, sisters, brothers, husbands, wives, servants, masters, rulers, subjects—the web is seamless and unending. When we talk of virtue, patience, courage, joy, we talk of what supports it. When we talk of tyranny, lust, and treason, we talk of what destroys it."[12] Virtue, patience, courage, joy—these are some of the attributes of androgyny, of a way of life that leads to social unity and harmony out of an inner-achieved unity and harmony. Mere ceremony is the enemy of life.

The tragedy of King Lear is that he comes to a realization of this too late in his life. In the beginning, he demanded the forms of love, not knowing its inner substance. All he required was "Ay" and "No" to everything he said, instead of truth, as in "good divinity." He discovered too late in life that he was "not ague-proof." Now he can accept death because he understands love and the conditions of nature.

I agree with Mack that, "in his last speech, the full implications of the human condition evidently come home to Lear. He has made his choice, and there will be no reward," but I do not agree with Mack (and most critics since Bradley) that Lear cannot hold "this painful vision unflinchingly before his consciousness" and that Lear dies under the illusion that Cordelia still lives. Some critics hold that the illusion is ironic, indicating an absurd universe, and others insist that the illusion is symbolic of a beneficent one; to Mack, Lear's final illusion is simply "one we need not begrudge him on his death bed" (114–16).

But I believe that the logic of this text, as well as the general tone of the Shakespeare canon, suggests that Lear dies under no illusion of any sort, but in full acceptance of death, "Never, never, never, never, never," and in full realization of the need of love to support life, "Pray you, undo this button. Thank you, sir."[13] From the time he has carried Cordelia's body on stage, Lear has never let her go and his whole attention has been on her lips, not just to see if she lives but in recollection of her love and the now frustrated significance of her existence; he now knows that she was, in herself, a dowry. "Her voice was ever soft,/Gentle and low, an excellent thing in woman." His final act is the unselfish one of reminding us still alive of the value of love: "Look on her, look, her lips,/Look there, look there."

When Lear says that "her voice was ever soft,/Gentle and low, an excellent thing in woman," his words do not give offense—he could have said "man" because he is talking about an androgynous quality of humankind. In an earlier life he could not have said "man" in this context; then he held that women and children should be seen and not heard in this, a man's world. Now he has awakened to the music and majesty of the human voice. The values of life exceed strutting, fretting, and being heard. His former life was an empty life, filled with empty words. He had not actually listened to

Goneril and Regan as they proffered love, nor to any of the ay- and no-sayers of his court; he had only subconsciously censored their phrases for propriety—for what they ought to say.

At the beginning of the play Cordelia had spoken what she felt, not (on a pragmatic basis) what she *should* have said at that time, in that place. But she felt more than just truth; she felt anger and jealousy, all diffused. Pet daughter, kid sister, will no one see me for what I am? The frustration is all too believable, but who, besides Goneril and Regan and Edmund, can really believe that she gets what she deserves? Easy to say in a classroom or a book. But she, as does Lear, "learns"—oh, what a harsh word—"no cause, no cause."

In the beginning, Cordelia did tell the truth, but only the truth. She did not speak what she really felt: disgust with her sisters and love for her father. Her answer to Lear's need did not come from her heart but from her head. She, in a way, had responded to Lear's question in a cause-and-effect manner, as had her sisters. But surely we come away from *King Lear* having experienced at some level of our consciousness that human intercourse should not be conducted on a cause-and-effect level, but should stem from within, as in the human intercourse of blessing and forgiving. In this, we, too, as we leave the theater, should obey "the weight of this sad time" and learn to "speak what we feel, not what we ought to say."[14]

Prospero tells us that in his ordeal Miranda was "a cherubin . . . that did preserve me." In Lear's case, Cordelia could have been his preserver, and that he realizes as much kills him, but he dies imploring us to live better. Speak what we feel, not what we ought to say; to act with an androgynous integrity, not from and to our socially defined orientation. This is the lesson Cordelia, even, learns and the one we must learn, as did Lear, from her.[15]

The merger of masculine and feminine becomes a dominant theme in the romances, but is most poignantly expressed here in this Pietà that closes the play. Manly Lear with dead Cordelia cradled in his arms cries "womanly" tears and speaks in a voice that is "ever soft, gentle, and low"—"an excellent thing" in man or woman. If we patiently watch and listen to this wise, fond, foolish, old man, perhaps we too may experience a vision of potential personal wholeness without first having to see so much or live so long.

11

Prospero and the Art of Humankindness

From 1601 through 1604, after the grand achievement of the romantic comedies, Shakespeare seems consciously to have moved into an experimental phase.[1] Those chorus speeches in *Henry V* are Shakespeare's ironic account of the art of dramatic poetry, and they imply that Shakespeare was dropping the genre of "history" (which had been his to develop and which had been very good to him) because it was too restricting for his imagination—it did not provide sufficiently an "imaginative ground plot of a profitable invention." Shakespeare moved into a "serious" phase, writing commanding, searching, cerebral drama, but drama which seems never to have found completed lines of development: *Julius Caesar*, *Hamlet*, *Troilus and Cressida*, *Measure for Measure*, and *All's Well That Ends Well*, each, at one time or another in the twentieth century, has been called one of Shakespeare's "Problem Plays."[2] Certainly each, in the Ibsen-Shaw sense, focuses on a social, ethical "problem" which refuses to be settled neatly, and each is a critical "problem" in and of itself; none falls neatly into a conventional category. Because these five plays are doubly problematic they have given and will continue to give free reign to critical inquiry and scholarly exploration.

In *Othello*, *Macbeth*, and *King Lear*, the plot lines are clear and the stories are resolved within a familiar generic context. With plot and genre under control Shakespeare can focus on character; he tries to sound the deeps of humankindness. Each play, varied and busy, is ultimately controlled by a base-level plot that is a sort of return to the morality play, which Theodore Spencer long ago saw as a main source and inspiration for Shakespearean drama. But each play deals with everyman and mankind through a person of highly particularized, complicated humanity.

Othello is pulled by his good and evil angels; the issues and themes are white and black, salvation and perdition. Othello's head and heart do not grow into accord; he is pulled apart, not sealed in self-sufficient wholeness. Macbeth moves from a kind of wholeness to a perverted independence; he knows his actions are wrong, but thinks he can get away with them. In attempting to better himself, he damns himself. Lear, a man who thinks that the social, ceremonial parades and progresses of life are life, misses the inner life: his own, his family's, his people's. Purged of his over-concern with surface values, he discovers the value of essential human worth, and, too late, seeks to renew his life on the basis of that invention.

In *Othello*, *Macbeth*, and *King Lear*, the action of the through-line sweeps across the boards to encompass and to possess us. This does not happen in *Timon of Athens*, *Coriolanus*, and *Antony and Cleopatra*. They are each part history, part tragedy, and part comedy.[3] They are plays, they are drama; they entertain and amuse, but in infuriatingly curious ways. They are strained, full of conscious bickering and deflation. As a result, each is essentially comic, as had been *Troilus and Cressida*. But, like *Troilus*, they are not ritualistic, festive, or purgative. They present no sense of The Comedy, the ultimate human comedy that life is, but only is when seen through the eyes of sustained comic disinterest.

1
The Four Comic Tragedies

All of this is changed in Shakespeare's last plays, the four romances, *Pericles*, *Cymbeline*, *The Winter's Tale*, and *The Tempest*, which prove beyond doubt that one can maintain comic detachment and simultaneously stimulate human warmth and genuine concern; they are, indeed, comic tragedies.[4] By 1608, at age 44, Shakespeare seems no longer to have been acting, was writing barely a play a year, and was spending more time in Stratford. The money was rolling in, for he was still a major shareholder in England's most successful—artistically and commercially—company of players. Edward Bond has his own version of these years, as did nineteenth-century critics with their theories of Shakespeare's decline, both artistically and emotionally.

In our century, we have grown mature enough to sense something positive in the difference of these plays, and we too speculate about Shakespeare in his last years in his theater. By 1608, Shakespeare was a grandfather, and four generations were still alive, although his mother was to die in September. Not only was his life literally broadened—in 1608 the Kings Men took up the Burbage lease at the Blackfriars, permitting them to play year-round in two different locations, day and night, in two theaters different from one another physically and in traditions. Thus, the demands on his artistic life were broadened. At one time much was made of Shakespeare's having to write for the one-time rival private theater. Shakespeare's last plays are indeed both public and private, but not in the restricted sense of theater, public and/or private, for, as many critics have come to record, these last four plays are written in a new key. The elements of the romances are not new: they call up historical worlds (although not strictly historically), they revive themes and motifs from the romantic comedies, and they invoke the same ultimate human values as do the tragedies. But, as Dame Frances Yates pointed out in her final book, these plays share a new note, one of "reconciliation."[5]

Alfred Harbage, my late master, felt a "sense of creative poise" in these plays which "seems to emanate increasingly from the very heart of the works." He went on to say:

> Shakespeare himself is *in* them, as he was *in* the great tragedies, but his mood is not the same; whether or not the man has found peace of mind, the artist chooses to contemplate those aspects of existence which contribute to peace of mind—the general phenomena of creation and growth, rebirth and renewal, and particular instances of restoration, redemption, fulfillment, providential intervention, realized hopes and sheer good luck. Characters are reconciled to their lives and each other in a way which reconciles us to life. The material is identical with the material of the tragedies—the deadly sins are on the prowl—and we feel, as in the tragedies, that the human condition is being allegorized, but the allegory invites a new interpretation. In the tragedies, good resists evil, whose ministers are finally expunged, but at the cost of dreadful suffering and waste. In the romances the resistance is more passive, yet less costly, and good succeeds evil instead of merely surviving it. These are plays of the second chance.[6]

The romances can be called "plays of the second chance" because they imply that we can learn from life, that we can learn to do better, act better, be better, that we can profit from experience, other people's and our own. They suggest that there is a process in life which can evolve in a kind of collective progress. These plays celebrate life—the beginning, the course, the ending, and the renewal all over again, but a renewal that is informed.[7] They are the first plays to emphasize the generations of life—in both meanings of the word generation. There is nothing "bleeding heart" or "fuzzy minded" or "merely intellectual" about them. They are *visionary*, but visionary in the purest sense of vision, *visio intellectus*, a seeing implying a reading and understanding and acceptance of life, all of life, whole life.[8] Evil is here.[9] *Pericles* begins amid skulls which serve as a bed for an incest that is educated, calculated, and continued. In *Cymbeline* the king is blind, Iachimo is a callous manipulator. In *The Winter's Tale* Leontes is a sick fool, Autolycus is a self-serving rogue. And the shadowed are here: Lysimachus, Posthumus, Polixenes. But above all, the good are here as well: Marina, Imogen, Paulina, Hermione, and Perdita. And so also in *The Tempest* we have the evil Sebastian and Antonio, the muddled Alonso and Prospero, and the good and innocent Ferdinand, Miranda, and Gonzalo, that choral "good old man," a familiar figure who throughout Shakespeare's plays holds firmly and without embarrassment to a vision of humankind that is optimistic—an androgynous vision which reaches far beyond the confines of concern and care for self.[10]

Above all—rather: beneath all—Shakespeare's four comic tragedies celebrate the myth of androgyny, the attempt to realize personal wholeness unimpeded by societal hindrance. This is not a return to a 1960s "do your own thing"; rather it simply means to be able to define yourself, and to be defined by others, *not* by who you are or what you do, but by what you are—the what you are within who you are and what you do. It is in this sense that the romances are both private and public plays. Because they are plays, the danger of solipsism is cancelled, for a play, by definition, is jointly "self" and "other"—audience and actor, actor and audience. Being in the audience or being on the stage, the self-and-other interaction is present, for the attending to a play and the presenting of a play are both parts of an ensemble activity. And with *these* plays, the barriers between audience and actors are invisible because the plays are so unreal. On one level, Shakespeare is saying, if you believe this you will believe anything; but, of course, this way he can make us believe everything.[11] These plays—filled with spirits, magic, and the metaphysical—are so unreal they are like dreams—both full of the unbelievable—except to the dreamer. These are not the stories of everyday life, or of historic episodes, or of the great and famous brought low. These are just tales—old tales, fairy tales, winter's tales.[12]

The Tempest is Shakespeare's last grand effort, valedictory in quality, a farewell—by consensus, a "last and final" play.[13] It is hard not to hear Shakespeare speaking to us through Prospero.[14] Whatever the voice and intention, while *King Lear* may be Shakespeare's greatest play, *The Tempest* is Shakespeare's most perfect—balanced, whole, contained, and measured. The poetry is supreme, the range of characters great and varied, and the plot even displays a perfect neoclassical unity of action, place, and time. Shakespeare is saying to Jonson and the others who are laying down the lines for future drama, see I can do it, too—it's easy. But the whole play is wonderfully Elizabethan, full of comedy, love, and, above all else, searching thought. In fact, it could be called the last Elizabethan play.[15] In *The Tempest*, as in the other three romances, gender and generational differences are overcome through synthesis and merger into "something rich and strange."[16]

2
The Tempest

The high Renaissance in England is framed by Marlowe's *Dr. Faustus* and *The Tempest*.[17] Both Faustus and Prospero were "reputed . . . for the liberal arts/Without parallel"; both went beyond the established curricula, "being transported/And rapt in secret studies." But Faustus lost faith in the efficacy of study, tired of the life of the mind, and turned to the world. Prospero remained "all dedicated/To closeness, and the bettering of my mind," finding that "my library/Was dukedom large enough." When Prospero was expelled from Milan, Gonzalo,

> of his gentleness,
> Knowing I loved my books . . . furnished me
> From mine own library with volumes that
> I prize above my dukedom.
>
> (1.2.165–68)

Faustus could not become a great Renaissance magus because he lost faith in the books in his own library, whereas Prospero was successful because he did study all the books in his library.[18] Prospero was able to force the storms because he had discovered in his books the secrets of nature.[19]

The secrets of nature were written into the Book of Nature by the Grand Author; hence, books about that large book collectively contained all one needed to know on earth about nature. Gonzalo stowed Prospero's books, Caliban knows the books were key to Prospero's power, and finally Prospero comes to the symbolic conclusion that he must drown his books. Prospero will not forget what he has learned from his books, but the books represent his having isolated himself from society. Faustus, at the end of his graduate school days, had turned from his books in order, he thought, to fulfill himself. So now, at the end of his life, Prospero will turn from his books, not for theological reasons, but for human ones: his studies have removed him from the pale of mankind and he knows that he must return to Italy, human as he is, to be once again the Duke of Milan.[20]

At the beginning of the play, in his long, embarrassed confession-narration to Miranda, Prospero, as just quoted above, had said of his books that they are things that "I prize above my dukedom." The tense is all important, for it emphasizes that Prospero changes his mind later and sees life from a new point of view by the end of the play, where he no longer prizes his books above his dukedom, the symbol of society, of humanity. In changing his mind, Prospero completes himself; he becomes an androgyne. He learns the lesson of another art, the art of humankindness.[21]

In isolation from humanity, first in Milan, then on the island, Prospero, by mastering the secrets of nature, became the Magus which the learned dreamed of becoming.[22] He succeeded where Faustus failed; he became "a spirit in form and substance" through Ariel, who is not just a symbol of that achievement, but is that achievement. Ariel is not human (has no body, no sex) but a spirit, yet a spirit in form and substance because of the physical reality of Prospero. They are one and the same, while separate and different. Ariel is (in him/her/itself) the realization of Prospero's knowledge, and Ariel is, in turn, the actualization of Prospero's power, which is actualized knowledge. Theirs is a totally symbiotic working relationship. Separated, Ariel resumes existence as a free-spirited descendant of Titania and Oberon. Separated, Prospero retains his knowledge, but loses his power to accomplish acts above and beyond the human realm. But during the play Ariel is, in MacLuhan's sense, the extension of Prospero as magus, his Paracelsian astral self.

Part of Ariel's job from the beginning of the play has been to serve as the agency of Prospero's revenge-plot against Alonso (King of Naples), Sebastian (Alonso's younger brother), and Antonio (Prospero's younger brother and the present Duke of Milan). At the beginning of a long last scene of the play (5.1), on Prospero's request, Ariel describes how the three are confined in a nearby grove:

> The King,
> His brother, and yours abide all three distracted,
> And the remainder mourning over them,
> Brimful of sorrow and dismay; but chiefly
> Him that you termed, sir, the good old Lord Gonzalo.
> His tears run down his beard like winter's drops
> From eaves of reeds. Your charm so strongly works'em,
> That if you now beheld them, your affections
> Would become tender.
>
> (5.1.11–19)

The last sentence is stated without emotion as a matter of fact. Ariel as an extension of Prospero knows the master; they think alike because they think Prospero's thought. It is natural that Ariel would and could serve as a conscience.

Prospero is obviously taken aback.[23] The feedback has introduced a new loop, one unlooked for. "Dost thou think so, spirit?" Then follows one of those moments which can only be called Shakespearean: "Mine would, sir, were I human." Ariel has been so well programmed from a fully developed model of humanity that his response to the question asked is based upon the information that to be human includes tenderness, mercy, remorse, sympathetic tears.

Prospero pauses—"and mine shall"—pauses again. Then asks a key rhetorical question:

> Hast thou, which art but air, a touch, a feeling
> Of their afflictions, and shall not myself,
> *One of their kind*, that relish all as sharply
> Passion as they, be *kindlier* moved than thou art?
>
> (21–24; emphasis added)

Prospero makes the identification of kind and resolves to be more humanly motivated ("kindlier moved") than Ariel, the creature not of kind, but of artificial intelligence. To be kindlier moved means to be moved as a human being should be moved—by the heart as well as by the head. Prospero is learning the art of humankindness:

> Though with their wrongs I am struck to th' quick,
> Yet with my nobler reason 'gainst my fury
> Do I take part.

He is learning that he must control his own private cosmos.[24] Reason is noble, for, God-given, it is angelic in nature, is ennobling of man among animals, all of whom have the passion of "fury." In the next sentence Prospero and Shakespeare speak doubly: "The rarer action is/In virtue than in vengeance"—yes, much the better, higher, nobler action—but, oh, so seldom exercised within the realm of human conduct. The androgynous vision itself is rare: an ideal which can inform action, but too seldom does.

Prospero sends Ariel to release the prisoners: "My charms I'll break, their senses I'll restore,/And they shall be themselves" (31–32). In changing his mind about revenge, Prospero seems to realize that his magic, innocent as it may be in origin and intent, interferes with the essential right of people to self-maintained integrity, to "be themselves." Magic enslaves. And, in order also for himself to be wholly himself, he must free himself; he must cease his manipulation of raw matter, the rough stuff of magic, this "rough magic":[25]

> But this rough magic
> I here abjure; and when I have required
> Some heavenly music (which even now I do)
> To work mine end upon their senses that
> This airy charm is for, I'll break my staff,
> Bury it certain fathoms in the earth,

And deeper than did ever plummet sound
I'll drown my book.

Prospero draws his final magic circle for the Alonzo group: "*They all enter the circle which Prospero had made, and there stand charmed.*" The restoration of the unity of mind is accomplished by the perfect harmony of the androgynous music of the spheres which pierces the circle of their heads, the home of the brain, the seat of the rational soul:

A solemn air, and the best comforter
To an unsettled fancy, cure thy brains,
Now useless, boiled within thy skull!

In order to show that Gonzalo needs no reclamation and that Prospero himself is regaining his sympathetic emotions, Shakespeare begins with Gonzalo:

Holy Gonzalo, honorable man,
Mine eyes, ev'n sociable to the show of thine,
Fall fellowly drops.

The ensuing restoration of sense is described as an awakening, but in terms that recall the meeting of Light and Darkness in primordial, unisexual creation myths:

The charm dissolves apace;
And as the morning steals upon the night,
Melting the darkness, so their rising senses
Begin to chase the ignorant fumes that mantle
Their clearer reason.

(61–68)

As oppressive magic disappears, the natural magic of heavenly reason infuses and informs the earthly self:

Their understanding
Begins to swell, and the approaching tide
Will shortly fill the reasonable shore,
That now lie foul and muddy.

(79–82)

This is the new beginning, the re-creation of the form of humanity out of earth and filled full of the divine breath of reason—matter informed—body and soul, the astral self in control of the earthly self. This is a natural baptism and a secular rebirth, the end of apocalypse.

When Prospero addresses Antonio we can see his own reclamation through his reaffirmation of "remorse and nature":

> Flesh and blood,
> You, brother mine, that entertained ambition,
> Expelled remorse and nature, who . . .
> Would here have killed your king, I do forgive thee,
> Unnatural though thou art.
>
> (74–79)

Prospero now acts naturally, not supernaturally. His forgiveness, triggered by remorse, restores the bonds of nature. Prospero is ready to step back into the circle of humanity, the ultimate magic circle:

> Not one of them
> That yet looks on me or would know me. Ariel,
> Fetch me the hat and rapier in my cell.
> I will discase me, and myself present
> As I was sometime Milan.
>
> (82–86)

But to be fully himself, he must free himself of Ariel: "Quickly, spirit!/Thou shalt ere long be free" (86–87).

Complementing and reinforcing Prospero's growth into a new awareness of his true self is Prospero's change in attitude toward Caliban at the beginning of the play to a different one at the very end. When bookish, scientific Prospero, product of European humanism, was cast up with Miranda on this lonely island, the only human inhabitant was a twelve-year-old, Caliban, a creature of darkness, an Adam-in-reverse, offspring not of God and the Holy Spirit, but of the devil and a witch. Prospero, with his mastery of the elements through the applied power of his learning, was a product of highly cultivated nurture. Caliban, existing in a sort of pre-Darwinian state, was a product of totally uncultivated nature, the ooze of nature—earthy, smelly, instinctive, merely existential. Paracelsian matter. Prospero—white Western European that he is—immediately claimed the island to be his, and—pedant that he is—immediately set about the education of Caliban by exposing him to the power of the word. Caliban's commentary on this experience, using the language of the English Bible, shows us a version of Adam's initial experience when he was sole human inhabitant of his "island" paradise:

> When thou cam'st first,
> Thou strok'st me and made much of me; woudst give me
> Water with berries in't; and teach me how
> *To name the bigger light, and how the less,*
> That burn by day and night; and then I loved thee
> And show'd thee all the qualities o' the isle,
> The fresh springs, brine-pits, barren place and fertile.
>
> (1.2.332–38; emphasis added)

Receiving loving humankindness, Caliban returned sociable love. But when he was drawn by Miranda's developing womanhood to extend sociable to sexual love, his "god" cursed him and, as with Adam when sexual desire disturbed the peace of Paradise, there was an angry expulsion from Prospero's cell to nightly imprisonment in a rock.

Prospero for some twelve years held school for Caliban and Miranda. During that period of the growth and development of his daughter in body and mind, Prospero obviously found Caliban capable. He says that he kept Caliban "in service" during this time, which does not mean in slavery, but is the sixteenth-century term which designates the custom of "housing" in one's own home during early adolescence a male-child from a home just below one's own on the social scale; in return for services rendered, the temporary "master" promised the well-being and supervised the upbringing of the boy, who would receive beyond food, clothing, and education the further benefit of possible advancement up the social ladder. Being sheltered in a home "better" than his could give rise to great expectations.

We do not know the circumstances of Caliban's sexual overture—and violation is inexcusable at any level, even verbal, even leering, even ineffectual groping—but given the cultural and physical environment in and around Prospero's cell, Caliban's sexual arousal is, on a crude biological level, somewhat "natural." And, given the "late" arrival of physical adolescence in girls four centuries ago, the event probably just recently took place. Howsoever, Prospero's reaction was obviously quick and extreme. No correction. School was over. And Caliban now regrets his previous kind acts and the loss of his previous solitude:

> Cursed be I that did so! All the charms
> Of Sycorax—toads, beetles, bats, light on you!
> For I am all the subjects that you have,

Which first was mine own king.

(339–42)

This is a most human touch; Caliban had been happy both when he had been his own master and when he had received and returned sociable love. But for Prospero Caliban has suddenly become subhuman and, therefore, can no longer respond to kindness, cannot become good:

> Thou most lying slave,
> Whom stripes may move, not kindness! I have used thee
> (Filth as thou art) with humane care, and lodged thee
> In mine own cell till thou didst seek to violate
> The honor of my child.

Prospero has forgotten, or needs to suppress, the fact that sexual drive is part of our humankindness. When Caliban, in effect, throws the fact of human sexuality right back in Prospero's face ("O ho, O ho! Would't had been done!/Thou didst prevent me; I had peopled else/This isle with Calibans"), Prospero's injured manhood and endangered fatherhood lead him to the angriest outburst in the play, yet one that loudly proclaims the need of and the benefit from nurturing nature—but leads further into a bold questioning of that claim in an equally loud counterclaim by Caliban that nurturing nature is needless and destructive. Prospero (*not* Miranda, as the First Folio indicates)[26] flings back at Caliban:

> Abhorred slave,
> Which any print of goodness wilt not take,
> Being capable of all ill! I pitied thee,
> Took pains to make thee speak, taught thee each hour
> One thing or other: when thou didst not, savage,
> Know thine own meaning, but wouldst gabble like
> A thing most brutish, I endowed thy purposes
> With words that made them known.

(351–58)

The whole role of learning, of human development, of education—the whole thrust of humanity to comprehend life, to make it meaningful—to label, to isolate separate factors and then to try to understand their various relationships—civilization, culture, progress, advancement of learning—all are caught here. And Prospero grants that Caliban "didst learn," but he has expelled Caliban from his home and confined him in prison because of Caliban's expression of a sexual drive:

But thy vile race,
Though thou didst learn, had that
in't which good natures
Cannot abide to be with.

(358–60)

"Vile race" must mean human race, descent from Setebos and Sycorax, or personal make-up; "good natures" must mean human race, nurtured natures, or well-mannered people (namely, my daughter and I)—but any way that one divides and pairs the two terms, "vile race" and "good natures" describe humankind, as Prospero will later remember. Yet Caliban now has the last word in this present exchange:

You taught me language: and my profit on't
Is, I know how to curse. The red plague rid you
For learning me your language!

(363–65)

No matter what myth we use, we have eaten from the tree of knowledge and have lost our innocence, that state of private individual security ("I . . . first was my own king") where we did not have any conscious interaction with our environment: did not build fires, did not use tools, did not wear clothes to soften the privation of our own human existence. Yet, we were kingdoms unto ourselves. Somehow we have moved on. We have invented love and the uses of language, but they do not always lead to contentment. We look back with yearning to a "golden age." Sometimes it does seem that all we have learned is how to curse.

Arrogant Prospero, himself full of curses, does not recognize any bonds with Caliban. He rejects him as subhuman. But Prospero is quite wrong. Caliban's nature has been nurtured.[27] He recognizes trash as trash, which the "human" Stephano and Trinculo do not, and his thrice repeated instruction to seize, possess, and burn Prospero's books is more than a blind anti-intellectualism: he knows there is a cause and effect relationship between the knowledge in the books and Prospero's power. But the strongest evidence for Caliban's humanity is the familiar report of his dream:

Be not afeard: the isle is full of noises,
Sounds and sweet airs that give delight and hurt not.
Sometimes a thousand twangling instruments
Will hum about mine ears; and sometimes voices
That, if I then had waked after long sleep,
Will make me sleep again; and then, in dreaming,

The clouds methought would open and show riches
Ready to drop upon me, that, when I waked,
I cried to dream again.

(3.2.132–40)

Caliban's dream haunts us, for we all have had it in one form or another. It is the dream of a fuller life. There is a harmony surrounding life which we want to pull in and make part of us. The hope of realization keeps us moving. We know we can experience contentment because we have, somewhere, sometime. We cry to dream again. Caliban's dream is the private, unaccommodated dream of human wholeness.[28]

Gonzalo's dream is a social, sophisticated version.[29]

Because Gonzalo is a choral figure, he has lines that are emblematic—"Here's a maze trod indeed/Through forthrights and meanders" (3.3.2–3), "All torment, trouble, wonder, and amazement/Inhabits here" (5.1.104–05), "Whether this be/Or be not, I'll not swear" (122–23)—but his experience of life is firmly anchored in reality: of the "*several strange Shapes, bringing in a banquet*," Gonzalo comments,

though they are of monstrous shape, yet note,
Their manners are more gentle, kind, than of
Our human generation you shall find
Many—nay, almost any.

(3.3.31–34)

Against this observation of things as they are and as they should be, we can interpret Gonzalo's "gentle, kind" vision, had he "plantation of this isle":

I' th'commonwealth I would by contraries
Execute all things; for no kind of traffic
Would I admit; no name of magistrate;
Letters should not be known; riches, poverty,
And use of service, none; contract, succession,
Bourn, bound of land, tilth, vineyard, none;
No use of metal, corn, or wine, or oil;
No occupation; all men idle, all;
And women too, but innocent and pure;
No sovereignty . . .
All things in common nature should produce
Without sweat or endeavor. Treason, felony,
Sword, pike, knife, gun, or need of any engine
Would I not have; but nature should bring forth,

Of its own kind, all foison, all abundance,
To feed my innocent people . . .
I would with such perfection govern, sir,
T'excel the golden age.

(2.1.143–64)

Gonzalo does not speak in contradictions, nor even in paradoxes. His problem is that of one who goes about to describe a myth or dream. He is restricted by a binary inability to describe that which simply is. He must speak figuratively. His vision, of "such perfection" that it would "excel the golden age," reaches beyond the silver age of Jove and the golden age of Saturn to the bosom of Dame Nature: "Nature should bring forth,/Of its own kind, all foison, all abundance." And we are back in Spenser's "Garden of Adonis." At such a vision of social justice, laugh who will. People like Sebastian and Antonio can never entertain a vision of androgyny, and some find it easier to laugh with them than at them. But they, not Gonzalo, are the ones to be pitied. They are prisoners of time and place; they, not Caliban, are creatures "on whose nature/Nurture can never stick."

The third dream in *The Tempest* (in the circle of the play events move in threes) is also androgynous: Prospero's dream. D. G. James makes a persuasive case in *The Dream of Prospero* that the whole play can be considered the dream of Prospero (a possibility I suggested for *Dr. Faustus*; and indeed, both plays can be accounted interior experiences, journeys inside the heads of the main characters). Less controversial would be the designation of the wedding masque as Prospero's dream. Certainly, it is the projection of his thoughts on marriage, his own myth of creation. Certainly, here we see magician as artist, artist as magician, making something appear out of nothing, giving airy nothings local habitation and names.

Caliban's dream is that of the individual, the private yearning for a freer, fuller life. Gonzalo's dream is that of society, the collective yearning for a freer, fuller living of lives. Prospero's dream is the link between the two—the dream of the shared life in which one loses one's self in order to find one's self in another, in which one plus one equals one, in which one finds the unity and harmony of androgyny. The clouds open up and show riches; we hear heavenly music and see Gonzalo's commonwealth being prepared by goddesses and nymphs for the new Adam and Eve. Then "*certain Reapers, properly habited*" enter and "*join with the Nymphs in a graceful dance; toward the end whereof Prospero starts suddenly and speaks*":

I had forgot that foul conspiracy
Of the beast Caliban and his confederates

Against my life; the minute of their plot
Is almost come. Well done! Avoid! No more!

(4.1.139–40)

(The stage direction describes the action: "*after which to a strange, hollow, confused noise, they heavily vanish*"). This noise, like Lear's storm, is in Prospero's mind. As the reapers enter, Iris tells them to "make holiday" and to "encounter" the nymphs "in country footing." Prospero's mind is playing Freudian tricks on him: "reapers" is pronounced "rapers," "encounter" and "country" encompass cunt, and "footing" and fucking are closely associated. Once more Prospero must confront male sexuality, and once more male sexuality confronting his daughter—this time with his conscious approval—but not his unconscious. Ferdinand's and Miranda's remarks make clear the extent to which Prospero is passionately angered. The thought/sight of the country dance suggested sex, suggested Caliban, but it is not because of Caliban that Prospero cancels his masque; it is because of sex.

When Prospero becomes aware that Miranda and Ferdinand are looking amazedly on him, he tries to calm them by explaining to them and to himself that his just-presented "revels"—actors, plays, theaters, life itself—were all dream. Then he ends,

Sir, I am vexed.
Bear with my weakness: my old brain is troubled.
Be not disturbed with my infirmity.
If you be pleased, retire to my cell
And there repose. A turn or two I'll walk
To still my beating mind.

(158–63)

The problem is not Caliban's revolution—that is easily taken care of. The problem is sex. He has to work this out in his "still beating mind," for it is his problem, in his mind, as his remarks to Ferdinand make clear: "My old brain is troubled." Prospero, the magician/alchemist, is undergoing the process of vexation, and we soon see what the vessel of his mind will produce. Unable to admit honestly his subconscious hate of Ferdinand's love, he sublimates his grief over the coming loss of his maiden daughter by once again hammering out against Caliban:

A devil, a born devil, on whose nature
Nurture can never stick: on whom my pains,

Humanely taken, all, all lost, quite lost!
And as with age his body uglier grows,
So his mind cankers.

(188–92)

Only after he accepts the fact of his daughter's marriage, and after he forgives his enemies, can Prospero finally admit that Caliban is not a monster, is not "unnatural," but is only King Lear's "unaccommodated man," "the thing itself," "a poor, bare fork'd animal" (*Lear* 3.4.106–08) —like Prospero himself.[30] Prospero learns the lesson of humankindness, by coming to know himself, by accepting sex as part of nature, by discovering tenderness and forgiveness, by having recourse to his natural virtue instead of following a falsely nurtured vengeance. When Prospero reenters the human circle by appearing in his ducal gown, his astral and his earthly begin to function together. The extent of his reformation or reintegration is marked by his final comment on Caliban. When the three "low life" join the ever increasing group after Gonzalo's last choral speech, Prospero says to Alonso, "Two of these fellows you/Must known and own"; and he adds, "this thing of darkness I/Acknowledge mine" (5.1.274–76). He now realizes that Caliban is not his subject but his kin and kind, part of his family.

The complete scholar of his day, the complete scientist-humanist who had mastered all of the arts, Prospero had not become wise because, in isolating himself from humanity, he had lost touch with his own humanity. He had not accepted the foolish nature of his own common being. He forgot (or because of incestuous turbulence within he tried to make himself forget) that he, too, carried the seat of folly hanging between his own legs. Shakespeare here uses the language of the ritual of paternal recognition and acceptance of offspring in order to indicate that Prospero has experienced an enlargement of his own understanding.

This seemingly casual remark of recognition is apt to run quickly past a modern audience unused to the custom of paternal acknowledgment to which it refers (and especially if the actor himself has no awareness of the ritual). Yet, one need only to call to mind *The Winter's Tale*; when Leontes refuses to accept as his own the newborn child whom Paulina brings to him for blessing, we witness a vivid, though negative, example of the act of acknowledgment in Shakespeare. Although their etymological relatednesses are no longer considered philologically valid, the words "kinder," "kind," "knee," "knowledge," "generate," and "generation" were all associated in the Middle Ages and Renaissance; such association created a unified, powerful moment when a man took a child on his knee, examined its features, and stated that he was the father, that he was the one who had known the mother, that he had generated this member of a new generation; in short, he says: "This child I acknowledge mine."

When Prospero acknowledges his bond to humanity by fittingly adopting Caliban as a kind of son—"this thing of darkness I/Acknowledge mine"—Shakespeare signals that Prospero has come to the understanding that he cannot be whole unless he recognizes the totality of his own human nature, and this twofold act of recognition, this act of humility, shows a nature no longer to be feared, a nature now full of "the milk of human kindness." By giving up the practice of the art of magic, the farthest reach of applied learning, Prospero gains unity of mind through mastery of the art of humankindness.

But he may not remain on the island. He has no business being here, for his business is being Duke of Milan. Because of our still romantic attitude toward nature, especially natural islands, we tend to think that leaving the island is a come-down, a bummer, too bad, old fellow. But Prospero must go home again. He has been a truant. He has come to terms with himself as a rational animal—as a male and father and as a thinking human. And now he must complete his fulfillment by resuming his place in society—a place which he cannot choose, only accept or reject, being Duke of Milan.[31]

His library in Milan had been "dukedom large enough" to occupy him, but at the cost of his occupation. Learning is good personally but must be made socially beneficial through the practice of "civic humanism." The higher calling is neither the active life over the contemplative, nor vice versa. The only calling is the fully active life fully informed. Prospero does not and should not reject his learning; he should use it for effective government carried out in the common good, the welfare of all. That is his obligation: to work toward the realization of Gonzalo's dream.

If he should fail—no one has succeeded yet—there is still hope in the next generation—and the next and the next. Through couples such as Miranda and Ferdinand life is given that "second chance" which Alfred Harbage spoke of. Miranda is described by Ferdinand as, "O you/So perfect and so peerless, are created/Of every creature's best," and Ferdinand by Miranda: "I might call him/A thing divine; for nothing natural/I ever saw so noble." Adam and Eve. The allegory is so obvious that Shakespeare did not have to give Ferdinand this speech during the masque:

Let me live here forever,
So rare a father and a wife[32]
Makes this place Paradise.

(4.1.122–24)

"This place": the island, the stage, London, the world. This can be so, for it is all in the mind. When "*Prospero discovers Ferdinand and Miranda playing at chess*" inside Prospero's cell, the miracle of life can begin anew. Even Sebastian can be overcome: "A most high miracle." Through Miranda we experience the potent wonder of life:

> O, wonder!
> How many goodly creatures are there here!
> How beauteous mankind is! O brave new world
> That has such people in't!

And the world is newly given to Miranda and Ferdinand to help humanity on its way to fulfilling Gonzalo's dream. Yes, it is all new for her.

Gonzalo's "epilogue" to all of this ritual of recognition and promise of hope and harmony is fittingly "biblical":

> Was Milan thrust from Milan that his issue
> Should become kings of Naples? O, rejoice
> Beyond a common joy, and set it down
> With gold on lasting pillars: in one voyage
> Did Claribel her husband find at Tunis,
> And Ferdinand her brother found a wife
> Where he himself was lost; Prospero his dukedom
> In a poor isle; and all of us ourselves
> When no man was his own.
>
> (206–14)

Prospero's art had allowed the Alonzo group to find themselves ("their senses I'll restore,/And they shall be themselves"), but mastery of a final art allows Prospero to come unto himself: the art of humankindness.

When Prospero acknowledges that he is not whole unless he recognizes the full range of his own human nature, this act of recognition, this act of humility marks a step taken toward the attainment of true wisdom beyond his vast accumulation of knowledge. Caliban, too, learns from the action of the play. Like his "sister" Miranda, he is overwhelmed by the gathering at Prospero's cell:

> O Setebos, these be brave spirits indeed!
> How fine my master is! I am afraid
> He will chastise me.

But Prospero is in a forgiving vein, and promises pardon. Caliban promises amendment:

I'll be wise hereafter,
And seek for grace. What a thrice-double ass
Was I to take this drunkard for a god
And worship this dull fool!

Through their reactions, we can tell that both Prospero and Caliban are gaining wisdom, the peace which passes all understanding. Sapience is a long way off, but androgyny is along the way.

The play is not yet over when Shakespeare gives the deserted stage to Prospero for an epilogue. The "chorus" had not been a character in *Romeo and Juliet* or in *Henry V*; therefore, no ambiguity is associated with the direct choral address of the audience in those two plays. Puck and Rosalind had been in their plays, and each actor pulls away from character a bit to speak his epilogue. But Prospero stays in character and in costume, which we all too easily can forget if we rush to substitute "Stratford" for "Milan." This is the only time, then, that Shakespeare wrote an "epilogue" which actually extends the play, for here he asks the audience to take a part. The audience must now become the magus if the play is to be resolved by a "happy ending," and the only power we will need we have: our generous humankindness. When we applaud we are incorporated within the play and the play is incorporated within us.[33]

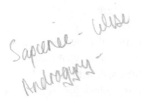

Sapience - Wise
Androgyny -

PART IV

End Matter

12

"Unity of Mind": Shakespeare's Androgyny

> *"A Man's life, of any worth, is a continual allegory—and very few eyes can see the Mystery of his life—a life like the scriptures, figurative . . . Lord Byron cuts a figure—but he is not figurative. Shakespeare led a life of Allegory: his works are the comments on it—"*
>
> *John Keats, February 18, 1819*

Some two hundred years ago, Samuel Johnson remarked that William Shakespeare had pleased many and pleased long because of his just representations of general nature. Johnson was praising Shakespeare's classical ability to classify the vast variety of classes (types and kinds) that form the human parade. Shakespeare captured in his art all the categories of human nature.

Two generations later, John Keats responded more to the unique characteristics of each character in Shakespeare than to how each represented a type to be found in life. Keats was fascinated by Shakespeare's ability to get inside his creations, his capability of so negating his own sense of person that he dwelled in what he created. (Keats called it Shakespeare's "negative capability.") Keats reveled in the gusto and fire that he experienced in Shakespeare, who, he said, took as much joy in creating an innocent heroine such as Imogen in *Cymbeline* as he did in a paranoid destructive Iago in *Othello*.

Taken together, the remarks of Johnson and Keats suggest the range and depth of Shakespeare, his neoclassical ability to limn the outlines of every type and his romantic ability to suggest the private, distinguishing characteristics of each human within each type.

Shakespeare's characters stem from his androgyny. We can sense that Keats sensed as much through our reading of his random remarks on Shakespeare in those marvelous letters. But it was Coleridge who first put the label on Shakespeare on September 1, 1832, when he casually commented in *Table Talk* that "the truth is, a great mind must be androgynous." Virginia Woolf in *A Room of One's Own* (1929) turned to Coleridge, and again and again to Shakespeare, in her essay to find the basis of creativity; her phrase for androgyny was "unity of mind." H. D. (Hilda Doolittle) in *By Avon River* (1949) describes movingly how she also found Shakespeare to be a kindred spirit, male in sex though he may have been, for she could feel how her androgynous spirit rose out of and hovered above her sex to meet Shakespeare's creative, androgynous spirit.[1]

Keats, of course, responded instinctively to the integrity of Shakespeare's work (the real things of this world are the "Sun, Moon, and Stars, and passages of Shakespeare"), and in so responding Keats sensed the uniqueness of Shakespeare. I use the word unique *not* as a colloquial term of adulation (that, too), but as a term for isolation (that hope each of us harbors that each of us is unique). When Keats said that "Shakespeare led a life of Allegory: his works are the comments on it," he implied that the works of Shakespeare are primarily private, that they are inventions of the mind, that they are fore-conceits conceived in the zodiac of Shakespeare's wit, conceptions of a far-from-idle brain, metaphorical parts of "a continual allegory." In short, Keats implied that Shakespeare was, in the best and fullest sense, a dreamer: one who internalizes life. But he also recognized the obvious: Shakespeare wrote down his dreams—for himself, and for a few others.[2]

Those few others were the members of the companies for which he created scripts. The intended readers of Shakespeare's texts were, then, players who translated Shakespeare's letters into action, gesture, and spoken words to be digested visually and aurally by the public. Shakespeare was published (made public) by the players over a number of years during which culture was still dominantly oral-aural. Only after Shakespeare's death, perhaps anticipating the recession of a reliance on the oral-aural as a mode of transmission of tradition, did the players publish Shakespeare through the printing press, and Shakespeare's oral comments on his life became ours. But during his lifetime, Shakespeare's publication was primarily through performance.

It is often remarked that Shakespeare did not have to write so fully, so multidimensionally in order to have been a successful playwright. Such an observation misses an essential point: Shakespeare had no choice, so to speak, in the matter of writing as he did, for he was not first of all a playwright, but a writer, a writer albeit whose work took the form of scripts for public performance. This is natural enough. We tend to forget that the sixteenth-century emphasis on literacy (*bonae litterae*) took place not within what was predominantly a print culture, but within what was still predominantly an oral culture. In Shakespeare's day one went to *hear* a play, not to *see* one. Words were written to be spoken. (The wide-ranging works of Sidney spring to mind.) The transitional nature of Renaissance culture, that crossing of the threshold from medieval to early modern, is perfectly captured in the fact that the finest achievement in art in England was by a writer of plays. Literacy and orality in league.

Shakespeare's plays are so fine not because he was a player and a playwright but because he was a writer. He loved words, he mastered language and syntax, he sensed that writing is a turning in before it is a turning out. Writing is a playing-out, both in the sense of joy (the "delight in conceiving an Iago [as well] as an Imogen") and a playing-out in the sense of lines going gradually through your hands as much under their own force and control as yours. Lines of writing run courses that cross back on themselves, leave signs and posts, develop linkages and feedback loops to inform, reinform, and reinforce what is being discovered by the writer during the act of writing. Because writing has a preserved beginning, one can go back, change, adjust; because writing is durational, one can point ahead, refer back, plant signals.

This is the basis of Shakespeare's art: writing. Writing—even though his "publication" was not by print, but by performance. Shakespeare is a meeting point of orality and literacy, for in making scripts he created literature, those detached, self-contained comments on life with lives of their own. He took from and built on oral tradition of all kinds, yet he subjected those traditions to literature, to literate analysis, to the scrutiny of literacy, through the act of writing. Ben Jonson objected to the way Shakespeare composed because he could not comprehend the process. Shakespeare was the first modern; Jonson was truly, thoroughly neoclassic. Rhetorically doctrinaire, Jonson objected that Shakespeare did not discipline himself to the genre at hand: drama. But Shakespeare's experience of writing was radically new. He wrote freely for himself, limited only by the demands of the stage. His plays are extensions of him; they are the allegory of his life, his figurative life. We do not need to "see the mystery of his life," because we can always study "the comments on it," the works themselves.

We do not know why Shakespeare gave up the practice of the art of drama. Perhaps he found writing scripts too restrictive—"I'll break my staff [and] I'll drown my book." Perhaps he even found writing restrictive—too demanding, too possessive, too isolating. He may have wanted to live a freer, fuller life. We wish we knew. The absence of any written material of any substance continues to haunt us, Stratfordians and anti-Stratfordians alike. But whether or not he quit writing, retire from the theater he did, and in 1613, in the first season after that retirement, the Globe theater burned down during a performance of *Henry VIII*, the pageant play Shakespeare left for others to finish. This fire symbolizes the end of Shakespeare's professional career, and it symbolizes as well the end of all that that great Globe Theatre had inherited: a public theater of the people.[3]

Others have analyzed at length the causes of this death, but the life of that theater of the people had been its preservation and presentation of the traditional values and essential truths embedded within oral tradition. This, especially, is the world which is evoked in Shakespeare's last plays, plays full of legend, dream, and rituals of life. These plays entertained King James, but they show the grounded strength of the theater that grew up during Elizabeth's reign. Shakespeare's plays do not just tell stories, old stories, winter's tales, folklore; Shakespeare's plays figured forth the myths and rituals that sustain these stories, tales, and lore. Shakespeare's plays are not of an age, but of all time, because they deal with deep myth and natural ritual. And they do so because they grew from the heart of a creative writer.

Shakespeare's plays celebrate the humanists's dream of human fulfillment, the art of humankindness, because his personal vision of nature and art was androgynous, as Keats, Coleridge, Woolf, and H. D. all sensed. To me, Shakespeare was a quiet, observant, tolerant, smiling person who did not have to preach, to thump his own chest, to announce how great he and his art were, because his very writing gave him a sense of fulfillment, a sense of calm, a sense of achievement. Robert Ornstein captures well the effect that Shakespeare can have on us:

> If through Prospero Shakespeare makes a personal statement, it is about the price one may have to make for great artistic achievement. We think of Shakespeare as one who, more than any other great writer, understood and enjoyed other people and was very much involved with and at home in his world. His masterpieces were, nevertheless, the work of an unassuming observer, an alert sympathetic listener, not a striking conversationalist; he was lovingly remembered by his colleagues for his gentleness, not his brilliance. He lived most intensely and fully perhaps in the hours he spent writing his plays and poems. When he laid down his pen, he no doubt found joy in the company of family and friends, but it is not likely that the ordinary experience of life was as vivid—as real—to him as the dream of art that ended with Prospero's farewell to Ariel.[4]

Through Shakespeare's writing we sense a fully centered person, even while his actual life remains a mystery transfused in the metaphors of his art. His life is figurative, a continual allegory, for he had, ultimately, "that within which passeth show." Look not on his picture but his book.

There one will find that Shakespeare's perspective on women is far more positive and egalitarian than the conservative, patriarchal, medieval view (even Marilyn French grants so much), and that Shakespeare, as do Sidney and Spenser, advocates an androgynous philosophy for society, where men and women of all ages and various social positions can freely explore and express a wide range of character traits and behaviors which society traditionally divides along sex lines by masculine and feminine. Sidney, Spenser, and Shakespeare all make the choice of the new Hercules in favor of accepting within both the male and the female in the essay toward androgyny.

But what happened to this androgynous awareness? The seventeenth century, the coming of the modern world—call it what you will—stomped on it. Androgyny is a cultural myth; that is to say, it is an artificial creation. Its parts are figures of analogy and similitude based on the ground-plot of a world-view that is concentric—circles within circles within circles. But the linearism of seventeenth-century science broke the circle, and its attendant rationalism destroyed analogy. As Blake so well knew, science and rationalism cannot tolerate the universe in a grain of sand, but demand sequential relationships, hierarchy, and history. Even today, we speak of the most curved of all processes, evolution, in terms of ascent and descent, higher and lower. Although Aristotle and others had had a sense of evolution, the Elizabethans did not, although, like the Native American, they had a habit of mind better fitted to really comprehend the concept than do we immigrants of western culture. Because of their trust in analogy as a means (not a proof or end) to truth, the Elizabethans were born comparatists, and they sought relationships not just up and down some chain of being, but all around. Because the Ptolemaic commonplaces of medieval thought became dynamic in the Renaissance, androgyny is found at the still point of the ever-moving concentric worlds of that Renaissance.

Androgyny is the expression of the vision of unity, wholeness, harmony, and perfection which was being sought in the confines of the human. Like the Renaissance pastoral, androgyny is a secular dream, without which life remains partial, uncompleted, fragmented, and unrelieved. Writers (i.e., thinkers) in the sixteenth century in England, from Hawes through Sidney, Spenser, and Shakespeare to Donne, came close to expressing and defining this vision, before the seventeenth century, so to speak, changed the rules of the game.[5] A necessary concomitant of a re-emergent sense of androgyny was a change in the milieu which began to destroy the age-old belief that woman was in mind inferior to man since the souls of men and women are equal and sexless. The full emergence and liberation of woman did not take place, but almost did, before seventeenth-century men clamped shut the doors of equal rights and status more tightly than had men in the Middle Ages.[6] But what signaled a favorable environment for potential liberation of humanity in the sixteenth century was the general movement of Renaissance thought as understood by Sidney, the presence and achievement of Queen Elizabeth as celebrated by Spenser, and the plays of Shakespeare.

Appendix I
Three Prisoners of Gender

The three "case histories" discussed here show: 1) the fears of a male traditionalist, 2) the anger of a female separatist, and 3) the power which the mind-as-gender has over the body-as-sex.

1

The New York Times Book Review (3/9/80) notwithstanding, Robert May's *Sex and Fantasy: Patterns of Male and Female Development* (N.Y.: Norton, 1980) is riddled with contradictions and inconsistencies, but May's main failure is an essential one: psychiatrically trained as he is, he does not know the basic difference between sex and gender: that sex is biological and physiological while gender is social and psychological (see his three-page introduction). His last-chapter attack on the women's movement ("The Dream of Androgyny," 163–77) is a fine example of fright, irresponsible scholarship, and muddle-headed criticism. But the book as a whole is an excellent argument in favor of the personal and social value of the androgynous vision: all of May's "clinical" evidence proves that "normal" genderization is a tendency to reinforce sexual differentiation and, thereby, leads to social and psychological division, discord, and decay. By the end of the book, he acknowledges that the two myths he opened with, Phaeton and Persephone, depict single-sex worlds and that his case studies of "Pride" and "Caring" are pathological: "One of the underlying themes in the preceding pages has been that an extreme version of either the male or the female fantasy pattern is not fit to live in . . . A split between the sexes . . . exacts a price" (149). He then goes on (149–61) to discuss the pathology of overgenderization (my term) and concludes:

Imagine a relationship between these caricatures of Caring and Pride, the

> masochist and the phallic narcissist. She has all the responsiveness, tenderness, patience, and willingness to give. He has all the open self-assertion, competitive energy, initiative, and bravado. Each thus confirms the other's conscious self-definition. At the same time each has the opportunity to explore and learn to manage this polar Other. She can unconsciously partake of his aggression and he of her ability to become attached and dependent. But it is a precarious balance. If the partaking, the living through the other, goes too far it then touches on those feared inner images: the greedy rapist inside her and the tattered victim inside him. Then anxiety surges up and the partner must be demeaned and cast aside. In all but the most lucky circumstances such a pattern obscures any vision of a relationship where *both* people are active and responsive by turns and both are relatively at ease with the two sexes inside them.

To me, this last sentence sounds like androgyny. It did to May as well, for he opens his attack on the women's movement in the next chapter with, "The words at the end of the last chapter may sound to some ears like another voice added to the recent growing chorus that is singing the praises of 'androgyny.' It is not; at least not in the way the term has begun to be used" (163). Because May's bias is male and "Calvinist," his exposition of androgyny is distorted, defensive, and dishonest.

2

Janice G. Raymond, too, felt compelled at the end of her *The Transsexual Empire: The Making of the She-Male* (Boston: Beacon Press, 1979) to attack androgyny. The "transsexual empire" is *manned* by the medical/surgical/psychiatric groups which through drugs, operations, and therapy turn genetic X–Y's into artificial "women," and vice versa. As her subtitle suggests, Raymond's concern, though, is with the "she" males, for they, as birth-to-death X–Y's, remain part of the patriarchal conspiracy to keep women down: "*Transsexualism at this point constitutes a 'socio-political program' that is undercutting the movement to eradicate sex-role stereotyping and oppression in this culture*" (p. 5; Raymond's italics). Furthermore, surgically altered men infiltrate the women's movement and assume positions of leadership: "It is a critical time for woman-identified women. Medicalized transsexualism represents only one more aspect of patriarchal hegemony. The best response women can make to this is to see clearly just what is at stake for us with respect to transsexualism and to assert our own power of naming who we are" (177).

Beneath the anger, beneath the rhetoric, Raymond's basic point is absolutely valid: that any X–X or X–Y in the twentieth century would, in mature years, voluntarily seek a "sex change" proves how established are the socio-psychological gender stereotypes of male and female—society's condition is indeed pathological. At first Raymond's solution was to offer "An Ethic of Androgyny," not just of would-be "transsexuals," but for all of us. But as she "examined the androgynous tradition and its uses in recent literature, problems of etymology, history, and philosophy arose that were not evident at first glance. These necessitated the choice of a different ethical vision, which I have called *integrity*. The word *integrity* means an original unity from which no part can be taken away—thus an original wholeness of personhood not divided by sex-role definitions" (155).

No advocate of androgyny would quarrel with this concept of *integrity*, except to note that the word has little resonance and a good bit of antonymous connotation ("be sincere, no matter how hard you have to try"). Indeed, the way Raymond defines integrity certainly looks as if she has, so to speak, merely substituted it where she had initially written androgyny:

> An intuition of integrity . . . is characteristic of the texture of be-ing (becoming) and prior to cultural definitions of masculinity and femininity. It is an original state that does not reside in a static historical past. Rather, integrity is the constant unfolding of a personal and social process that has the potentiality of generating for all of us a future vision of becoming, beyond a gender-defined society.
>
> This original state of be-ing, this condition of integrity, may indeed have been what the androgynous myths of the primal person were pointing toward . . . The real mytho-historical memory may have been that of an original psychosocial integrity where men were not masculine, nor women feminine, and where these definitions and prescribed norms of personhood did not exist.
>
> The real Fall may not have been the division into biological sexes but the separation into oppressive sex roles and stereotypes. Such a separation has cleft humanity into two static states of being. What the myths of the Fall from androgynous humanity into maleness and femaleness may more fully tell us about is humanity's initial loss of the intuition of integrity in which human development has been channeled into a two-track system of masculinity and femininity. Thus "salvation" is not achieved by the union of the two but by transcending masculinity and femininity. (163–64)

All of this is fine, particularly Raymond's version of "the Fall." Too bad her radical separatist position forces her, as had May, to give a definition of androgyny that is distorted, defensive, and dishonest: "In appearance, the words *androgyne* and *androgen* are quite similar. In fact, *androgyny* is sometimes spelled *androgeny*. Thus to speak of androgynizing humanity comes dangerously close to androgenizing or "male-izing" humanity. This, of course, was one mode of androgyny that was expressed in the Gnostic tradition. However, an *androgenous* or male-ized humanity is no more myth, nor is it simply a clever play on words, in light of some of the statements in John Money's work on sex differences" (160).

3

John Money, his various groups at Johns Hopkins, and like groups across the country are the transsexual imperialists. Without entering the battle over the morality of encouraging "sex change" and the ethics of "gender clinics," one can gather and sort much relevant information about sex and gender from the three decades of pioneering work carried out by Money and his associates. In general, I side unhesitatingly with Raymond: reinforcement of sexual stereotyping runs counter to the collective well-being of society. Anyone who has known, or read about, or seen on television a "public transsexual" has recognized the more-Catholic-than-the-Pope kind of extreme behavior of a convert—better to remain covert. But most of Money's work is not with the attention-seeking Christine Jorgensens and Jan Morrises, who were physically normal at birth and beyond puberty. Raymond ignores the ultimately more dramatic work being done at Johns Hopkins and elsewhere with those few out of five and a half billion of us who are not conceived as simple X–X or X–Y, or whose prenatal development is not able to follow normal patterns because of external hormones induced into the embryo. Nor does Raymond note Money's latest attitude toward gender development: "Gender identity is not immanent in the genes nor in prenatal hormones." His position is clear: "The major theoretical point in this chapter is that it is necessary for investigators of human behaviour to abandon the unicausational models of physics and chemistry, and rid themselves of the conceptual pitfalls of instincts, drives, and motivation (which have the same conceptual status as phlogiston) and to get down to identifying the actual mechanisms of behaviour."*

Money can come to such conclusions about gender because of such experiences as this:

> As an example, there was the man who first came to Johns Hopkins when he was twenty-four years old. Even with his medical history open on the desk, it is hard for the experienced medical professionals who have followed his case to believe that he was ever anything but a normal male. Nothing in his appearance, manner, gestures, or conversation betrays the fact that genetically and gonadally he was born female. He had looked like a boy at birth, although there were no testicles and the penis was somewhat deformed. He was labeled male and raised as a boy on the assumption that the testicles were there but had not descended. Since his family was quite relaxed about nudity, he had recognized at an early age

---

* John Money and Mark Schwartz, "Biosexual Determinants of Gender Identity Differentiation and Development," in Hutchinson. Money has summarized his work, and his personal conclusions drawn from that work, in *Love and Love Sickness: The Science of Sex, Gender Difference, and Pair-bonding*; from his preface on, Money emphasizes the need to distinguish carefully between sex and gender.

> that he was not as well equipped genitally as his father and brothers, but it never occurred to him to doubt that he was a boy who would become a man and marry a woman. By the age of seven he had singled out a little girl as his sweetheart.
>
> As he approached puberty, his breasts started to develop and his body began to round out. Those who believe that anatomy is destiny would expect these anatomical developments to be reflected in his outlook. On the contrary, he regarded his breasts as a deformity and wanted only one thing of the medical profession—to be rid of them. An exploratory operation at that time revealed ovaries, a uterus, and a vagina that opened internally into the urethra near the neck of the bladder, but no male reproductive system. Even when the boy understood, as he described it, that "they'd found some kind of female apparatus in there by mistake" and that he would never be able to sire offspring, his concept of himself as a male remained unshaken; it never seemed to him that he might "really" be a girl. The female organs were removed, eliminating the menstrual process which had just begun, and he was put on replacement male hormones to stop breast development, distribute his body fat in a masculine pattern, and direct masculine bone growth. His voice soon began to deepen and his beard to grow.
>
> At nineteen this man had a passionate love affair with a girl, and the following year he met and fell in love with the girl he later married. Before they became engaged he told her the facts about himself as he understood them, and they both discussed the situation with his doctor. After he had a minor operation to position his penis more favorably for intercourse, they went ahead and married. His penis responds readily, and although it is only two inches long when erect, they overcame that handicap so that from the start their sex life was satisfactory to them both. Like many honeymoon couples, they made love daily at first, and in this respect their honeymoon lasted more than six months. Two years after their wedding he reported with dreamy sincerity, "We think we're the luckiest people in the world." (*Signatures*, 59–61.)

What this story proves, if proof is still necessary, is that sex is genetic; gender is social, psychological, and cultural. Susan W. Baker, a psychoendocrinologist, after having recently surveyed the latest scholarship of "Biological Influences on Human Sex and Gender," concludes: "Gender identity will be concordant with the rearing regardless of the chromosomal, gonodal, or prenatal hormonal situation. This principle is so well established from clinical experience that it should not be in jeopardy" (*Signs* 6 [1980], 94).

Appendix II

Renaissance Unified-Field Theory

To try to name all of the branches of sixteenth-century Renaissance thought, one would end up like Polonius trying to name the genre of Renaissance drama. In both cases, the possible combinations are endless. Shakespeare's point was that there is really only one genre: drama. It is tempting, and it would be a great deal of fun, to link up in doublets and triplets such items as Christian, Hermetic, Platonist, alchemical, Gnostic, cabalist; mathematical, geometric, astronomical, musical; and the names of noted explorers of the mind and the real and imagined schools they "established" or influenced. My point is, however, that there may be many branches but they all grow from the same tree: Renaissance science. Because of the rise of modern science we can no longer use the Renaissance term for thought leading to knowledge and understanding of underlying principles: "science." But the story I wish to tell comes from Renaissance science, a unified body of thought that we can now understand only by breaking it down into components. I wish to emphasize unity and coherence; labels would get in the way.

The first picture (Figure II–1) shows the mistiness of myth, for it suggests both that a unisexual force lies behind the mating of Mercury and Venus which (like the mating of Mars and Venus) leads to the birth of a Cupid, who is often thought of as unisexual (and certainly so, in later myth when he "married" Psyche). But then the picture reverses itself and Cupid unites Hermes and Aphrodite who create the original hermaphroditic human.

In the second picture (Figure II–2), hermaphroditic creation is "Christianized" with reliance on the Cabala and Gnostic doctrine, but merged with Hermeticism and alchemy through the ambiguously named Albertus Magnus (1193–1280) who was both a bishop and an alchemist/magus. Thus, he was God creating humankind and God's representative blessing humankind, and the alchemist creating the rebus which leads to perfection, the "Y," which is the original word, Yahweh, and is, therefore, the source of humankind, created in the Divine Image, the mystical "Y," the first letter of the word too sacred to be uttered. (See James A. Weisheipl, ed., *Albertus Magnus and the Sciences* [Leiden: Brill, 1980].)

The original creation of humankind is celebrated in the symbolism of marriage, as seen in the third picture (Figure II–3), where man and woman, tied together by a "true-love's knot," become the tree of life, both spiritually in Christ and actually in nature, and thus are blessed both by Moses, society's lawgiver, and by the Satyr, whose presence validates nature's sexual energy.

The fourth picture (Figure II–4) is secular but not unspiritual. Here the magus, the learned person, can replicate all of life through the square (the four elements), the triangle (the body, the soul, the spirit—the secular Trinity), and the circle (unity and harmony). His tools—inventions of his mind—make the magus like God.

In the fifth picture (Figure II–5), the compass of the magus becomes the compass of God, the Maker of the Magus. From the bottom, with the tree of life coming out of her/his head and the subjection of the beast under foot, the hermaphrodite leads both directly and circuitously to the godhead, which in turn projects and controls the masculine and feminine principles of the world, which in conjunction create humankind in the person of the hermaphrodite symbolized both at the bottom of the picture and in the very middle in the form of the rebus, the unisexual symbol of wholeness, completion, perfection—the center of the universe—often called the macrocosmic child: the child of the universe (and associated with the egg and eternity, and with the philosopher's stone). Humankind is not only at the center of the universe, the universe is centered in humankind, which is what Mephostophiles reminded Faustus.

Fludd's version of all this in the sixth picture (Figure II–6) both celebrates and denigrates humanity. Compared to God and to Dame Nature who create by word and deed the entire cosmos, the human is a mere ape, but only the human animal among all of the others could invent God's compass to measure and recreate God's various versions of the micro- and macrocosmos. Fludd's scheme represents the Renaissance unified-field theory of all science. (See Edward William Tayler, *Nature and Art in Renaissance Literature* [New York: Columbia University Press, 1964], 11–37.)

Sources:

II–1 Michael Maierus. *Atlantus fugiens*. Frankfort, 1617, p. 95.

II–2 Michael Maierus. *Symbola aureae mensae duodecim nationum.* Frankfort, 1617, p. 238.

II–3 Barthélemy Aneau. *Picta poesis.* Lyons, 1552, p. 14.

II–4 Michael Maierus. *Atlantus fugiens.* Frankfort, 1617, p. 115.

II–5 *Museum Hermeticum* (*reformatum et amphificatum*). Frankfort, 1678, Figure IV, following p. 803.

II–6 Robert Fludd. *Utruisque cosmi maioris scilicet et minoris metaphysica, physica atque technica historia.* Oppenheim, 1617, 2 vols., I, 3–4.

II–1: The Issue of the Hermaphrodite

II–2: God and Man as Magus

II–3: The Spirituality and Sexuality of Marriage

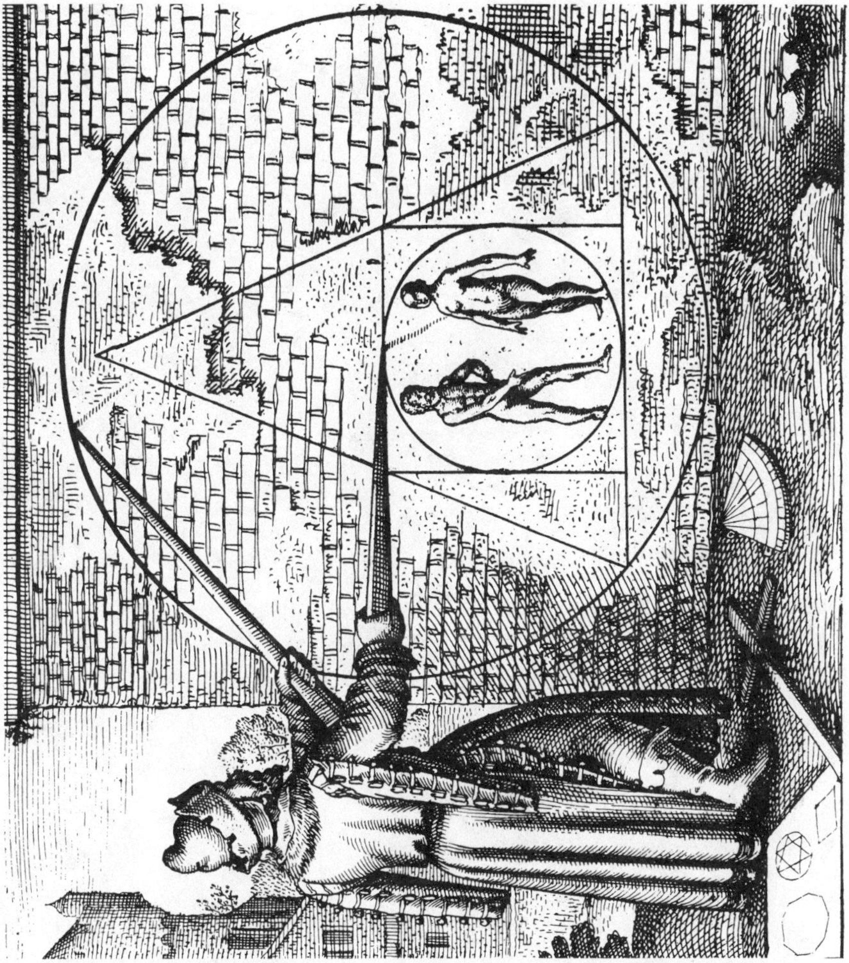

II–4: HUMAN RECLAMATION OF THE GARDEN OF EDEN

II–5: THE MACROCOSMIC CHILD

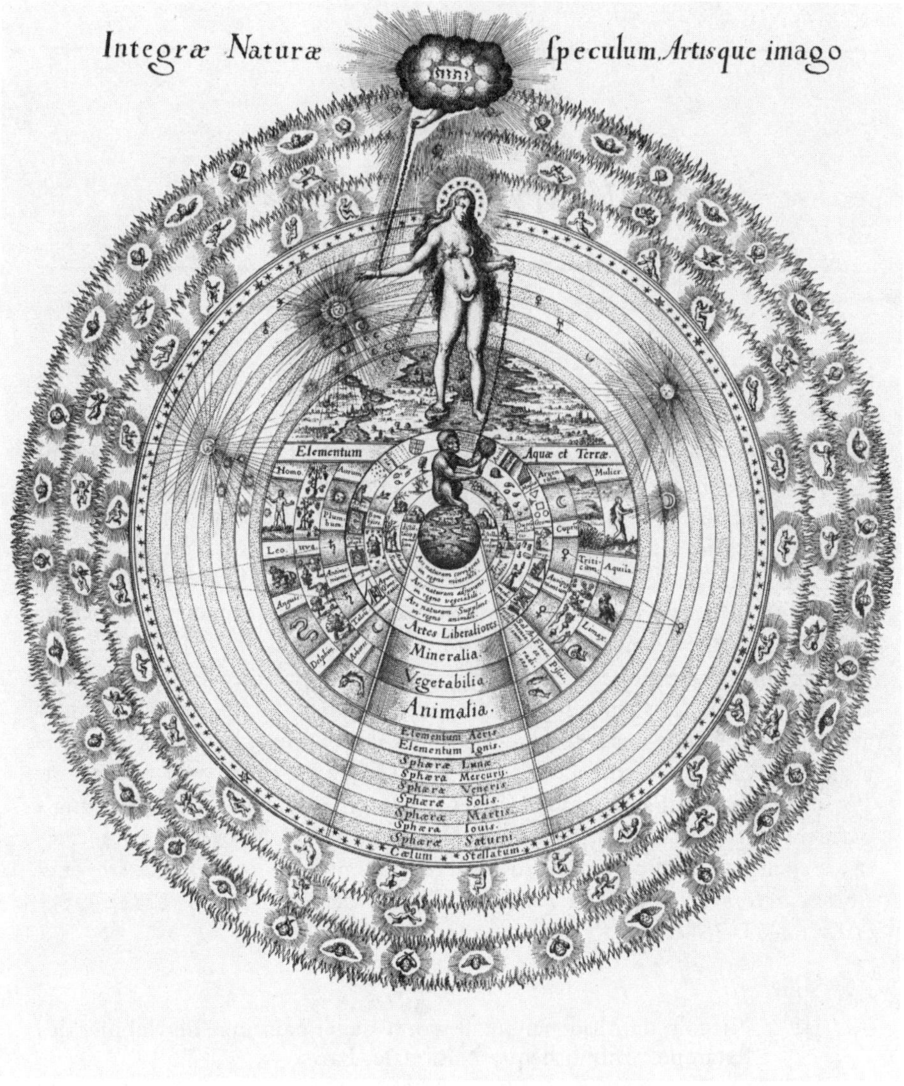

II–6: THE EXTERNALITY OF NATURE AND THE INTERNALITY OF ART

Appendix III

Androgynous Majesty

Because Françoise le Premier combines both Hermes ("Mercure") and Aphrodite ("Amour"), he is by definition a hermaphrodite. But, because he contains wisdom, eloquence, generosity, personal integrity, fortitude, justice, love, caring, and all other graces and virtues which make up the "perfect" human being, he is also by definition an androgyne. A unified composition of opposites, Françoise surpasses nature, as we experience it, and becomes the Dame/Father Nature of the *Two Cantos of Mutabilitie*.

Note the imagery of Perseus and, particularly, that the king is pregnant. On his back is the sheath for Mars's sword and/or the quiver for Diana's arrows (it does not matter) which leads to Diana's hunting horn, which is also a vulvaic cornucopia (allied to the Gorgon's mask which contains Proserpine) as well as a phallus (for it points to a vulvaic fold in the king's garment). For further explanation of Mercury (hence, Françoise) as Hermetic, alchemical, and as an androgyne, see Elémire Zolla, *The Androgyne: Reconciliation of Male and Female* (New York: Crossroads, 1981), especially 62–63, 76–77.

Source:

III–1 Niccolò da Modena. Small wood-panel painting. Le Cabinet des Estampes. Bibliothèque Nationale, Paris.

III–1: FRANÇOISE LE PREMIER AS MERCURY AND VENUS

Appendix IV

Circles within Circles within Circles

The four elements create the circle (the squaring of the circle by the magus) with the cosmic child (unisexual because presexual) at the center, in the first picture (Figure IV–1). In the second (Figure IV–2), the child has become sexed, and, in the seventeenth century, is securely male. In the third (Figure IV–3), George Ripley is more mystical than is Fludd, for at the center, at the still point of the turning world, that quintessence of dust is nothing and is everything, both a speck of dust and the symbol of the entire universe. Ripley's work is in the field of spiritual alchemy, the specialty of John Dee. Both Dee and Ripley sought, as did Faustus, to become a spirit in form and substance.

The fourth, fifth, and sixth pictures (Figures IV–4, 5, 6) represent in different ways this attainment: 4) the alchemical quest for and attainment of the philosopher's stone, 5) the complete philosopher or cosmic man who is so detached that he can understand the entire universe (with the earth in its center)—both God and man fulfilled—Hercules and his load, and 6) Sapience the Queen of Heaven—Elizabeth the Queen of Faerie land.

Sources:

IV–1 *Museum Hermeticum (reformatum et amplificatum)*. Frankfort, 1678, Figure II, following p. 803.

IV–2 Robert Fludd. *Utriuisque cosmi maioris scilicet et minoris metaphysica, physica atque technica historia*. Oppenheim, 1617, 2 vols., I, title page (lower half).

IV–3 John Goddard, "George Ripley's Wheel." *Theatricum chemicum britannicum*, ed. Elias Ashmole. London, 1652, between pp. 116 and 117.

IV–4 A. Labavius. *Alchymis*. Frankfort, 1606, Part II, Book IV, p. 51.
IV–5 Basilius Valentius. *Occulta Philosophia*. Frankfort, 1613, p. 47.
IV–6 Michael Maierus, *Atlantus fugiens*, Frankfort, 1617, p. 161.

IV–1: The Making of Humankind

IV–2: MANKIND MADE

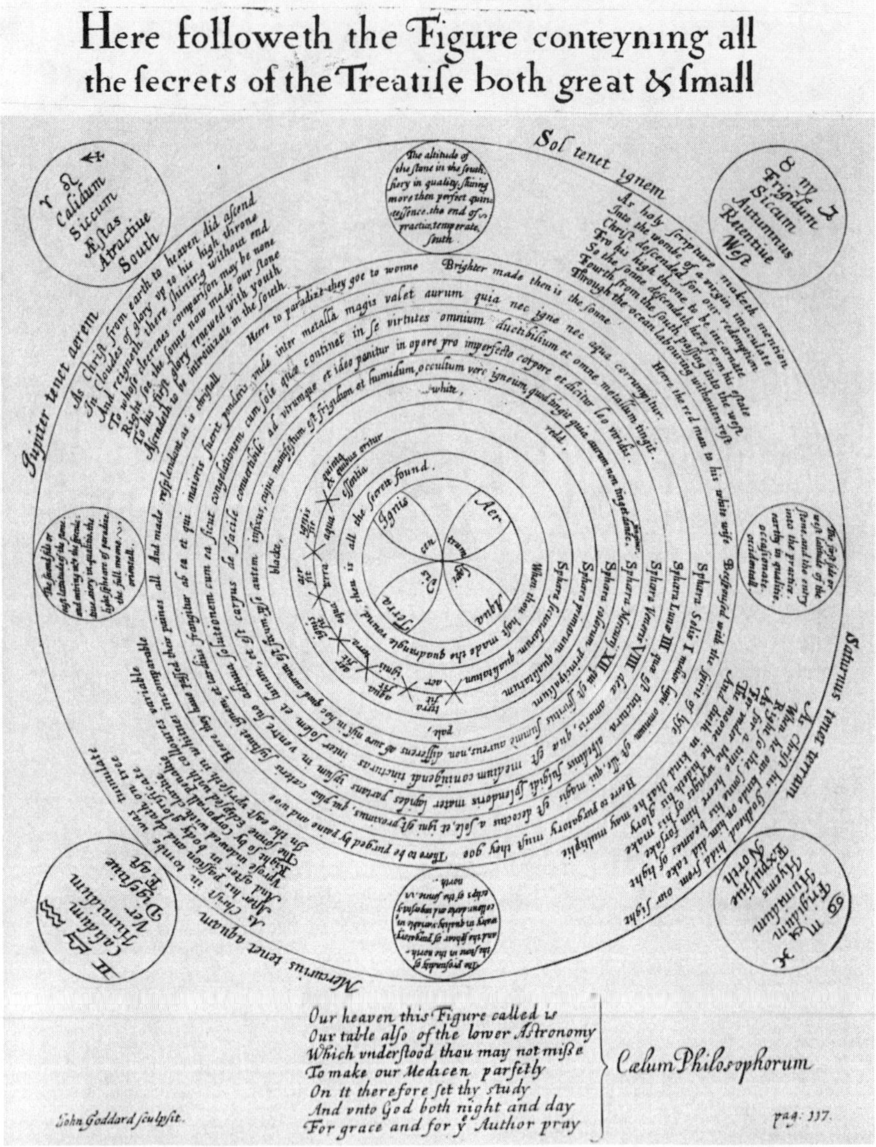
Here followeth the Figure conteyning all the secrets of the Treatise both great & small
Sol tenet ignem
Jupiter tenet aerem
Saturnus tenet terram
Mercurius tenet aquam
Calidum Siccum Æstas Atractiue South
Frigidum Siccum Autumnus Retentiue West
Ignis
Aer
Terra
Aqua
Our heaven this Figure called is
Our table also of the lower Astronomy
Which vnderstood thou may not misse
To make our Medicen parfetly
On it therefore set thy study
And vnto God both night and day
For grace and for ye Author pray
Cælum Philosophorum
John Goddard sculpsit.
pag: 117.

IV–3: The Still Point

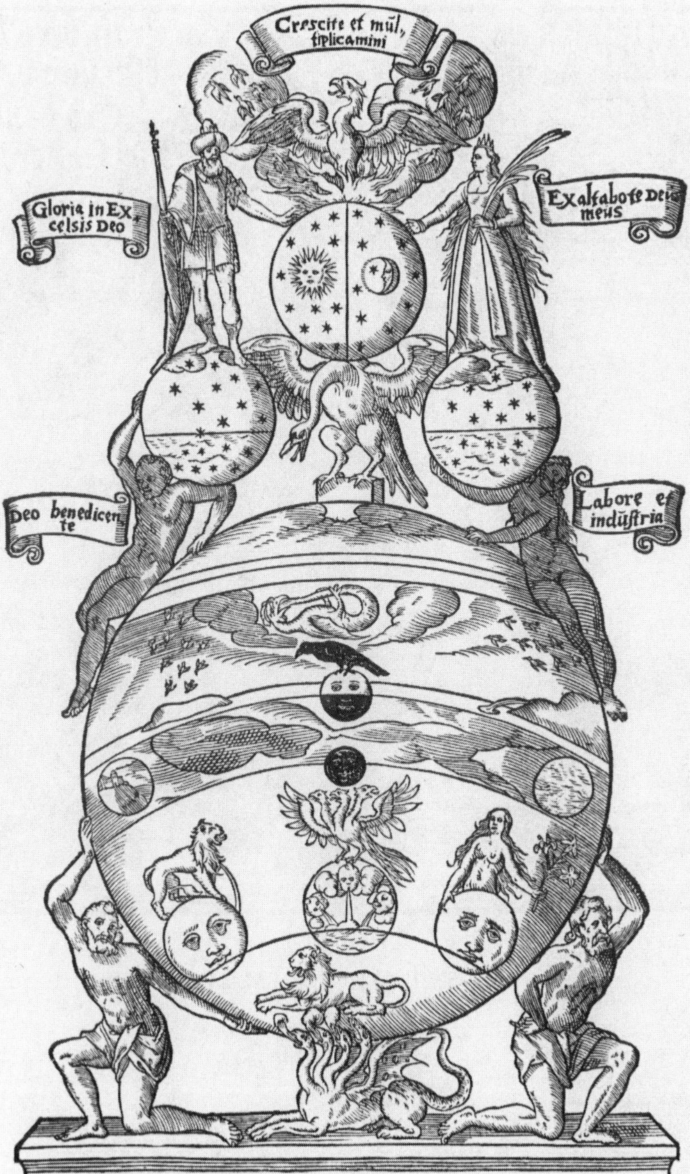

IV–4: The Philosopher's Stone

IV–5: THE COSMIC MAN

IV–6: THE HEAVENLY QUEEN

Appendix V

Versions of Venus and Cupid

No lesson in iconography is intended, nor will be attempted—just a few reminders, more the remarks of a museum guide than a lecture from an historian of art. (Or more like the lyrics from "The Sound of Music": "These are a few of my favorite things.")

In the first two pictures (Figures V–1, 2), we see the easy interplay of so-called pagan and Christian, the lack of tension between the mother and child by Cambiaso and by Rubens (both at the Art Institute of Chicago, but not side by side). Both are pleasant, domestic, secular, similar in mood as well as disposition—the adoring angel could be a visiting cupid. But the main point is simple: only a pre-"modern," non-"western," unsophisticated mind is sufficiently sophisticated to absorb and respond to myth without categorizing, analyzing, and explicating. Receiving pleasure from old stories is part of understanding myth.

Each of the third, fourth, and fifth pictures (Figures V–3, 4, 5) gives pleasure, but here, together, they suggest the range of significance of Venus. The "highest" Venus (heavenly beauty) is impossible to delineate, but is felt behind the Botticelli. Born full grown from castrated Saturn, she floats lightly on the sea of her "father"'s semen. Her actual "parentage" is suggested by the nearly hermaphroditic pairing on her right (a kind of Hermes and Aphrodite) (see Appendix II). On her left is her personification of terrestrial life—spring, flora, organicism, the garden of Venus. Thus, in one picture we can feel Venus as a unisexual, pre-creation source of life, as the procreative, formative power of life, and as created life.

The fourth picture for centuries was generally labeled "school of Carravagio," but recently has been given to Manfredi. Befitting its subject, the canvas is large and bold. Its composition is the circle of life, containing the paradox that out of concord and discord, pleasure and strife, love and hate, come concord and discord, pleasure and strife, love and hate—but the picture does indeed contain the paradox, so that the ultimate, lasting feeling is that of unity and harmony. We can feel that Venus loves both Mars (the worker of her smart) by her look and soft gesture of restraint and her son Cupid whose scattered, broken arrows headed with both silver (hate) and gold (love) she tries to gather. Mars, still attracted to Venus (notice the placement of his knee between her legs), hates himself for his "weakness" which he takes out on Cupid. Cupid is technically innocent because he is blind and is only a boy, frightened and crying—but "he" is also a god, the only feathered figure in the picture, and his expression is simultaneously mocking and mischievous—Cupid, the greatest of the gods.

Whereas the Manfredi, as does the Botticelli in a contrasting mood and manner, suggests the whole range of creation myths (night/day, earth/sky, pleasure/strife, woman/man, construction/destruction) from heavenly to earthly expressions, there can be no doubt about the Cranach, which says so eloquently and misogynously: If you seek the honey in the beehive you are apt to get stung. Pleasure, so to speak, has fallen out of the dance of the three graces to become the debased Venus, and taking with her all womankind, the daughters of Eve and Pandora.

We find Pleasure in the "Primavera" trying to look over Beauty's left shoulder to get "a good look" at Hermes/Mercury, whom Beauty and Venus intend for Chastity—but, of course, all of the "female" figures here are "Venus." This grand picture has been beautifully discussed by many, from Edgar Wind, *Pagan Mysteries* (100–10), to Stevie Davies, *The Idea of Woman* (13–15), but see especially M. L. D'Ancona, *Botticelli's Primavera: A Botanical Interpretation Including Astrology, Alchemy and the Medici.* Heavenly Venus (in human guise, unveiled) hovers (goddess-like, not touching the ground) in the center, taking in both Mercury looking in contemplation to heaven for inspiration and to Zephyrus bringing the life-forcing and life-forging breath from heaven. The picture comes as close as a painting can to the physical depiction of the myth of androgyny.

Sources:

V–1 "Venus and Cupid" (c. 1573) by Luca Cambiaso (1527–85). The Art Institute of Chicago

V–2 "Holy Family" (c. 1615) by Peter Paul Rubens (1577–1640). The Art Institute of Chicago

V–3 "The Birth of Venus" (c. 1482) by Botticelli. Florence, The Uffizi

V–4 "Cupid Chastised" (c. 1608) by Bartolomeo Manfredi

(1587–1620).
The Art Institute of Chicago

V–5 "Venus and Amor" (1537) by L. Cranach the Elder (1472–1553).
Amsterdam, Rijksmuseum Kröller-Müller

V–6 "Primavera" (c. 1477) by Botticelli.
Florence, The Uffizi

V–1: VENUS AND CUPID

V–2: HOLY FAMILY

V–3: THE BIRTH OF VENUS

V–4: Cupid Chastised

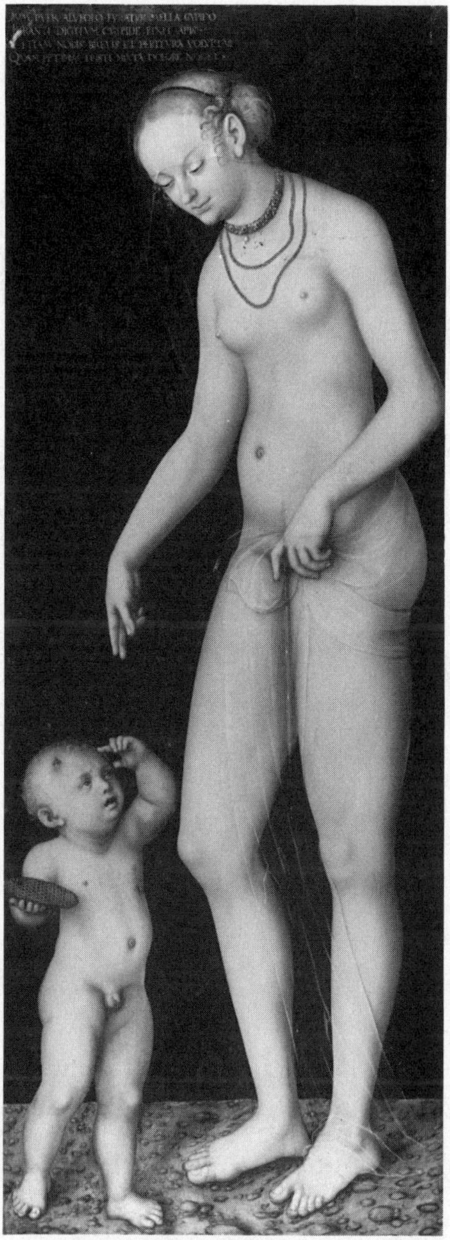

V–5: VENUS AND AMOR

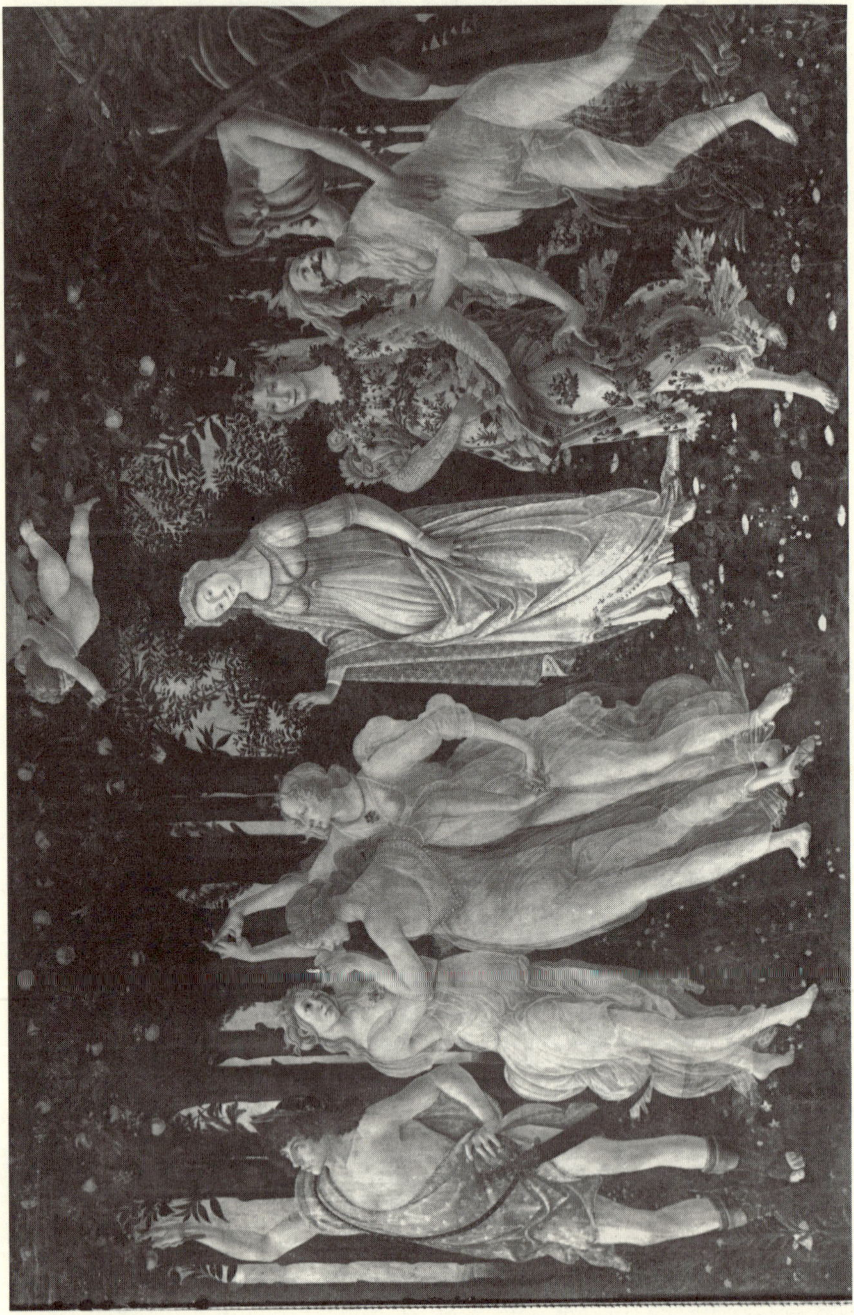

V–6: PRIMAVERA

Appendix VI

Deep Myth in DNA: Unity within Science and the Humanities

In chapter 3, I mentioned John Donne along with Marlowe, Sidney, Spenser, and Shakespeare as a male author who reflected a change of attitude toward women from one of sexual separation and male superiority to one of unity and parity. His "The Extasie" is his most intensified, compressed expression of his new vision of humanity, even though it is contained within the context of a satire on the Neoplatonic model of humankind as divided between body and soul—a yoking together of the earthly and the material with the heavenly and the spiritual. Living in a moment of extremely dramatic theoretical shift within the scientific world, Donne, wanting to say something significant about the nature of human life and instinctive human endeavor, had no sufficient model to work from, and had to exploit the old. Toward the end of his poem Donne becomes highly serious for a special moment when he overrides satire to talk about man and woman in the act of love; his words have both a literal and far-reaching allegorical significance:

> our blood labours to beget
> Spirits, as like souls as it can,
> Because such fingers need to knit
> That subtile knot, which makes us man.

In the image of two laboring before labor to create a set of rational fingers which will be capable of examining and understanding the paradoxical unity of body and soul, Donne catches simultaneously both the organic thrust of life and the human attempt to comprehend and even direct that thrust. (See

Virginia Ramey Mollenkott, "John Donne and the Limitations of Androgyny," *JEGP* 80 [1981].)

Thanks primarily to the romantic rebellion or revolution of the last two hundred years, we can almost accept the concept of the wholeness, the completeness of humankind; we can almost realize the entirely metaphorical nature of the phrase, "body and soul." But we, like Bacon and Donne, are still hemmed in by old models. (We still divide the learned world into scientists and humanists, assuming the one to be concerned with the material aspects of life, the other with the spiritual.) But "body" and "soul" are merely labels for aspects of the whole—aspects which in function feed back into the whole.

Robert Frost, in the fall of 1961, made his last of many visits to the Madison campus of the University of Wisconsin. The Department of English held a small luncheon in his honor, and, toward the end, one truly distinguished professor started holding forth on the number and diversity of learned and critical journals to which he subscribed. With all attention on him, he turned to Frost to ask, "And how many journals do you subscribe to, Mr. Frost?" In pretended puzzlement, Frost replied quietly, "Just one." "Oh," returned the learned scholar, "which one is that?" Frost paused, then answered through his special bemused smile: "*Scientific American.*"

Three years before, Frost gave a lecture at Harvard in which he talked about his poetry and spoke a few poems, especially those which were to appear in *A Cabin in the Clearing*. At the end, he spoke some old favorites, including "Mending Wall," after which he commented, "I've been asked many times what this poem means, and I've never said, but I might as well this once. The poem simply says that all life is cellular, constantly bonding and breaking." Frost knew that science and humanity are inseparable.

One of the most creative human achievements of the last several decades was the postulation and proof by James Watson, Francis Crick, Maurice Wilkins, and (we now know) Rosalind Franklin in the early 1950s of the form and function of the DNA double helix molecule within the cell as the basis of genetic coding and source of protein generation. In order to talk of cellular biology, molecular biology, biochemistry, or whatever name one places on the study of these infinitesimals, it is necessary to move inward to microscopic speculation, opposite to the outward macrocosmic speculation needed to see and conceive of outer space, where the distance, size, and temperature of the sun boggle the mind—93 million miles away from earth, in relative proportions of a speck of dust 10 yards away from an orange, and 20 million degrees F. at the center—where the nearest star to that star is 4 light years away (light travelling at 186,000 miles per second or 6 trillion miles a year), where there are a million planetary systems in our galaxy, where the diameter of our galaxy is millions of light years across (6 trillion miles times millions), and where there are billions of galaxies—all in what we casually refer to as "outer space."

Looking inward, the human body contains trillions of cells, an ejaculation of sperm contains millions of cells, and when you rub your thumb and finger together you brush off many thousands of cells. All life is cellular, and within *each* of those cells the processes of bonding and breaking are constant, patterned, and predictable.

Much is known, but as is the case with outer space, much remains unknown. We know that chemically compounded DNA is the biological basis of genetic evolution. We know that *within a single cell* there are over a million DNA molecules, such as the one sketched in Figure VI–1. We know that these millions of DNA molecules are constantly bonding in the twisting, spiralling dance of double-helical chains which cross and link, and, after complementary mating, break—or come "unzipped," to use the wonderful metaphor created by the new biologists. This is shown in the upper part of Figure VI–2. We know that before relinking or rebonding with other "unzipped" molecules these chains encode linear RNA molecules, as is shown in the lower part of Figure VI–2. Carrying the various genetic messages of life, these *messenger RNA molecules* seek entry to *macromolecules* called *ribosomes* floating around in the cell. A ribosome, which is shown in Figure VI–3, is much larger than a DNA or RNA molecule (to contain the thousands upon thousands of ribosomes of a size such as this enlarged one, a single cell would have to be over 100 feet in diameter). Ribosomes carry within them some RNA, some protein, and various other necessary components of life-stuff. Before the messenger RNA enters, the ribosome has already invited in other distinctly different RNA molecules which have been formed to receive unique triplet messages from the templates of the messenger RNAs. After mating with the messenger, each *transfer RNA* positioned in the ribosome transforms its own message into the generation of polypeptide molecules of protein which generate and regenerate the infinite and shifting variety of cells which constitute the physical basis of life.

Some few years ago, during a presentation of DNA—° RNA—° protein synthesis as just outlined, a biology professor illustrated her lecture using the blackboard. First she drew the DNA double helix as shown in Figure VI–1. Then she sketched the growth of a linear messenger RNA from off an unzipped DNA as is shown in Figure VI–2. Then, as in Figure VI–3, a ribosome which carries the stuff of life in two parts, the upper and larger part providing a home for the transfer of RNA molecules and a lower part seemingly designed to attract the messenger RNA, which enters at the point of the bonding of the two parts. The transfer RNA looks something like Figure VI–4 and the messenger RNA something like Figure VI–5. Their interaction within the ribosome, which is sketched in Figure VI–6, leads to the generation of protein out of the transfer RNA within the womb of the ribosome.

At this point in the lecture, someone shouted out, "Wait a minute," and ran down to the blackboard and put the two signs in Figure VI–7 on the board, and said,

Nature is a ribosome,
A macromolecule
Mating microcosms.

Some students laughed, most were confused, but all were curious. What had caused the outbreak was the resemblance of the transfer and messenger RNA molecules to mankind's primitive signs for woman and man, signs later given personification as Venus and Mars, archetypal figures of love and strife whose relationship produced Eros, the innate creative thrust of life toward unity and harmony. Venus and Mars, in one guise or another, have filled canvas and page as artist after artist has uniquely groped to project the mystic and mythic bonding and breaking interactions of woman and man. Artists' efforts can help us comprehend ourselves; understanding the submicroscopic biochemical process of life can also help us comprehend ourselves. The artist shows us our psychic self; the molecular biologist shows us our physical self. Perhaps two seemingly disparate ways of looking at the evolution of our strifefully harmonious species both lead back, and within, to the same androgynous origin—that "time" when Hermaphrodite and Androgyne were the same.

DNA → RNA → PROTEIN

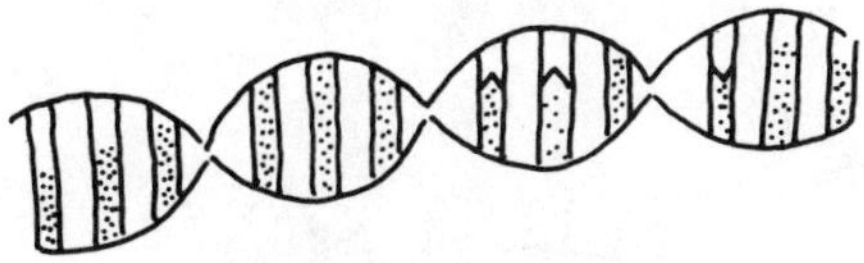

FIGURE VI–1: DNA

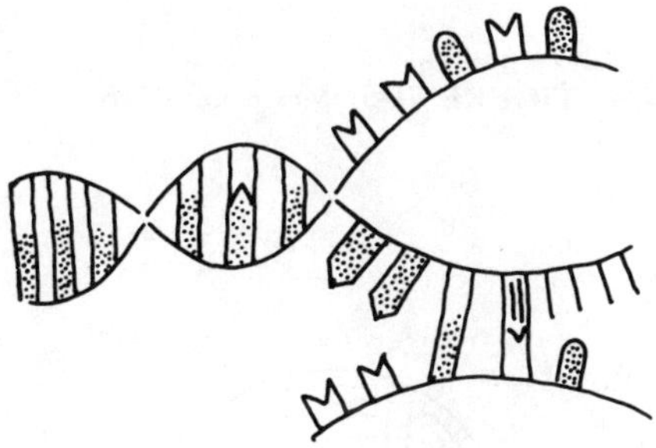

FIGURE VI–2: DNA and RNA

FIGURE VI–3: A Ribosome

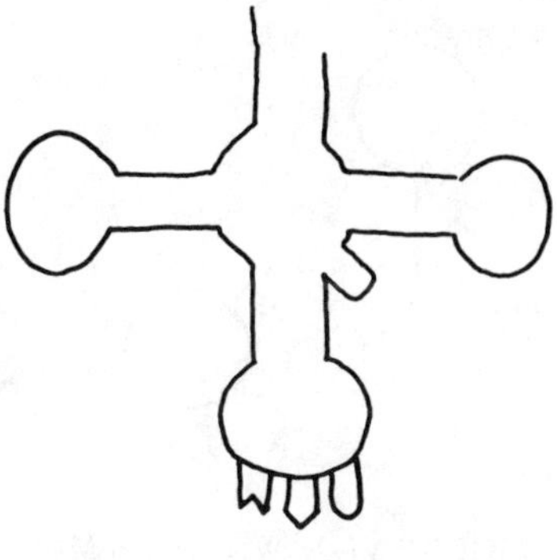

FIGURE VI–4: Transfer RNA

DNA → RNA → PROTEIN

FIGURE VI–5: Messenger RNA

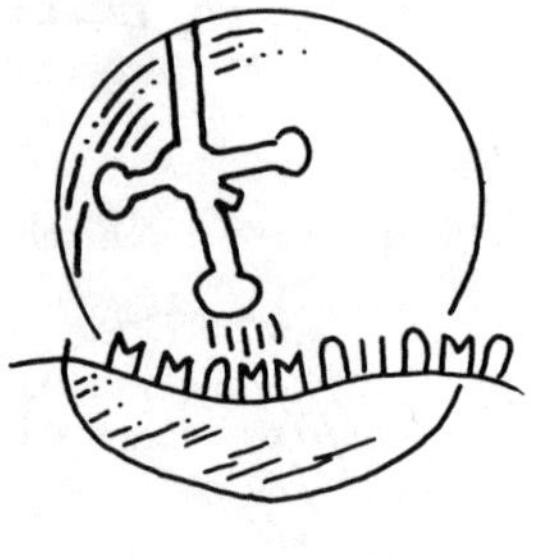

FIGURE VI–6: Ribosome, Transfer, and Messenger

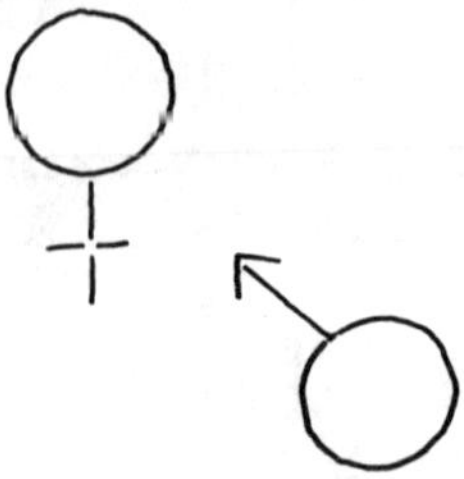

FIGURE VI–7: Woman and Man

Notes

1. Introduction: Discovering Humankindness

1. The assumptions which inform this seemingly simple opening paragraph are, of course, immensely complex and complicated. By nature, I am an offspring of the old historical scholarship and of the old New Criticism, which was an incestuous marriage, like that of the sun and the moon, for the even older New Humanism can be traced in both lines of the family. By nurture, I believe in human sameness and in cultural similitudes: deep myth and thick description.
2. See John T. Robinson, "Men, Morals and Meta-evolution," *Central Issues in Anthropology* 2 (1980), and Teilhard de Chardin, *The Phenomenon of Man.*
3. See Geoffrey Bush, *Shakespeare and the Natural Condition*; Edward W. Tayler, *Nature and Art in Renaissance Literature*; and chapter 10, below, on *King Lear.*
4. From "Nosce Tiepsum," *The Renaissance in England*, ed. Hyder Rollins and Herschel Baker.
5. See Dorothy Koenigsberger, *Renaissance Man and Creative Thinking*; and Amos Funkenstein, *Theology and the Scientific Imagination from the Middle Ages to the Seventeenth Century.*
6. Francis Bacon, "Of Goodness and Goodness of Nature," *Works, XII*, 118; but see also Robert Grams Hunter, *Shakespeare and the Comedy of Forgiveness*, for the tradition that our common shared humanity is, at base, evil.
7. See Terry Eagleton, *Shakespeare and Society*: "Human spontaneity must be contained within a pattern of responsibility, and the two are fused when men make this pattern their own, living it authentically; in this way, too, personal and social can be seen as aspects of a single life" (156), quoted from his chapter on the final plays.
8. Coleridge's remark is not just a casual one, for he had a long, continuing interest in alchemy (as would Jung), the processes of which figure forth a psychology of androgyny. Woolf, while recognizing Shakespeare's androgyny, was wise enough to go on to comment that the androgynous nature of Shakespeare's creativity does not necessarily lead to Shakespeare's having had a positive, egalitarian attitude toward women; she said that we can never know what Shakespeare was like in day-to-day matters.
9. Heilbrun, "Further Notes Toward a Recognition of Androgyny," and Harris, "Androgyny: The Sexist Myth in Disguise," *Women's Studies* 2 (1974), special issue on androgyny, ed. Cynthia Secor. When Heilbrun published *Reinventing Womanhood* in 1979 the word androgyny had been dropped from her vocabulary: the search for self-hood "must have a stronger psychological base, a wider foothold, than can be provided by female experience alone. The reinvention of womanhood, I think, requires chiefly an effort to widen its boundaries and enlarge its scope. If women can take as their own the creative possibilities, the

human aspirations once the property of men only, can they not also adopt male role models in their struggle for achievement? I believe that women must learn to appropriate for their own use the examples of human autonomy and self-fulfillment displayed to us by the male world" (95). Heilbrun's latest remarks in book reviews and at conferences almost signal outright rejection of her early recognition of androgyny.

10. Such a claim is a major argument in this book, and evidence will be offered; for the nonce, see Stevie Davies, *The Idea of Woman in Renaissance Literature: The Feminine Reclaimed*; Jerome Schwartz, "Aspects of Androgyny in the Renaissance," *Human Sexuality in the Middle Ages and Renaissance*, ed. Douglas Radcliffe-Umstead; and John N. King, "The Godly Woman in Elizabethan Iconography," *Renaissance Quarterly* 38 (1985). The massive research of Linda Woodbridge, *Women and the English Renaissance*, both supports and denies my claim.
11. Geoffrey Fenton, *Monophylo* (1572), uses the *Symposium* but departs somewhat from it, for he elevates love between man and woman above that of man and man, stating that true love is "a most excellent forme or plot, exceeding generally the consideration of man, and therefore did figure unto us an Androgina, by whom they ment a man composed of the Masculine and Feminine sexe, and be standing in his state of perfection, swelled in such mortall pryde agaynst the Gods, that by that meanes was afterwardes devided into two" (33–34). And Fenton goes on to define androgyny: Love "drawes us besides by a devine power, with such a strong indissoluble bonde (returning to the first Androgina of our father Adam) that he distils two spirites into one bodye, and . . . two spirits be made *one minde* in two bodies" (35; emphasis added).
12. "Man and Maid in *Twelfth Night*," *Journal of English and Germanic Philology* 80 (1981).
13. See also David Leverenz, "The Woman in Hamlet: An Interpersonal View," *Representing Shakespeare*.
14. *The Shakespearean Metaphor: Studies in Language and Form*, 62.
15. Yet, I do not hold that Shakespeare was dominantly possessed by an *Androgynous Vision* any more than he was dominated by a *Christian Vision*—he was too much the artist to be restricted by an -ism of any kind. Still, just as understanding that a basic sixteenth-century Christian ethic and many other strands of public thought, large and small, accepted and eccentric, run through his work can more fully open his play to our comprehension and delight, so also learning how to recognize the vision of androgyny that plays around the edges of, and pierces through here and there, the drama of Shakespeare can enrich our responses and heighten our appreciation—in the fullest meaning of those phrases.

    For the curious, the most extensive use of the word "kind" (and related words) to be found in one place is in *Gorboduc*.
16. Again, one could open here demonstrations better left for later, but a good beginning point is Charles Trinkhaus's thoughtful survey-article, "Humanism, Religion, Society: Concepts and Motivations of Some Recent Studies," *Renaissance Quarterly* 29 (1976), which emphasizes the *unity* of the various "philosophies."
17. Lucien Febvre, *The Problem of Unbelief in the Sixteenth Century: The Religion of Rabelais*: "Wanting to make the sixteenth century a skeptical century, a free-thinking and rationalist one, and glorify it as such, is the worst of errors and

delusions. On the authority of its best representatives it was, quite to the contrary, an inspired century, one that sought in all things first of all a reflection of the divine" (462–63).

18. The works of the late D. P. Walker are the essential explications of this topic.
19. "Of Education," *Milton's Prose*, ed. M. W. Wallace, 146.
20. There is not much evidence that men were willing to extend to women this opportunity of androgynous growth. Britomart is a notable exception, but then she is that exception, Queen Elizabeth.
21. D. G. James has stated that *The Tempest* is "a commentary on *King Lear*," *The Dream of Prospero*, 26. For *The Tempest* and *King Lear* as a pair for study, see also James P. Driscoll, *Identity in Shakespeare*, 155–57.
22. Wendy Doniger O'Flaherty in *Women, Androgynes, and Other Mythical Beasts* introduces the androgyne: "Androgyny is, at least for the moment, a trendy word in Jungian, feminist, and homosexual circles, to mention but a few: people are 'into' androgyny. This fact should not, however, obscure the importance of the androgyne as an enduring religious symbol; for when the primal screams and Rolfings and skateboards have taken their place with bloodletting and chastity belts, androgyny will still be with us. As a media term, however, it is often applied to a range of phenomena far broader than the specific symbolism under examination here" (283).

2. *Hermaphrodite and Androgyne: Myths of Sex and Gender*

1. Caroline Walker Bynum, *Holy Feast and Holy Fast: The Religious Significance of Food to Medieval Women*, and "The Body of Christ in the Later Middle Ages: A Reply to Leon Steinberg," *Renaissance Quarterly* 39 (1986); Elaine Pagels, *The Gnostic Gospels*; and W. D. O'Flaherty, *Women, Androgynes, and Other Mythical Beasts*, Chapter 9, "Androgynes."
2. Anyone who has ever waded into these waters of sex, gender, innate characteristics, and sex and social roles soon discovers how troubled and treacherous they are. Where to begin? Elizabeth Fisher, *Woman's Creation: Sexual Evolution and the Shaping of Society*, although clearly feminist in point of view, has a full, balanced general bibliography. Almost any work by John Money and his colleagues at the Gender Identity Clinic and the Psychohormonal Research Unit at Johns Hopkins University can be helpful, but a quick introductory read is Money and Patricia Tucker, *Sexual Signatures: On Being a Man or a Woman*. So also, almost any issue of *Signs* seems to cast a pertinent light on this huge area, especially "Woman—Sex and Sexuality," in two parts, summer (5) and autumn (6) 1980, but a good jumping off is Helen A. Lambert, "Viewpoint: Biology and Equality: A Perspective on Sex Differences," *Signs* 4 (1978), which offers a complete review of the science of the controversy. Another reliable general source is the *International Journal of Women's Studies*, especially 8 (1985), which contains two special issues, "Women in Groups: Sex Roles and Sex Differences," and "Sex Roles and Sex Differences [,] and Androgyny," but see also Sandra W. Pyke and J. Martin Graham, "Gender Schema Theory and Androgyny: A Critique and Elaboration," 6 (1983). *Sex Roles: A Journal of Research*, entering its third decade of publication, is itself a vast sea of information in which one could easily drown. But for one ready for a thorough immersion, dive into *Biological Determinants of Sexual Behavior*, ed. J. B. Hutchinson. This symposium, sponsored by the Medical Research Council Unit

on the Development and Integration of Behavior of Cambridge University, has a general introduction and index, is divided into four sections each with an introduction, and contains twenty-four essays, each heavy with referenced materials (for a total of 822 pages). The aim was to bring together the latest in both physiological and behavioral disciplines, with a special emphasis on the role of hormones in human development (mainly the brain) and behavior. I was struck by how often scientist after scientist commented that the tendency toward automatic labeling of hormones and behavior as male or female imposes whole sets of deductions on findings which might not otherwise be implied by the data if weighed without predilection. Another note sounded again and again was the warning of the danger of transferring, wholesale, the findings within the animal domains to the human because of the quantitative and qualitative difference in the nature, role, and function of the brain in human behavior as distinguished from all other mammals. (Both of these topics come up later in this chapter.) Finally, two excellent, balanced collections are *"Femininity," "Masculinity," and "Androgyny": A Modern Philosophical Discussion*, ed. Mary Vetterling-Braggin, and *Sexual Meanings: The Cultural Construction of Gender and Sexuality*, ed. Sherry B. Ortner and Harriet Whitehead.

3. In addition to note 2, see Suzanne J. Kessler and Wendy McKenna, *Gender: An Ethnomethodological Approach*.
4. Again, the literature in this subject is immense; a pioneering work is Alice Clark, *Working Life of Women in the Seventeenth Century*. More recent works are: Ruth H. Bloch, "Untangling the Roots of Modern Sex Roles: A Summary of Four Centuries of Change," *Signs* 4 (1978); Brian Easlea, *Witch Hunting, Magic, and the New Philosophy: An Introduction to the Debates of the Scientific Revolution, 1450–1750*; and, Carolyn Merchant, *The Death of Nature: Women, Ecology, and the Scientific Revolution*. An excellent summary essay is the "Introduction" by the editors of *Rewriting the Renaissance: The Discourses of Sexual Difference in Early Modern Europe*, Margaret W. Ferguson, Maureen Quilligan, and Nancy Vickers.
5. For a "canonization" of the field of feminist criticism of Shakespeare, see Richard Levin, "Feminist Thematics and Shakespearean Tragedy," *PMLA* 103 (1988), and see also the "Forum" exchange, *PMLA* 104 (1989).
6. A major dissenter is W. Thomas McCary, *Friends and Lovers: The Phenomenology of Desire*, who argues that the ideas and ideals of the age were so male-biased that they prevented even a hint being heard about gender equity.
7. For example, Sandra Bem, "Psychological Androgyny," *Beyond Sex Roles*; Anne Fausto-Sterling, *Myths of Gender: Biological Theories about Women and Men*; Ann Ferguson, "Androgyny As an Ideal for Human Development," *Feminism and Philosophy*; and Joyce Trebilcot, "Two Forms of Androgynism," *Feminism and Philosophy*. (The whole of *Feminism and Philosophy* is worth reference, reading, or study.)
8. See Dorothy Dinnerstein, *The Mermaid and the Minotaur: Sexual Arrangements and Human Malaise*; Gerda Lerner, *The Creation of Patriarchy*; Virginia Ramey Mollenkott, *The Divine Feminine: The Biblical Imagery of God as Female*; Nancy Tanner, *On Becoming Human*; William Irwin Thompson, *The Time Falling Bodies Take to Light: Mythology, Sexuality, and the Origins of Culture*; and Diane Wolkstein, ed., and Samuel Noah Kramer, trans., *Inanna, Queen of Heaven and Earth: Her Stories and Hymns from Sumer*.
9. See Betty S. Travitsky, *The Paradise of Women: Writings by Englishwomen of*

the Renaissance; Suzanne W. Hull, *Chaste, Silent, and Obedient: English Books for Women, 1475–1640*; Mary Beth Rose, ed., *Women in the Middle Ages and the Renaissance: Literary and Historical Perspectives*; Carole Levin and Jeanie Watson, eds., *Ambiguous Realities: Women in the Middle Ages and Renaissance*; and Katherine Usher Henderson and Barbara F. McManus, *Half Humankind: Contexts and Texts of the Controversy about Women in England, 1540–1640.*

10. Woodbridge's *Women and the English Renaissance: Literature and the Nature of Womankind* is now the definitive work on this question. Because she and I are running over the same course, perhaps it would be useful to indicate briefly where we differ. First of all, she treats "The Formal Controversy" as a literary genre, and she believes that literary genres cannot lead us to clear, exact, "true" pictures of actual social issues and conditions. Certainly, not entirely, but one need not be a New Historian to question her assumption. Then, although she discusses at length cross-dressing both in the streets and on the stage, she refuses to see androgynous potential in it, but lumps all cross-dressing under hermaphroditism and considers it therefore unnatural. And, finally, she eschews discussion of the influence of Elizabeth as Queen on the whole question of the nature of womankind.
11. *The Idea of Woman in Renaissance Literature: The Feminine Reclaimed.*
12. See Virgil B. Heltzel, *A Check List of Courtesy Books in the Newberry Library*; Francis L. Utley, *The Crooked Rib*; Carroll Camden, *The Elizabethan Woman*; Ruth Kelso, *Doctrine for the Lady of the Renaissance*; Katherine M. Rogers, *The Troublesome Helpmate*; and Pearl Hogrefe, *Sir Thomas Elyot, Tudor Women*, and *Women of Action in Tudor England.*
13. Joseph Swetnam's *Arraignment* is the most famous, but see also Sir Humphrey Gilbert, *Queene Elizabethes Achademy*; Thomas Salter, *A mirrhor mete*; and William Whateley, *A bride-bush* and *A Care-cloth.*
14. See the translation of Juan Luis Vives's *The Instruction of a Christian Woman* by Richard Hyrde (Margaret More-Roper's tutor); the translations of Agrippa's *The Nobility of Women* by William Bercher and David Clapham; James Sanford's translation of Agrippa on the vanity of learning; "I.D."'s translation of Aristotle's *Politics*; and the anonymous *Aristos seven planets governing Italie.* Lesser voices are: Robert Allott, *Wits theater of the little world*; William Cecil, Lord Burghley, *Advice to Queen Elizabeth* and his *Precepts*; Stephano Guazzo, *The ciuile conuersation*; Nicolas de Montreux, *Honors academie*; Thomas Watson, *Holsome and catholyke doctrine*; and *The glasse of godley love* (ed. F. J. Furnivall).
15. *Positions wherein those primitive circumstances be examined which are necessarie for the training up of children*, 132, 179.
16. *Praise of vertuous ladies*, 15, 18.
17. *The mirrour of good maners.*
18. *A treatise of Salomons marriage*, 40–41.
19. Lodowick Bryskett, *A discourse of civil life*; S. Leonard's translation of Tommaso Buoni, *Problems of beautie and all humane affections*; Alexander Nicchołas, *A discourse of marriage and wiving*; John Wing, *The crowne conjugall*; and Samuel Torshell, *The womans glorie.* I am staying out of the "Jane Anger" controversy, but for an account of the growing positive attitude toward women see John N. King, "The Godly Woman in Elizabethan Iconography," *Renaissance Quarterly* 38 (1985).
20. For discussions of aspects of feminist/androgynist thought in Erasmus and

More, see Dusinberre and Davies; for Colet, see Daniel Lochman; for Elyot, see Constance Jordan; for Hoby/Castiglione, see Woodbridge; for Bruno, see Yates and editions cited; and, as for Calvin and Hooker sharing a regard for the personhood of woman within marriage, see Lawrence Stone and A. J. Smith.

21. The essential biological processes of human development between conception and adolescence take place during the first nine months, as does female and male differentiation. That is, "normal" female or male inauguration takes place, as does partial, or pseudo-hermaphroditic, development. All humans produce their own hormones (from the Greek, "to stimulate") to assist in this process (and other processes after birth), and all humans produce the same hormones, mainly androgen and estrogen, in their sex and adrenal glands. Because testes produce relatively more androgen than they do estrogen, and because ovaries produce relatively more estrogen than do testes, androgens (as the root indicates) are known as the "male" hormone and estrogens the "female" (from the Greek for "gadfly": a sarcastic reference to supposed periodic female randiness, as if males were not, in general, constantly horny). An imbalance of these hormones in an X–X may prevent complete withering away of all signs of male organs of reproduction, and an imbalance of these hormones in an X–Y may fail to suppress all signs of female organs. Most of these few cases in men or women of arrested and divided development can be spotted or checked for at birth, but some become apparent only at adolescence. Some very few probably are never discovered, possibly even by the individual X–X or X–Y, who may even have undertaken a gender identity opposite from genetic (sexual) identity. (See Appendix I.)

22. I use the expression "so-called" in order to draw attention to the fact that in discussing scientific details, especially the unseen, scientists speak in metaphor, something most of them do not realize. For example, tell a zoologist, botanist, anthropologist, or molecular biologist that the term "natural selection" is not a fact, but a fiction that describes a fact, and you can start a mutually edifying discussion. "Natural selection" as a fiction of fact is allied to Dame Nature and the Great Goddess. My favorite "scientific" metaphor is the one used to describe the splitting of a completed double helix when it is ready to replicate itself twice by each half's new mating to create new double helixes: "unzipping." (See Appendix VI.)

23. *Signatures*, 40–41.

24. *Sex and Fantasy*, 85.

25. See Robert W. Goy and Bruce S. McEwen, *Sexual Differentiation of the Brain*; and Anne Fausto-Sterling, *Myths of Gender: Biological Theories About Women and Men*.

26. For sexism within, and the sexism of, science, see Ruth Bleier, *Science and Gender: A Critique of Biology and Its Theories on Women*, and *Feminist Approaches to Science*; Ruth Hubbard and Marian Lowe, *Genes and Gender II: Pitfalls in Research on Sex and Gender*; Evelyn Fox, *Reflections on Gender and Science*; Sandra Harding and Jean F. O'Barr, eds., *Sex and Scientific Inquiry*; Lynda Birke, *Women, Feminism and Biology*; and the entire issues of *Resources For Feminist Research/Documentation Sur La Recherche Feministe* 15 (1986) and "Restructuring the Academy," *Signs* 12 (1987). An interesting parallel development of sexism in the field of classics is discussed by Natalie Harris Bluestone in *Women and the Ideal Society: Plato's Republic and Modern Myths of Gender*, where she shows that Plato's actual egalitarianism was not allowed to survive the

generations of male sex-biased commentators; Bluestone uncovers a lost androgynous philosophy.

27. For reviews, reports, and critiques of sex and brain research, see the papers edited by J. B. Hutchinson, especially: Linda Plapinger and Bruce S. McEwen, "Gonadol Steroid—Brain Interactions in Sexual Differentiation," 153–218; Hutchinson, "Introduction," Part II: "Integration of Sexual Behavior: Physiological Mechanisms," 221–24; H. H. Feder, "Specificity of Steroid Hormone Activation of Sexual Behavior in Rodents," 395–424; and, John Bancroft, "The Relationship Between Hormones and Sexual Behaviour in Humans," 493–519. The papers and essays in *Genes and Gender II: Pitfalls in Research on Sex and Gender*, especially: Ruth Bleier, "Social and Political Bias in Science: An Examination of Animal Studies and their Generalizations to Human Behavior and Evolution," 49–69, and Susan Leigh Star, "Sex Differences and the Dichotomization of the Brain: Methods, Limits and Problems in Research on Consciousness," 113–130. Other pertinent books are: Julia A. Sherman, *Sex-Related Cognitive Differences: An Essay on Theory and Evidence*; Ronald A. LaTorre, *Sexual Identity*; Jacquelynne Parsons, ed., *The Psychobiology of Sex Differences and Sex Roles*; Mike Brake, ed., *Human Sexual Relations: Towards a Redefinition of Sexual Politics*; and Joseph H. Pleck, *The Myth of Masculinity*.
28. The philosophy of the nudist movement is that the trappings of gender prevent us from being ourselves and knowing others. Transvestism is also an attempt not to be limited by gender, but it runs the danger of one's becoming a stereotype of the gender crossed to, a mocking, shallow, awkward imitation.
29. "Transsexual" became in the 1950s the adjective and noun to label those people who underwent surgery to have organs of one sex removed or altered and artificial organs of the other sex implanted. The term so used is misleading and adds false dignity and beneficence to a procedure that is of highly dubious general human value. For a full definition and analysis, see Janice Raymond, whose work is discussed in Appendix I.

3. *Locating Androgyny in Sixteenth-Century England*

1. "Reason is the principal parte of the soule diuine and immortal, wherby man dothe discerne good from yll," Sir Thomas Elyot, *The Defence of Good Women*, 41.
2. Giovanni Battistee Nenna, *Nennio; or, A treatise of nobility . . . Done into English by William Jones* (dedicated to the Earl of Essex; prefatory poems by Spenser, Daniel, Chapman, and Angel Day), II, 47.
3. "In searching out, if God be the Soueraigne good, knowing it through Science, I seeke to vnderstand what God is. Afterwardes by Wisdome I comprehend the principles, and that which proceedeth of them wherof by good right, it is named the true knowledge of diuine and humane thinges," *Nennio*, II, 50.
4. *A Defence of Poetry*, 111.
5. Francis Bacon, "Of Goodness and Goodness of Nature," *Works*, XII, 118.
6. John Colet, *Commentary on First Corinthians*, 250. See also the first chapters in Theodore Spencer, *Shakespeare and the Nature of Man*.
7. The "spiritual mind" (the "heart of our heart and soul of our soul") is "one indivisible unity" which, like the sun, sheds its influence over all parts; Leone Ebreo, *The Philosophy of Love*, 204. See T. Anthony Perry, *Erotic Spirituality: The Integrative Tradition from Leone Ebreo to John Donne*. The idea of the

unity of all within all so permeates the Renaissance that no one label can cover it: Cabalist, Gnostic, Hermetic; or, in the case of Nicholas of Cusa who seems to have been his own master and pupil, perhaps "Christian" is the only appropriate label to apply (see Pauline Moffit Watts, *Nicolaus Cusanus: A Fifteenth-Century Vision of Man*). In introducing his book, *Mighty Opposites: Shakespeare and Renaissance Contrariety*, Robert Grudin emphasizes the unity of the thought about unity. In his chapter, "Late Medieval Nominalism and Renaissance Philosophy," Amos Funkenstein, *Theology and the Scientific Imagination from the Middle Ages to the Seventeenth Century*, 57–72, links Cusanus, Ficino, and Bruno through a shared vision of the world as an explication, a self-expression of God. One could add Ramon Lull, Johannes Reuchlin, Guillaume Postel. Call it "Christian-Hebraica" as Jerome Friedman does, or *Les Kabbalistes Chrétiens de la Renaissance*, as does François Secret.

8. See Terry G. Sherwood, *Fulfilling the Circle: A Study of John Donne's Thought*; Stephen Greenblatt, *Renaissance Self-Fashioning*; Jay L. Halio, "The Metaphor of Conception and Elizabethan Theories of the Imagination," *Neophilologus* 50 (1966); Harry Berger Jr., "'The Renaissance Imagination': Second World and Green World," *CRAS* 9 (1965); Arnold Stein, "On Elizabethan Wit," *RES* 1 (1961); and William Rossky, "Imagination in the English Renaissance: Psychology and Poetic," *Studies in the Renaissance* 5 (1957).
9. See Joseph Penquiney, Chapter 5, "The Bisexual Soul," in *Such is My Love: A Study of Shakespeare's Sonnets*; and Constance Jordan, "Woman's Rule in Sixteenth-Century British Thought," *RQ* 40 (1987).
10. *The Individual and the Cosmos in Renaissance Philosophy*, 40.
11. *Renaissance Thought: The Classic, Scholastic, and Humanistic Strains*, 132–138.
12. See A. J. Smith, *The Metaphysics of Love*.
13. See Leonard Barkan, *Nature's Work of Art: The Human Body as Image of the World*; Thomas C. Heller, Morton Sosna, and David E. Wellbery, eds., *Reconstructing Individualism: Autonomy, Individuality, and the Self in Western Thought*; and Howard I. Needler, "Of Truly Gargantuan Proportions: From the Abbey of Thélème to the Androgynous Self," *University of Toronto Quarterly* 51 (1982) (but see also Carla Freccero, "The Other and the Same: The Image of the Hermaphrodite in Rabelais," *Rewriting the Renaissance*).
14. *The boke named The gouernour*, 2: 88–89.
15. Charles Trinkaus, "Marsilio Ficino and the Ideal of Human Autonomy," *Ficino and Renaissance Neoplatonism*. See also, of course, *The Scope of Renaissance Humanism* and *In Our Image and Likeness*.
16. Renaissance cosmology is based on the analogy of the circle: "a circle that existed in the perfect spheres of the planets, in the circular globe, in the round head of man. This was not mere analogy to them; it was truth," Marjorie Hope Nicholson, *The Breaking of the Circle*, 7; and see also Rosemond Tuve, *Elizabethan and Metaphysical Imagery*.
17. See Dorothy Koenigsberger, *Renaissance Man and Creative Thinking*.
18. See E. H. Gombrich, "*Icones Symbolicae*: Philosophies of Symbolism and Their Bearing on Art," *Symbolic Images: Studies in the Art of the Renaissance*; and Michael Murrin, *The Veil of Allegory*.
19. For a recent encyclopedic account of this general movement see the forty-one essays collected in three volumes, *Renaissance Humanism: Foundations, Forms, and Legacy*, ed., Albert Rabil Jr.: 1, *Humanism in Italy*; 2, *Humanism Beyond Italy*; 3, *Humanism and the Disciples*. See especially Richard J. Schoeck, "Humanism in England," and Retha M. Warnicke, "Women and Humanism in

King Alfred's College of Higher Education
Winchester SO22 4NR

TO:

INTERNAL MEMORANDUM

FROM:

DATE:

p.11 (Sidney) — Indivdl choice + inner growth v. romance idea that identity comes from outer, soc^l achievement alone (FQ).

p.12-13: Humanity in Temp.

Sidney – poetry + learning directed twds. personal development
– how valid now in technocratic/comm^cl soc^y (secular)

England," Vol. 2. Although the overall account is varied, the general atmosphere of the three volumes is heavily "Kristellerian." For a seemingly dissident position, see the sharply worded volume by Anthony Grafton and Lisa Jardine, *From Humanism to the Humanities: Education and the Liberal Arts in Fifteenth- and Sixteenth-Century Europe* which, to this reader, does not so much undercut the "humanist" position as it merely points out that, as in all of life, the humanists's reaching exceeded their grasps, and that they were guilty, God bless us, of being inconsistent and even hypocritical. A more perceptive piece is Arthur B. Ferguson, "Humanism as a Mode of Perception: The Case of England," *Medieval and Renaissance Studies* 9 (1982).

20. Dennis Hay, "England and the Humanities in the Fifteenth Century," *Itinerarium Italicum.*
21. In addition to Trinkaus, see Arthur F. Kinney, *Humanist Poetics: Thought, Rhetoric, and Fiction in Sixteenth-Century England*; Thomas O. Sloane, *Donne, Milton, and the End of Humanist Rhetoric*; Rocco Montano, *Shakespeare's Concept of Tragedy: The Bard As Anti-Elizabethan*; James D. Tracy, "Humanism and the Reformation," *Reformation Europe*; Stevie Davies, "Introduction," *Renaissance Views of Man*; and the assumptions informing Joel B. Altman, *The Tudor Play of Mind.*
22. In *Love's Labor's Lost* both boys and girls receive instruction under Master Holofernes.
23. See Ian Maclean, *The Renaissance Notion of Woman: A Study in the Fortunes of Scholasticism and Medical Science in European Intellectual Life*, for a calm, clear discussion of the education of women. Ever since Dusinberre's positive claims, a controversy has raged over how widespread, how deep, and to what ends was the education of women. For opposition to Dusinberre, Maclean, and Davies, see Grafton and Jardine, the introduction to *Rewriting the Renaissance* (Ferguson, Quilligen, Vickers); and Janis Butler Holm, "The Myth of a Feminist Humanism: Thomas Salter's *The Mirrhor of Modestie*," *Ambiguous Realities* (but if you read Holm I would advise you also to read Salter, whose misogyny is so virulent and apparent that Holm actually has a non-case case).
24. See Nancy S. Streuver, *The Language of History in the Renaissance: Rhetoric and Historical Consciousness in Florentine Humanism*; Marion Trousdale, *Shakespeare and the Rhetoricians*; Jane Donawerth, *Shakespeare and the Sixteenth-Century Study of Language*; Victoria Kahn, *Rhetoric, Prudence, and Skepticism in the Renaissance*; and Margreta De Grazia, "Shakespeare's View of Language: An Historical Perspective," *Shakespeare Quarterly* 29 (1978), one of her many fine essays on language in the sixteenth century.
25. See Robert S. Westman and J. E. McGuire, eds., *Hermeticism and the Scientific Revolution*; Paolo Rossi, "Hermeticism, Rationality, and the Scientific Revolution," in *Reason, Experiment, and Mysticism in the Scientific Revolution.* For helpful summaries of Hermeticism (among a host of other good ones) see Ernest Lee Tuveson, *The Avatars of Thrice Great Hermes*; Thomas O. Calhoun, *Henry Vaughan: The Achievement of "Silex Scintillans*;" James Robinson Howe, *Marlowe, Tamburlaine, and Magic*; and John S. Mebane, *Renaissance Magic and the Return of the Golden Age.*
26. See Robert Mandrou, *From Humanism to Science 1480–1700*; Jack D'Amico, *Knowledge and Power in the Renaissance*; and Russell Fraser, *The Language of Adam: On the Limits and Systems of Discourse.*
27. See Brian Vickers, "Frances Yates and the Writing of History," *The Journal of Modern History* 51 (1979); and R. H. Stuever, ed., *Historical and Philosophical*

Perspectives of Science; but see also Vickers, ed., *Occult and Scientific Mentalities in the Renaissance.*

28. See also an earlier summary essay by Trinkaus, "Humanism, Religion, Society: Concepts and Motivations of Some Recent Studies," *Renaissance Quarterly* 29 (1976).
29. In addition to Koenigsberger and others just mentioned in the text and in the notes, see Jasper Hopkins, *Nicholas of Cusa's Dialectical Mysticism*; Brian P. Copenhaver, "Scholastic Philosophy and Renaissance Magic in the *De vita* of Marsilio Ficino," *Renaissance Quarterly* 37 (1984), and *Symphorien Champler and the Reception of the Occultist Tradition in Renaissance France*; Allan G. Debus, *Man and Nature in the Renaissance* and *The Chemical Philosophy: Paracelsian Science and Medicine in the Sixteenth and Seventeenth Centuries*; Walter Pagel, *Paracelsus: An Introduction to Philosophical Medicine in the Era of the Renaissance*; Martin Kemp, *Leonardo da Vinci: The Marvellous Works of Nature and Man*; David Summers, *Michaelangelo and the Language of Art*; John Charles Nelson, *Renaissance Theory of Love: The Context of Giordano Bruno's "Eroici furori*;" Nicholas H. Clulee, "Astrology, Magic, and Optics: Facets of John Dee's Early Natural Philosophy," *Renaissance Quarterly* 30 (1977); Peter French, *John Dee: The World of an Elizabethan Magus*; and Wayne Shumaker, *The Occult Sciences in the Renaissance: A Study in Intellectual Patterns.*
30. *Human* comes from *homo* (from *hemo*, O. L. for *of the earth*) plus *anus* (*belonging to*). Humanity's birth from Mother Earth (Gaia/Tellus) is signalled in *Adam* (from *adomah*, Hebrew, fem., for *earth*). (Eve, of course, means *spirit*.)
31. See D. P. Walker, *The Ancient Theology: Studies in Christian Platonism from the Fifteenth to the Eighteenth Century.*
32. See M. A. Screech, "Introduction," *An Apology for Raymond Sebond*, whose translation is cited in my discussion.
33. See Robert D. Cottrell, *Sexuality/Textuality: A Study of Montaigne's Essays*; and Richard L. Regosin, *The Matter of My Book: Montaigne's "Essais" as the Book of the Self.*
34. "Aspects of Androgyny in the Renaissance," *Human Sexuality in the Middle Ages and Renaissance*, 127.
35. See Sukanta Chaudhuri, *Infirm Glory: Shakespeare and the Renaissance Image of Man*; T. K. Seung, *Cultural Thematics: The Formation of the Faustian Ethos*; and John G. Burke, "Hermeticism as a Renaissance World View," *The Darker Vision of the Renaissance.*
36. See Walker and Debus.
37. *The Works*, ed. C. F. Tucker Brooke, line-numbered throughout, here 24–28.
38. See also Maclean.

4. *Sidney's Invention of a New Choice for Hercules: Androgyny*

1. June Jordan has discovered a streetwise young alter-ego named DeLiza who recites the following poem:

DeLiza Questioning Perplexities:

If Dustin Hoffaman prove
a father be a better mother than a mother

If Dustin Hoffaman prove
a man be a better woman than a woman

When do she get to see
a Betterman than Hoffaman?

2. Ed. Jean Robertson, 27.
3. Ed. Victor Skretrowicz, 69.
4. Woodbridge, 158–59, also discusses these passages, as well as refers to yet other discussions.
5. Jeff Shulman in "At the Crossroads of Myth: The Hermeneutics of Hercules from Ovid to Shakespeare," *English Literary History* 13 (1983), does just what his title says: examines the meaning of Ovid's stories about Hercules, the transmission of those stories over some 1,400 years, and Shakespeare's re-invention of Ovid for his own purposes in *Love's Labor's Lost*. Shulman builds on the basic "Ovidian idea that successful love requires a union of self and other, a union that negates both the Narcissus-like fear of self-loss and the Echo-like engulfment of personal autonomy" (83), and leads to the conclusion that "the hermeneutics of myth, the language of courtship, and the phenomenology of eros—criticism, art, and love—all require a labor that Hercules never imagined: the reconciliations of our most habitual modes of responding to reality, of the songs of the romantic and the realist, of Apollo and Mercury, in the harmonious marriage of opposites that the self and its society ought to be" (103). Pyrocles was well instructed in the choice of his new emblem.
6. See Jeanne Harrie, "Duplessis-Mornay, Foix-Candale and the Hermetic Religion of the World," *Renaissance Quarterly* 31 (1978); and Robert Kimbrough, *Sir Philip Sidney*, 25, 33–34.
7. That Sidney translated *De la Verité* we have the testimony of his literary executor, Fulke Greville; of Arthur Golding who said his translation published in 1587 took up where Sidney left off; and of Duplessis-Mornay's widow. Fueillerat found Sidney's hand only in the preface and the first six chapters of the Sidney-Golding and so printed only them in his pioneering edition of the work of Sidney in 1912 (reprinted without the poetry as *The Prose* in 1963). Katherine Duncan-Jones (and others) believes that Sidney's hand can be found nowhere in the 1587 publication, so her edition of the *Miscellaneous Prose* contains no translation of Duplessis-Mornay. How much, if any, "Sidney" is in the Sidney-Golding translation is still an open question, but because it is safe to believe that Sidney did receive, read (translate), and possibly translate in writing some or all of Duplessis-Mornay, I use the 1963 reprint of Feuillerat for my discussion of the ideas Sidney found in Duplessis-Mornay. (See K. Duncan-Jones, *Miscellaneous Prose*, 155–57.)
8. Civil war broke the placid world of Sidney scholars with the publication of Andrew D. Weiner, *Sir Philip Sidney and the Poetics of Protestation*; Barbara Lewalski, *Protestant Poetics and the Seventeenth Century Religious Lyric*; and Alan Sinfield, *Literature in Protestant England, 1560–1660*. Like most civil wars, both parties are "right," so right that on certain issues agreement will never be reached and compromise is out of the question. Attack and defense become meaningless. My friend and colleague, Weiner, abhors my "Sidney," and I abhor his. Interested onlookers must be left on their own to read and judge these mighty matters.

9. See Trinkaus, *In Our Image and Likeness*, for a discussion of the role of the will in the matter of "moving"; especially important is his discussion of Petrarch.
10. *The Poems*, ed. Wm. Ringler, 201.
11. Jonathan Crewe, in *Hidden Designs*, has surmised that Spenser became George Puttenham to write his own defense of poetry, *The Arte of English Poesie*.

5. *"Both male and female, both vnder one name"*

1. John Knox, *The First Blast of the Trumpet Against the Monstrous Regiment of Women*. See Constance Jordan, "Woman's Rule in Sixteenth-Century British Political Thought," *Renaissance Quarterly* 40 (1987).
2. Historians are fond of pointing out that Elizabeth I was not really a very good ruler, or whatever—they miss the point: she created with the help of those directly and indirectly around her a public presence which stirred great admiration. And *that* is what irritates the historians.
3. See Paul Johnson, *Elizabeth I: A Study in Power and Intellect*; Frances A. Yates, *Astraea*; Roy Strong, *The Cult of Elizabeth*; Alison Plowden, *Marriage with My Kingdom*; Louis A. Montrose, "'Eliza, Queene of shepheardes' and the Pastoral of Power," *English Literary History* 10 (1980), and "'Shaping Fantasies' Figurations of Gender and Power in Elizabethan Culture," *Representations* 2 (1983); and Frederick A. DeArmas, *The Return of Astraea*.
4. See Kent T. Van den Berg, *Playhouse and Cosmos: Shakespearean Theater as Metaphor*.
5. Robin Headlam Wells, *Spenser's "Faerie Queene" and the Cult of Elizabeth*.
6. Leah S. Marcus, "Shakespeare's Comic Heroines, Elizabeth I, and the Political Uses of Androgyny," *Women in the Middle Ages and the Renaissance*.
7. See Daniel T. Lochman, *The Ecstatic Embrace: Form and Content in the Major Works of John Colet*; and Benjamin G. Lockerd Jr., *The Sacred Marriage: Psychic Integration in "The Faerie Queene."*
8. John N. King, "The Godly Woman in Elizabethan Iconography," *Renaissance Quarterly* 38 (1985).
9. *Hermaphrodite: Myths and Rites of the Bisexual Figure in Classical Antiquity*, 45.
10. Although Lockerd, *Sacred Marriage*, takes a Jungian (and therefore by implication an alchemical) approach, his discussion of androgyny, 40–49, is weakened by his unwillingness to separate the androgyne from the hermaphrodite, which leads him to make this statement: "At the human level perfect androgyny is *physically* impossible" (49; emphasis added).
11. *The Poetical Works* (Oxford), 210 (the cancelled version of III. 43–47).
12. *English Literary Renaissance* 9 (1979), 63. See also, Donald Cheney, "Spenser's Hermaphrodite and the 1590 *Faerie Queene*," *PMLA* 87 (1972); and Harry Berger Jr., "*The Faerie Queene* III: A General Description," *Criticism* 11 (1969).
13. The following account is my own, but of course I have learned from Panofsky, Seznec, and Wind. For beautiful accounts of the energizing, bonding powers of love in all of this, see John Charles Nelson, *Renaissance Theory of Love*, and A. J. Smith, *The Methaphysics of Love*.
14. The temptation is great to diverge into a discussion of our collective need for a "total explication" as reflected in the book review and Sunday magazine sections of the "leading" English-language newspapers, which offer us several times a year books and profiles under such headlines as: "The Threshold of God's

Thoughts," "A Theory of Everything," "Britain's Whole Earth Guru," "Reality with Witches in It," and "An All-Inclusive System."

15. See Robert Grosseteste, *On Light*, and the discussions by N. H. Clulee, *Renaissance Quarterly* 30 (1977); and David C. Lindberg, *Theories of Vision from al-Kindī to Kepler*.
16. See also Thomas Hyde, *The Poetic Theology of Love: Cupid in Renaissance Literature*.
17. See Erich Neumann, *The Great Mother*.
18. *The Idea of Woman*, 12–15. See also her fine discussion of the *Two Cantos of Mutabilitie*.
19. For a perceptive account of how aware of and close to nature Spenser was, see Carolyn Merchant, *The Death of Nature: Women, Ecology, and the Scientific Revolution*, especially Chapter 1, "Nature as Female."
20. See Kimbrough, *Sidney*, 63–68.
21. *John Lyly: The Humanist as Courtier*.
22. Richard N. Ringler, whose article on the Faunus episode is cited in the next chapter, wrote his doctoral thesis (Harvard, 1961) entirely on the *Two Cantos*; my titling of the trial comes from him. He shows in his thesis, in addition to a great many other things, how thoroughly Spenser uses and plays with the language of law throughout the *Two Cantos*.
23. Whereas Lockerd believes that Nature's "brief and gentle reply comes from an utter certainty" (183), Kenneth Gross, *Spenserian Poetics: Idolatry, Iconoclasm, and Magic*, believes that Nature's judgment is weak, empty, and foolish and that Spenser gets out fast so no one will notice (251–52). Russell J. Meyer, "'Fixt in heauens hight': Spenser, Astronomy, and the Date of the *Cantos of Mutabilitie*," *Spenser Studies* 4 (1983), believes that the cantos are a self-contained personal statement and make a fit conclusion to *The Faerie Queene*. I agree. In fact, I would suggest that, as is often noted, Book I is in small a completed epic (Redcrosse/Arthur/England and Una/Gloriana/Elizabeth), so also I would suggest that, like "Venus and Adonis" and "Hero and Leander," the so-called "two" cantos are really all one piece, a completed poem better called "Mutabilitie and Jove" and left undivided (except by the Faunus episode which, as do the Horses and the Mercury episodes in Shakespeare and Marlowe, reflects back thematically and attitudinally on the main story line). Spenser opened with a micro-epic and ended with an epyllion.
24. *The Tempest* (Arden), xxiv.
25. Just how deep that philosophy was is suggested by Spenser's reference to "that great Sabbaoth God," which is not just an evocation of Revelation and Judgment, but is also an evocation of ecstatic enlightenment, or complete understanding, or total fulfillment. See Francis T. Fallon, *The Enthronement of Sabaoth: Jewish Elements in Gnostic Creation Myths*.

6. *Making Myth: Spenser, Marlowe, Shakespeare*

1. See G. Wilson Knight, *The Mutual Flame: On Shakespeare's "Sonnets" and "The Phoenix and The Turtle*," for Shakespeare's strong interest in androgyny.
2. See Barbara L. Parker. *A Precious Seeing: Love and Reason in Shakespeare's Plays*, especially Chapter 1, for an encyclopedic account of love as rational. (Curiously, Parker never mentions this poem.)
3. For an excellent reminder that the "Garden of Adonis" episode (badly named) is

not a set, detached piece, but has Britomart at its center, see Lauren Silberman, "Singing Unsung Heroines: Androgynous Discourse in Book 3 of *The Faerie Queene*," *Rewriting the Renaissance*.

4. *The Poetry of Edmund Spenser*, 204–35.
5. Chapter 4, *Shakespeare and the Common Understanding*.
6. *The Motives of Eloquence*, 91–93.
7. For Venus's self-deception, see Heather Dubrow, *Captive Victors: Shakespeare's Narrative Poems and Sonnets*.
8. "The Faunus Episode," *Modern Philology* 63 (1965).

7. *"Half sleep, half waking"*: A Midsummer Night's Dream

1. See Edward Berry, *Shakespeare's Comic Rites*.
2. See Jackson I. Cope, *The Theater and the Dream: From Metaphor to Form in Renaissance Drama*.
3. See Marjorie B. Garber, *Dream in Shakespeare: From Metaphor to Metamorphosis*; and John Arthos, *Shakespeare's Use of Dream and Vision*.
4. See C. L. Barber, *Shakespeare's Festive Comedy*; and Northrop Frye, *A Natural Perspective*.
5. One could go on to list the further reaches of association which these four trigger, but another must be noted. A student of mine, Bette Duff, in a paper on "Alchemical Imagery in Shakespeare's *A Midsummer Night's Dream*," points out that "Titanos" is a popular name for the Philosopher's stone: indeed Titania says she will be an alchemical philosopher for Bottom: "I will purge this mortal grossness so/That thou shalt like an airy spirit go" (3.1.145–46).
6. In addition to Garber's excellent chapter on *A Midsummer Night's Dream* in her *Dream in Shakespeare*, see her *Coming of Age in Shakespeare*. See also William C. Carroll, *The Metamorphoses of Shakespearean Comedy*; and Joseph Westlund, *Shakespeare's Reparative Comedies: A Psychoanalytic View of the Middle Plays*. Joan Stansbury, "Characterization of the Four Young Lovers in *A Midsummer Night's Dream*," *Shakespeare Survey* 35 (1982), talks of difference but not change.
7. Carl G. Jung, *Psychology and Alchemy*. (See also Sonnet 135.) An early, reliable account of alchemy is John Read, *Prelude to Chemistry: An Outline of Alchemy, Its Literature and Relationships*. Full and wonderfully illustrated is Johannes Fabricius, *Alchemy: The Medieval Alchemists and Their Royal Art*. Good introductions are: John S. Mebane, "Renaissance Magic and the Return of the Golden Age: Utopianism and Religious Enthusiasm in *The Alchemist*," *Renaissance Drama* 10 (1979); Bettina L. Knapp, *Theatre and Alchemy*; and, especially, Charles Nicholl, *The Chemical Theatre* because it is so fully illustrated.
8. Paul's second letter to the Corinthians.
9. See Alvin B. Kernan, *The Playwright as Magician*.
10. Ruth Nevo ends her book on *Comic Transformations in Shakespeare*: the comedies "take a tolerant and genial view of the vital spontaneities, the imperious instincts, the recalcitrant emotions and the chaotic appetites and desires. Respecting these, they set out to remedy disorder, tension and deficiency by individual hazard, individual inventiveness and creativity. And so if they are 'romantic' it is not only because they deal with lovers, but because they represent a dazzling, if brief adventure in the discovery and exploration of what is humanly possible."

8. *Explorations in Disguise:* As You Like It *and* Twelfth Night

1. This remark stands in stark contradiction to the last two sentences in her book: "The lively women they ['Renaissance authors'] created show that their hearts were very impressed with (and often quite fond of) exuberant English Woman exactly as they found her. Though they write of Grissills for their peace, in the Rosalinds their pleasure lies" (327). (I purposely choose not to discuss the assumptions which inform both quotations, in the text and here.)
2. The basic reason that boys could play girls in the theater is that the audience accepted the convention of all-male professional companies. It is that simple. The audience had never experienced anything else. Now, *why* it was the convention, and what were the implications and ramifications of the convention are valid questions to pursue, and an exciting literature on the topic is developing. See Stephen Orgel, "Nobody's Perfect," and Steve Brown, "The Boyhood of Shakespeare's Heroines, or Did Cleopatra Squeak?" and "' . . . and his ingle at home': Notes on Gender in Jonson's *Epicoene*." (*Epicoene*, by the way, could not have been written for any other than an all-male company [in this case, all boy]: all the women on stage have to be female impersonators or else you give away the game, as happened in the 1989 production by the Royal Shakespeare Company.) See also Mathew H. Wikander, "As Secret as Maidenhead: The Profession of the Boy-Actress in *Twelfth Night*," *Comparative Drama* 20 (1986–87), and Victor Oscar Freeburg, *Disguise Plots in Elizabethan Drama: A Study in Stage Tradition*.
3. In addition to Dusinberre, see Irene Dash, *Wooing, Wedding, and Power: Women in Shakespeare's Plays*; and Marianne Novy, "Shakespeare's Female Characters as Actors and Audience," *Love's Argument*. The clinching proof of the playability of Shakespeare's women is the fact that they are still being played. The only complaint one hears from actresses is that there are not enough roles in Shakespeare for women.
4. Nancy K. Hayles, "Sexual Disguise in *Cymbeline*," *Modern Language Quarterly* 41 (1980), would agree with this statement concerning the disguise itself and Imogen's lack of any psychological curiosity concerning the implications of that disguise; however, Hayles presents a searching reading of *Cymbeline* which suggests that the whole play offers an androgynous reading of life in Jungian terms of the search for "psychic wholeness." On this level, the disguise plays a significant part: "The bifurcation between male and female becomes a metaphor for the bifurcation between dream-life and waking life, as the commingling of genders in the androgynous Fidele is made to coincide with Imogen's entry into a state of combining aspects of the conscious and unconscious mind" (242). As will be clear in chapter 11, I, too, believe that an atmosphere of androgyny plays through *Cymbeline* and all of the last plays, especially *The Tempest*.
5. Woodbridge also isolates Rosalind and Viola for discussion; Rackin extends her analysis to include Portia. Both writers posit that this particular form of androgyny could only have taken place in the 1590s. By the early 1600s with James on the throne and the "Hic-Muliers/Haec-Virs" controversy raging the atmosphere was too charged with difference.
6. Barbara Everett, "*Much Ado About Nothing*," *The Critical Quarterly* 3 (1961): 322.
7. Text edited, translated, and introduced by Sears Reynolds Jayne, *The University of Missouri Studies* 19 (1944), 160.

8. Albert R. Cirillo, "*As You Like It*: Pastoralism Gone Awry," *ELH* 38 (1971): 25. Margaret Boerner Beckman, "The Figure of Rosalind in *As You Like It*," *SQ* 29 (1978), has noted the "male/female coincidence in Rosalind's character" and believes that "Rosalind ends the play as a magician because throughout the whole play she has made extraordinary, seemingly impossible—and thus 'magical'—conjunctions between contrary things. Her own person is a seemingly impossible reconciliation of opposites. The magic she performs brings contrarieties together and harmonizes them. The 'strange things' she does, then, are not incidental to the play, but rather a logical development from what she has been doing all along" (44).
9. Almost as if to emphasize that Rosalind does not *change*, but *grows*, Shakespeare introduces the "bloody napkin," the "swoon," and the "counterfeit to be a man" business with Oliver at the end of 4.3; swagger as she may throughout the middle action, Rosalind never loses touch with the tenderness that marked her reactions to the wrestling in the opening action. Woodbridge finds this belittling. I disagree: would to goodness that men would learn to faint at the thought of violence and sight of blood.
10. I like the idea (Royal Shakespeare Company, 1980) that Rosalind casts Corin to play Hymen, first because it implies that Rosalind wrote and staged her own star-piece (she is magician as playwright creating something out of nothing), and second because it is in keeping with the poetic innovations of the 1590s of secularizing and humanizing metamorphoses.
11. *As You Like It* opens in the time-bound world of society (what is "the new news at the new court?") but moves into the timeless world of the clock-less forest (where "golden time *con*-vents"). The linear, hierarchical tendency of western society is reflected in Jaques's seven ages of man speech which does not belong in the circular, egalitarian forest. The social world is, in the worst sense, masculine, typified by the wrestling and the brothers against brothers; the forest is, in the best sense, feminine, a place of coming together, close-knitting, of caring and curing. Man the phallic destroyer is tamed, when encircled by the vulvaic forest.
12. Nancy K. Hayles, "Sexual Disguise in 'As You Like It' and 'Twelfth Night'," *Shakespeare Survey* 32 (1979), says of the epilogue: "The unlayering of the disguise is linked with a reconciliation between the sexes as the boy actor speaking the epilogue appeals separately to the men and women in the audience. Within the play these two perspectives have been reconciled, and the joint applause of the men and women in the audience re-affirms that reconciliation and extends it to the audience" (67). Albert R. Cirillo makes this happy observation: "If the Forest has been a magic circle for the characters in the play, so has the play been for the audience . . . By stepping out of the play, as if out of the fiction, [Rosalind] exercises the genuine force of her magic on us by bringing us *into* the fictional. The play is our Arden" ("Pastoralism Gone Awry," 38).
13. See Maura Slattery Kuhn, "Much Virtue in *If*," *Shakespeare Quarterly* 28 (1977), for an argument that Rosalind remains dressed as a boy during the closing action of the play, including the epilogue.
14. Leslie Fiedler, *The Stranger in Shakespeare*, 47, believes that Rosalind's final curtsy was intended to set the gallants' homosexual hearts astirring. Lisa Jardine would agree with him. In contrast, see Catherine Belsey.
15. See Heilbrun, *Toward A Recognition of Androgyny*, 34–35, and her notes on 180–81, for a discussion of twins and psychological androgyny. Shakespeare was, of course, himself the father of opposite-sex twins.

16. See William W. E. Slights, "Maid and Man in *Twelfth Night*," *Journal of English and Germanic Philology* 80 (1981).
17. The heterosexual resolution of the plot should not be taken as a signal that only a heterosexual mating can stimulate one's potential for androgyny. Sebastian is referring to the procreative bias of Nature, but as we know from *Troilus and Cressida*, and from life, nature draws "bias and thwart."
18. See Phyllis Rackin, "Shakespeare's Boy Cleopatra, the Decorum of Nature, and the Golden World of Poetry," *PMLA* 87 (1972), for an excellent discussion of the function and effect of this speech within *Antony and Cleopatra*.
19. That the sex of the character cancels the sex of the actor is indirectly proved by an article about Cleopatra which both assumes and implies her extra-dramatic existence. L. T. Fitz (Linda Woodbridge), "Egyptian Queens and Male Reviewers: Sexist Attitudes in *Antony and Cleopatra* Criticism," *Shakespeare Quarterly* 28 (1977). Fitz suggests "that many male critics feel personally threatened by Cleopatra and what she represents to them" (298); how real can you get! The naturalness and normalcy of a boy actor's playing a woman character is casually indicated in *Hamlet* when Hamlet banters with the company of players upon their arrival at Elsinore, and in the opening of *The Taming of the Shrew* when the lord gives directions for his page Bartholomew's playing of Sly's "wife." His long speech, 104–37, clearly sets up a comic situation where laughter will stem not from the fact that a boy is making over Sly, but that Sly will believe he is a lord because he will believe that a noble lady is his wife.

9. *Myth and Counter-Myth in* Macbeth

1. I have left out the long marriage of Henry VI and Margaret, and I pass by the story of mature love in *Antony and Cleopatra* not because they technically never marry but because they are psychologically incapable of marriage. Neither can give or yield self. Cleopatra may call Antony "husband," but not until he is dead and gone.
2. After Brutus says, "You are my true and honorable wife," there follows the potentially denigrating, "I grant I am woman" speech by Portia which is capped by the claim that she is "stronger than my sex" because she once stabbed herself in the thigh in order to give "strong proof of my constancy." The revelation of her masculine side when she gave herself the wound of Adonis to prove her love and to preserve her chastity could be called an androgynous act, but only is in a vague, blurred manner. I think it shows, rather, the confusion of gender identity that plagued that period of transition from Elizabeth to James, which Woodbridge, Rackin, and Garber explore.
3. *Othello* is a perfect illustration of Marjorie Garber's thesis in *Coming of Age in Shakespeare* that "the Shakespearean novice, like his or her counterpart in society, must be separated from a former self before he or she can be integrated into a new social role" (26), for Othello and Desdemona are surely novices. (The soldier as a case study in arrested development is perfectly illustrated by Lt. Col. Oliver North, who had the world's largest sandbox to play in in the basement of the White House.)

   The constantly asked critical question, was this marriage ever consummated, is itself pertinent evidence in support of the point I am making. The critical literature on homosexuality, castration-fear, and misogyny in *Othello* is fascinating but still far from complete.

4. Marjorie Garber, *Shakespeare's Ghost Writers: Literature as Uncanny Causality*, 97.
5. See Coppélia Kahn, *Man's Estate*.
6. Harry Berger Jr. in "Text against Performance in Shakespeare: The Example of *Macbeth*," *The Power of Forms in the English Renaissance*, joins other new critics (whom he calls collectively "textual athletes") in the belief that "the conceptions implied in the locution 'the world of the play,' divert attention from what should be the primary object of interpretive curiosity, namely, the *community* of the play, and that it is the community rather than the author which creates its world" (59). I am not entirely sure I follow Berger here, but there is a "world of the play" in *Macbeth*, and as "Jacobean" as the play is, the play is also the world of Scotland before 1066 which Shakespeare found in Holinshed's *History of Scotland*. Shakespeare's borrowing from Holinshed is really not so much in the usually identified sources, but in the total atmosphere he absorbed from Holinshed's whole history. In a most real way *Macbeth* is "The True Chronical History of Scotland."
7. José A. Benardete, "Macbeth's Last Words," *Interpretation* 1 (1970), sees the play as entirely an issue of manly versus womanly. But see Irene Dash, *Wedding, Wooing, and Power*, for a more sensitive reading of sex-role opposition throughout the play.
8. Richard Horwich, "Integrity in *Macbeth*: The Search for the 'Single State of Man'," *Shakespeare Quarterly* 29 (1978), and Vincent F. Petronella, "The Role of Macduff in *Macbeth*," *Etudes Anglaises* 32 (1979), recognize Macduff as the representative of wholeness and completeness in the play. But in contrast, see Berger who goes after Macduff with disdain and scorn from the beginning all the way through to the end, even refusing to cite "But I must also feel it as a man." Peter Erickson, *Patriarchal Structures in Shakespeare's Plays*, does mention "But I must also feel it as a man," yet does not feel that it enlarges Macduff, who represents "distorted masculinity" in "his excessive violence in decapitating Macbeth" (192). Since the decapitation takes place off stage, after Macbeth has been killed, I do not see how Erickson is in a position, so to speak, to make his claim; furthermore, how does one measure *excessive* violence in a decapitation?
9. The qualifying of "androgynous" with "very" shows that Levin does not understand the concept of androgyny; clearly to him an androgyne is merely a stereotypically limp-wristed, ineffectual, soft, wet, twerpy male: an androgyne only does "nice" things.
10. Marina Warner, *Joan of Arc: The Image of Female Heroism*, especially Chapter 7, "Ideal Androgyne."
11. Janet Adelman, "'Born of Woman': Fantasies of Maternal Power in *Macbeth*," *Cannibals, Witches, and Divorce*, touches on this point in a far-ranging, closely argued essay (the notes to which provide a "variorum" discussion of "sex-and-gender" criticism of the play). Adelman, as one of the anti-Macduff party, criticizes Macduff for having "inexplicably abandoned his family" (108). I do not want to argue with Adelman; I recognize the brilliance of her essay, even while not being much in sympathy with her kind of reading of drama texts. Yet, I do think that she and Berger are not opening themselves to the logical necessities of the plot of the play with regard to Macduff's so-called inexplicable abandonment of his family. The explanation is simple: Macduff has taken on the cause of Scotland versus Macbeth. He goes to England to persuade the return of the rightful king. This is hardly abandonment. True, he does not take his family with

him, which would have endangered them more through the attention the act would have drawn than would leaving them at home, protected. Here is his "mistake"—he neither knew that Macbeth had suborned one of the Macduff retainers nor did he realize the monstrous extent of Macbeth's degeneration. Perhaps, also, he should have told his wife what he was up to; he obviously thought that she, he, the cause, would all be safer in secrecy. Ross thinks so, by the way he tries to calm his cousin, Lady Macduff, whose banter with her son after Ross leaves shows that her "anger" with her husband was more act than real—she was petulantly exaggerating when she says that, "He loves us not,/He wants the natural touch." Certainly Macduff's reaction to the news of his family's slaughter shows the depth of his love and the extent of his "natural touch," his humankindness.

12. Note the Medusa-head in the portrait of François le Premier in Appendix III. In addition to Garber's fine chapter, see Laurie Schneider, "Ms. Medusa: Transformations of a Bisexual Image," *The Psychoanalytic Study of Society* 9 (1981).
13. See Theodore Spencer, *Shakespeare and the Nature of Man*, and Geoffrey Bush, *Shakespeare and the Natural Condition*.
14. Garber refers to the witches throughout as androgynous, but she would strengthen her case that they are monstrous if she would label them properly. Berger gets it right: "In addition to being withered and childlike they are also . . . bearded women—not androgynes but bemonstered manlike images of the feminine power that threatens throughout the play to disarm the pathologically protective *machismo* essential to the warrior society" (68).
15. See Dennis Biggins, "Sexuality, Witchcraft, and Violence in *Macbeth*," *Shakespeare Studies 8* (1975).
16. Charles G. Labrizzi, "*Macbeth* and the 'Milk of Human Kindness': A Note," *Massachusetts Studies in English* 5 (1978), reads the phrase merely as meaning that Macbeth has just now been filled with honors from king and country.
17. Alice Fox, "Obstetrics and Gynecology in *Macbeth*," *Shakespeare Studies 12* (1979), 127–41, points out that "visitings of nature" can mean menstruation; and Jenjoy La Belle, "'A Strange Infirmity': Lady Macbeth's Amenorrhea," *Shakespeare Quarterly* 31 (1980), adds that "make thick my blood" is a plea for menstrual cycles to cease. (See also Alice Fox, "How Many Pregnancies Had Lady Macbeth?" *University of Dayton Review* 14 (1979–80).
18. Suicide is able to take place because, with the drying up of the heart, vital spirits can no longer rise to the brain to activate, invigorate, and charge the rational soul.
19. See Inga-Stina Ewbank, "The Field-like Queen: A Note on 'Macbeth' and Seneca's 'Medea'," *Shakespeare Survey* 19 (1966), reprinted in *Aspects of Macbeth*, ed. Muir and Edwards (Cambridge: Cambridge University Press, 1977). (See also W. Moelwyn Merchant, "His Field-like Queen," in the same sources.)
20. See Richard Ide, "Theatre of the Mind: An Essay on *Macbeth*," *English Literary History* 42 (1975).
21. Robert N. Watson, *Shakespeare and the Hazards of Ambition*: "By misdefining his 'manhood' at his wife's instigation, Macbeth loses not only his procreative manliness, but also his human self-hood" (131). Robert M. Wren, "The 'Hideous Trumpet' and Sexual Transformation in Macbeth," *Forum* 4 (1967), believes that Macbeth becomes "a moral hermaphrodite, bearing the vices of both sexes and the virtues of neither, a creature unnatural, almost a non-nothing, 'what is not'" (21).

22. Many editors annotate this as "let's get dressed"; for a sensitive exploration, see Cleanth Brooks, "The Naked Babe and the Cloak of Manliness," *The Well Wrought Urn*, 22–49, esp. 37.
23. I have yet to witness a Macbeth who does not rush through this speech, anxious to get it over with.
24. Girls who became pregnant at very young ages were believed to give birth to extremely weak babies, who were most likely themselves to be girls.
25. H. R. Courson, *The Compensatory Psyche: A Jungian Approach to Shakespeare*, believes that, "We feel their 'kindness,' that is their spiritual link to their species and to God, an intrinsic selfhood beneath the deeds they have committed and prior to their effort to pervert the 'magister interior' Augustine claims abides in all of us. That selfhood, Jung would suggest, if held back by conscious orientation will walk like a ghost along the parapets of our dream world, indeed can explode into waking nightmare, as in the case of both Macbeths." See also Paul Jorgensen, *Our Naked Frailties*, 214–15, and G. Wilson Knight, "The Milk of Concord: An Essay on Life-Themes in *Macbeth*," *The Imperial Theme*, 125–53.
26. French, 244 (see her entire essay, 241–51). Although French finds Lady Macbeth "the factor responsible for Macbeth's" crime, Joan Larsen Klein, "Lady Macbeth: 'Infirm of purpose'," *The Woman's Part: Feminist Criticism of Shakespeare*, believes that Lady Macbeth, though sinning, remains subservient and docile throughout the action of the play, a conclusion also reached by B. J. Bedard, "The Thane of Glamis Had a Wife," *University of Dayton Review* 14 (1979–80).
27. See also Lachlan McKinnon, *Shakespeare the Aesthete: An Explanation of Literary Theory*, 70–72.

10. Lear and Cordelia: "Cosmic Man" and "Heavenly Queen"

1. In the second half of this century *King Lear* surpassed *Hamlet* as the most respected of his tragedies among North American academics, and I suggest that the same shift has taken place in the United Kingdom as the century comes to a close. Michael Long, among many, speaks eloquently of the reason for the appeal of *King Lear*: it "is a play about general Law which is archetypal, a play in which the figure of the King is an archetypal imagining of everything that it is to be social man. *King Lear* is about 'the world'," *The Unnatural Scene*, 161. A recent "reading" of the play by Graham Holderness, Nick Potter, and John Turner, Chapter 6, "*King Lear*," *Shakespeare, The Play of History*, 89–118, powerfully embraces both the deeply negative and the deeply positive aspects of the play, reminding us once again of its mythic depths and contemporary significances. I recommend the essay because it does not debate small (and great) issues as it addresses the greatness of this work of art.

   Since I do not wish to be here diverted into contemporary critical debates about *King Lear* and humanism and *King Lear* and feminism (my opinions and feelings certainly are not hidden), allow me to leave the debate to others. On the issue of essentialist or classical liberal humanism there is Jonathan Dollimore, *Radical Tragedy: Religion, Ideology and Power in the Drama of Shakespeare and his Contemporaries*, recently opposed by Arthur Kirsch, "The Emotional Landscape of *King Lear*," *Shakespeare Quarterly* 39 (1988). On the issue of patriarchal suppression there is Kathleen McLuskie, "The Patriarchal Bond: Feminist Criticism and Shakespeare: *King Lear* and *Measure for Measure*,"

Political Shakespeare: New Essays in Cultural Materialism, which can be matched against a recent reassessment by Claire McEachern, "Fathering Herself: A Source Study of Shakespeare's Feminism," *Shakespeare Quarterly* 39 (1988), which also focuses on *King Lear*. Another essay not so easy to obtain but worth the trouble of a search is a work earlier than the four above: Kathy L. Kirik, "An Inquiry into Misogyny in *King Lear*: The Making of an Androgyny," *Journal of Evolutionary Psychology*, 1979.

2. For an alchemical reading of the play, see Charles Nicholl, *The Alchemical Theatre*; and for splendid Jungian readings, see James P. Driscall, *Identity in Shakespearean Drama*, and H. R. Coursen, *The Compensatory Psyche*.
3. See Alfred Herbage, "Introduction," *King Lear, The Pelican Shakespeare*.
4. In addition to Spencer and G. Bush, see the still important Robert Speaight, *Nature in Shakesperian Tragedy*; John F. Danby, *Shakespeare's Doctrine of Nature: A Study of "King Lear"*; and D. G. James, *The Dream of Learning: An Essay on "The Advancement of Learning," "Hamlet," and "King Lear."*
5. Marjorie Garber, *Coming of Age in Shakespeare*, 23–24.
6. When we are caught making fools of ourselves, the function of the fool is to tap us on the head with his bauble, the bauble being in the shape of a penis, the head of which is the seat of folly—one touch of nature makes the whole world kin. Shakespeare was Robert Armin's most accomplished pupil, and Shakespeare showed his appreciation by presenting Armin with one of theater's choice parts.
7. For Cordelia as a type of Christ, see Paul N. Siegal, *Shakespeare's English and Roman History Plays: A Marxist Approach*, 40–43; Harry Morris, Chapter 3, "*King Lear*: The Great Doom's Image," *Last Things in Shakespeare*; and Derek Cohen, *Shakespearean Motives*, 15.
8. John Danby suggests that Cordelia has within her pure nature as in natural theology; he reminds us that "Kinde" is Middle English for Nature and that "kindness [is] a natural characteristic of man" (131). At this point it is helpful to recall the Gnostic tradition that the bisexual earth is the offspring of the incestuous sacred marriage of the sun (male) and the moon (female).
9. Jan Kott and William Elton almost gleefully take this to be the whole point of the play.
10. 4.3.30, 4.4.23, 4.6.200. Also, because Cordelia means Dear Heart, the step to Sacred Heart is not a big one.
11. Of this scene, Joseph Summers, "'Look there, look there!' The Ending of *King Lear*," *English Renaissance Studies*, remarks: "From Cordelia's 'No cause, no cause', Lear makes a discovery more astonishing than any of the earlier ones: love is as gratuitous as evil; it has nothing to do with deservings; it is long suffering and kind, returns good for evil, and perceives 'no cause' for hatred or revenge" (86). And Marjorie Garber, *Coming of Age*, comments: "There is 'no cause' for her to hate him, despite his actions in the past, because the bonds of love and blood which bind her to him are not susceptible to change by reason of circumstance. This is what she had tried to tell him by her silence, and failed. Here she speaks, and speaks what might at first be taken for a falsehood—for in one sense at least she does have 'cause'. But her action in speaking, and her willingness to speak to the question behind the question, mark a change, if not in her moral rectitude and purity of love, then in her capacity to translate that love into a social act of reintegration. Just as her failure to reply in the first scene led to a separation of father and child, so her spoken answer here leads to an incorporation, a new bond, the formation of a new social unit, however brief and

fragile. It is this ability to come to terms with the world around her, its social necessities as well as its moral issues, that I have in mind when I speak of 'maturity'" (24).

12. Maynard Mack, *King Lear in Our Time*, 110–11.
13. The pauses, the movements, the gestures, the blocking of this moment are all important and remind us most emphatically that a script needs actors (and a director) before the full impact of meaning can be generated for an audience. See David Bevington, *Action is Eloquence: Shakespeare's Language of Gesture*; Jean E. Howard, *Shakespeare's Art of Orchestration: Stage Technique and Audience Response*; and Philip C. McGuire, *Speechless Dialect: Shakespeare's Open Silences*, of which this is a main one McGuire analyzes.
14. Kirsch, "Emotional Landscape": "There is no scene in Shakespeare that represents the wrench of death more absolutely or more painfully; and the scene is not merely the conclusion of the action of the play, it is its recapitulation, the moment in which the whole of it is crystallized" (156).
15. See Garber, *Coming of Age*.

11. *Prospero and the Art of Humankindness*

1. See Madeleine Doran, *Endeavors of Art: A Study of Form in Elizabethan Drama*; and Howard Felperin, *Shakespearean Representation: Mimesis and Modernity in Elizabethan Tragedy*. (All of us who write on Shakespeare presume to write the history of his "development.")
2. This is reviewed in Robert Kimbrough, *Shakespeare's "Troilus and Cressida" and its Setting*.
3. See Virgil K. Whitaker, *The Mirror up to Nature: The Technique of Shakespeare's Tragedies*.
4. Which is the opposite of a tragicomedy. See Stephen Orgel, "New Uses of Adversity: Tragic Experience in *The Tempest*," *In Defense of Reading* (an excellent article from which Orgel has recently pulled somewhat back; see "Prospero's Wife," *Representing the English Renaissance*, as well as his new Oxford edition, for a "skeptical" reading of the play); and Barbara Mowat, *The Dramaturgy of Shakespeare's Romances*.
5. Dame Frances Yates, *Shakespeare's Last Plays: A New Approach*, 78. See also Daniel Horowitz, *Shakespeare: An Existential View*.
6. Alfred Harbage, *William Shakespeare: A Reader's Guide*, 438. See also another Harbage disciple, Norman Rabkin, *Shakespeare and the Problem of Meaning*: "In the last plays . . . he asks us to accept an overlay of patterns, paradoxically embracing the contradictory gestalts of art and nature, which leads to a new kind of acceptance" (140).
7. Joseph Westlund, *Shakespeare's Reparative Comedies*: "The late comedies confirm that Shakespeare's works consistently address our reparative impulses. They introduce destruction and loss so as to contain and regain them: not just for the characters, but for us" (186).
8. See Northrop Frye, "Introduction," *The Tempest, The Pelican Shakespeare*. See also Terry Eagleton, *Shakespeare and Society*.
9. See R. G. Hunter, *Shakespeare and the Comedy of Forgiveness*.
10. See Barbara Meyerhoff, "The Older Woman as Androgyne," *Parabola* 3 (1978). See also David G. Brailow, "Prospero's 'Old Brain': The Old Man as Metaphor in *The Tempest*," *Shakespeare Studies* 14 (1981); and James Driscoll, *Identity in*

Shakespearean Drama, 153.

11. See Daniel Seltzer, "The Staging of the Last Plays," *Stratford-Upon-Avon Studies* 8 (1967).
12. The temptation to linger over *The Winter's Tale* is great. Because it is Hermetic, the implications of androgyny are everywhere; see Stevie Davies, "Woman as Magus," *The Idea of Woman*, 165–74; Myra Glazer Schotz, "The Great Unwritten Story: Mothers and Daughters in Shakespeare," *The Lost Tradition: Mothers and Daughters in Literature*; D'Orsey W. Pearson, "Witchcraft in *The Winter's Tale*: Paulina as 'Alcahueta y vn Poquito Hechizera'," *Shakespeare Studies* 12 (1979); Patricia S. Gourlay, "'O my most sacred lady': Female Metaphor in *The Winter's Tale*," *English Literary Renaissance* 5 (1975); and Thomas McFarland, *Shakespeare's Pastoral Comedy*. See also Louis Martz, "Shakespeare's Humanist Enterprise: *The Winter's Tale*," *English Renaissance Studies*; and Charles R. Lyons, *Shakespeare and the Ambiguity of Love's Triumph*, 187–213.
13. D. G. James, *The Dream of Prospero*, 1–4; Ernest B. Gilman "'All eyes': Prospero's Inverted Masque," *Renaissance Quarterly* 33 (1980), 230; G. Wilson Knight, *The Crown of Life: Essays in Interpretation of Shakespeare's Final Plays*, throughout.
14. R. A. D. Grant, "Providence, Authority, and the Moral Life in *The Tempest*," *Shakespeare Studies* 16 (1983), an excellent piece of work.
15. Joseph H. Summers, "The Anger of Prospero: *The Tempest*," *Dreams of Love and Power*; D'Orsey W. Pearson, "'Unless I Be Relieved by Prayer': *The Tempest* in Perspective," *Shakespeare Studies* 7 (1974); Harry Berger Jr., "Miraculous Harp: A Reading of Shakespeare's *Tempest*," *Shakespeare Studies* 5 (1969).
16. See also Nancy K. Hayles, "Sexual Disguise in *Cymbeline*," *Modern Language Quarterly* 41 (1980); and William Barry Thorne, "*Cymbeline*: 'Lopp'd Branches' and the Concept of Regeneration," *Shakespeare Quarterly* 20 (1969).
17. See chapter 3, above, and James, *The Dream of Prospero*, 59.
18. Selected literature on the magus: E. M. Butler, *The Myth of the Magus*; Frank Kermode, ed., *The Tempest* (Arden); Alvin Kernan, ed., *The Alchemist* (Yale); Barbara Howard Traister, *Heavenly Necromancers: The Magician in Renaissance Drama*; Anthony Harris, *Night's Black Agents: Witchcraft and Magic in Seventeenth-Century English Drama*; Robert R. Reed, *The Occult on the Tudor and Stuart Stage*; K. M. Briggs, *Pale Hecate's Team: An Examination of Beliefs on Witchcraft and Magic among Shakespeare's Contemporaries and His Immediate Successors*; Jacqueline E. Latham, "The Magic Banquet in *The Tempest*," *Shakespeare Studies* 12 (1979); and John S. Mebane, "Renaissance Magic and the Return of the Golden Age," *Renaissance Drama* 10 (1979).
19. The ability to raise storms was common to the magus, the learned woman (witch), and the spirit world (fairies).
20. James, *The Dream of Prospero*, 125, reminds us that Prospero's "I'll . . . retire me to my Milan" means no more than "I'll return home" (where two-thirds of his thoughts will *not* be on his death but will include ways to practice civic humanism).
21. Such, of course is the thesis of this chapter, but in light of so many recent performance-choices to make Prospero an angry, bitter, broken old man from beginning to end, here are some who believe that Prospero does grow: those in notes 13, 14, 15, above; Driscoll, *Identity in Shakespearean Drama*; Speaight,

Nature in Shakespearian Tragedy; Westlund, *Shakespeare's Reparative Comedies*; Garber, *Coming of Age*; Patrick Grant, *Images and Ideas in Literature of the English Renaissance*; Terry Comito, "Caliban's Dream: The Topography of Some Shakespeare Gardens," *Shakespeare Studies* 14 (1981); David C. Brailow, "Prospero's 'Old Brain': The Old Man as Metaphor in *The Tempest*," *Shakespeare Studies* 14 (1981); and K. M. Abenheimer, "Shakespeare's Tempest: A Psychological Analysis," *The Design Within*.

22. James, *The Dream of Prospero*, makes the interesting suggestion that Prospero did not become a magus until after he completed his studies in his cell on the island. This is fitting, for it suggests the parallel of Prospero's life and Sycorax's.
23. "The idea had never occurred to him—he has been so preoccupied with justice . . . Here the philosopher King, so stern and solitary, so little given to forgiveness, returns to the community of men," Speaight, *Nature in Shakespearian Tragedy*, 177.
24. See Brailow, "Prospero's 'Old Brain'."
25. Shakespeare juxtaposes "rough magic" against "heavenly music"; the one invokes disturbing influences, the other invokes beneficent influence. We are right at the threshold point separating unnatural and natural magics.
26. The speech designation in the First Folio is an error: the language of the speech does not "fit" Miranda; she was too young when she first came to the island to receive education, let alone give it; never, before or after this speech, does Miranda show any anger, let alone *this* amount of anger; the speech is totally "in character" for Prospero—he has been quite angry and continues quite angry; the exchange is between Caliban and Prospero with Miranda as audience; and, finally, had Miranda made this Prospero-like outburst, her proud parent would probably have patted her on the head and backed her by repeating and verifying the accuracy of what she had said, but Shakespeare gives Prospero no such speech. As disappointing as it is to justly outraged feminism and to any actress cast as Miranda, this is not Miranda's speech, but Prospero's. For a thoroughly convincing argument in support of this position see Peter Lindenbaum, "Prospero's Anger," *Massachusetts Review* 25 (1984), especially 165–66.
27. "Caliban exists for us inside and out, and there is no more to be said about him. There is no strange riddle of his existence, no dark and subterranean mystery which the author is travailing to bring to light. Having conceived him, Shakespeare simply accepts him, as he might accept the person standing beside him in the street"; John Bayley, *The Characters of Love: A Study in the Literature of Personality*, 288. See also Sister Corona Sharp, "Caliban: The Primitive Man's Evolution," *Shakespeare Studies* 14 (1981).
28. D. P. Walker, *The Decline of Hell: Seventeenth-Century Discussions of Eternal Torment*, finds Caliban's account to be an anticipation of seventeenth-century Neoplatonism, especially the Platonist dream-experience of wholeness. (See Henry More, *Conjectura Cabbalistica* [1653].) See also Comito, "Caliban's Dream," but in stark contrast, see Norman Holland, "Caliban's Dream," *The Design Within*.
29. See Lucien Febvre, *The Problem of Unbelief in the Sixteenth Century: The Religion of Rabelais*, 110–15, for an account of the cabalist vision of Guillaume Postel of the return of a golden age that sounds remarkably like an account of Gonzalo's dream. (For more on Postel see Marion L. Kuntz, *Guillaume Postel, Prophet of the Restitution of All Things: His Life and Thought*.) See also Driscoll, *Identity*, 160–61; James, *The Dream*, 113; Eagleton, *Shakespeare and Society*, 163–64.

30. The "fork" is not the legs, but where the legs begin to fork: the groin.
31. See James, 150; Speaight, 188; Kermode (li); Brailow, 300–02; Driscoll, 168; and R. A. D. Grant.
32. I agree that the third letter in this word in the First Folio is not an "s" but a broken "f."
33. For a brilliant discussion of how the epilogue ties together all of the elements in the play see Margreta de Grazia, "*The Tempest*: Gratuitous Movement or Action Without Kibes and Pinches," *Shakespeare Studies* 14 (1981).

12. "Unity of Mind": Shakespeare's Androgyny

1. John Keats, *Selected Poems and Letters*, ed. Douglas Bush; S. T. Coleridge, *The Table Talk and Omniana of Samuel Taylor Coleridge*, ed. T. Ashe; Virginia Woolf, *A Room of One's Own*; and H. D., *By River Avon*, whose last stanza is (25):

    And suddenly, I saw it fair,
    How Love is God, how Love is strong,
    When One is Three and Three are One,
    The Dream, the Dreamer and the Song.

2. "Shakespeare revealed almost nothing of his real identity, yet his mighty imagination disclosed the whole self in its plays and took the world onto its stage. He seems to have intended to show that the self is like a play and the world like a stage"; Driscoll, *Identity in Shakespearean Drama*, 182–83.
3. See Alfred Harbage, *Shakespeare and the Rival Traditions*; Robert Weimann, *Shakespeare and the Popular Tradition in the Theater*; and Michael D. Bristol, *Carnival and Theater: Plebian Culture and the Structure of Authority in Renaissance England.*
4. *Shakespeare's Comedies: From Roman Farce to Romantic Mystery*, 246. See also J. A. Bryant Jr., *Shakespeare and the Uses of Comedy.*
5. Alice Clark, *Working Life of Women in the Seventeenth Century*; Roberta Hamilton, *The Liberation of Women: A Study of Patriarchy and Capitalism*; and Carolyn Merchant, *The Death of Nature: Women, Ecology, and the Scientific Revolution.*
6. Linda Woodbridge, *Women in the English Renaissance*; Margaret W. Ferguson, Maureen Quilligan, and Nancy J. Vickers, eds., *Rewriting the Renaissance: The Discourses of Sexual Difference in Early Modern Europe*; and Stanley Chojnacki, ed., "Recent Trends in Renaissance Studies: The Family, Marriage and Sex," *Renaissance Quarterly* 40 (1987) (introduction, three essays, comment, bibliography).

Bibliography

Abbreviations

ELH	(formerly *Journal of English Literary History*)
PMLA	the publications of the Modern Language Association of America
RQ	*Renaissance Quarterly*
SEL	*Studies in English Literature, 1500–1900*
SQ	*Shakespeare Quarterly*

Abenheimer, K. M. "Shakespeare's Tempest: A Psychological Analysis." *The Design Within*, ed. M. D. Faber. New York: Science House, 1970: 499–518.

Adelman, Janet. "'Born of Woman': Fantasies of Maternal Power in *Macbeth*." *Cannibals, Witches, and Divorce: Estranging the Renaissance*, ed. Marjorie Garber. Selected Papers, English Institute, 1985. Baltimore and London: Johns Hopkins University Press, 1987: 90–121.

———. "'Anger's My Meat': Feeding Dependency and Aggression in *Coriolanus*." *Shakespeare: Pattern of Excelling Nature*, ed. D. Bevington and J. L. Halio. Newark: University of Delaware Press, 1978: 108–124.

Agrippa, Henry Cornelius. *Of the vanitie and uncertaintie of artes and sciences: Englished by James Sanford*. London, 1575.

———. *De Nobilitae E. Praecellentia Foeminei* (1529). See Clapham.

———. *Three Books of Occult Philosophy or Magic. Book One: Natural Magic*, ed. Willis F. Whitehead (1897, based on English ed. of James French, London, 1651). New York: Samuel Weiser, 1971.

Alberti, Leon Batista. *The Family in Renaissance Florence*, trans. Renee Neu Watkins. Columbia: University of South Carolina Press, 1969.

Allen, Don Cameron. *Mysteriously Meant*. Baltimore: Johns Hopkins University Press, 1970.

Allen, Sally G. and Joanna Hubbs. "Outrunning Atalanta: Feminine Destiny in Alchemical Transmutation." *Signs* 6 (1980): 210–29.

Allott, Robert. *Wits theater of the little world*. London, 1599.

Altman, Joel B. *The Tudor Play of Mind: Rhetorical Inquiry and the Development of Elizabethan Drama*. Berkeley: University of California Press, 1978.

D'Ancona, Mirella Levi. *Botticelli's "Primavera": A Botanical Interpretation Including Astrology, Alchemy and the Medici*. Florence: L. S. Olschki, 1983.

Anderson, Linda. *A Kind of Wild Justice: Revenge in Shakespeare's Comedies.*

Newark: University of Delaware Press, 1987.

Anger, Jane. *Iane Anger her Protection for Women To defend them against the scandalous reportes of a late Surfeiting Louer, and all other Venerians that complaine so to bee ouer cloyed with womens kindnesse*. London, 1589.

Archambault, Paul J. and Marianna M. Mustacchi, eds. *A Renaissance Woman: Helisenne's Personal and Invective Letters*. Syracuse: Syracuse University Press, 1985.

Ariosto, Lodovico. *Ariostos seven planets governing Italie* . . . London, 1611.

Aristotle. *Aristotles politiques, or discourses of government. Tr. out of Greeke into French . . . by Loys Le Roy, called Regius. Tr. out of French into English [by I. D.]*. London, 1598.

Arthos, John. *Shakespeare's Use of Dream and Vision*. Totowa, NJ: Rowman & Littlefield, 1977.

Auerbach, Erich. *Mimesis: The Representation of Reality in Western Literature* (1946), trans. Willard R. Trask. Princeton: Princeton University Press, 1953.

Bacon, Francis. "In felicem memoriam Elizabeth Angliae Reginae." *Opera Omnia*, 4 vols. London: Thomas Osborne, 1730. II, 389.

———. *The Works*, ed. James A. Spedding, Robert Leslie Ellis, and Douglas Denon Heath. 14 vols. London: Longman, 1857–74.

Baker, Herschel. *The Dignity of Man: Studies in the Persistence of an Idea*. Cambridge: Harvard University Press, 1947.

Baldwin, T. W. *Shakespeare's Small Latine & Lesse Greeke*. 2 vols. Urbana: University of Illinois Press, 1944.

Bamber, Linda. *Comic Women, Tragic Men: A Study of Gender and Genre in Shakespeare*. Stanford: Stanford University Press, 1982.

Barber, C. L. *Shakespeare's Festive Comedy*. Princeton: Princeton University Press, 1959.

Barber, C. L. and Richard P. Wheeler. *The Whole Journey: Shakespeare's Power of Development*. Berkeley, London: University of California Press, 1986.

Barish, Jonas. *The Antitheatrical Prejudice*. Berkeley: University of California Press, 1981.

Barkan, Leonard. *The Gods Made Flesh: Metamorphosis and the Pursuit of Paganism*. New Haven: Yale University Press, 1986.

———. *Nature's Work of Art: The Human Body as Image of the World*. New Haven: Yale University Press, 1975.

Baron, Hans. *The Crisis of the Early Italian Renaissance* (2nd ed). Princeton: Princeton University Press, 1966.

Bayley, John. *The Characters of Love: A Study in the Literature of Personality*. London: Constable, 1960.

Beckman, Margaret Boerner. "The Figure of Rosalind in *As You Like It*." *SQ* 29 (1978): 44–51.

Bedard, B. J. "The Thane of Glamis Had a Wife." *University of Dayton Review* 14 (1979–80): 39–43.

Belsey, Catherine. "Disrupting Sexual Difference: Meaning and Gender in the Comedies." *Alternative Shakespeares*, ed. John Drakakis. London: Methuen, 1985: 166–190.

———. *The Subject of Tragedy: Identity and Difference in Renaissance Drama.* London: Methuen, 1985.

Bem, Sandra. "Psychological Androgyny." *Beyond Sex Roles*, ed. Alice G. Sargent. St. Paul, MN: West Publishing Co, 1977: 319–25.

Bercher, William. *The nobility of women* (1559), ed. R. Warwick Bond. London: Roxburghe Club, 1904.

Berger, Harry, Jr. "*The Faerie Queene* III: A General Description," *Criticism* 11 (1969): 234–61.

———. "Miraculous Harp: A Reading of Shakespeare's *Tempest*." *Shakespeare Studies* 5 (1969): 253–83.

———. *Imaginary Audition*. Berkeley: University of California Press, 1989.

———. "Orpheus, Pan, and the Poetics of Misogyny: Spenser's Critique of Pastoral Love and Art." *ELH* 50 (1983): 27–60.

———. "The Renaissance Imagination: Second World and Green World." *Centennial Review of Arts and Sciences* 9 (1965): 26–78.

———. "Text against Performance in Shakespeare: The Example of *Macbeth*." *The Power of Forms in the English Renaissance*, ed. Stephen Greenblatt. Norman, OK: Pilgrim Books, 1982: 49–79.

Bergeron, David M. *Shakespeare's Romances and the Royal Family*. Lawrence: University Press of Kansas, 1985.

Benardete, José A. "Macbeth's Last Words." *Interpretation* 1 (1970): 63–75.

Berry, Edward. *Shakespeare's Comic Rites*. Cambridge, New York: Cambridge University Press, 1984.

Berry, Ralph. *Shakespeare and the Awareness of Audience*. New York: St. Martin's Press, 1985.

———. *Shakespeare's Comedies: Explorations in Form*. Princeton: Princeton University Press, 1972.

———. *The Shakespearean Metaphor: Studies in Language and Form*. Totowa, NJ: Rowan & Littlefield, 1978.

Bevington, David. *Action is Eloquence: Shakespeare's Language of Gesture*. Cambridge: Harvard University Press, 1984.

Biggins, Dennis. "Sexuality, Witchcraft, and Violence in *Macbeth*." *Shakespeare Studies* 8 (1975): 255–77.

Birke, Lynda. *Women, Feminism and Biology*. New York: Methuen, 1986.

Blau, Joseph Leon. *The Christian Interpretation of the Cabala in the Renaissance*. Port Washington, NY: Kennikat Press, 1944.

Bleier, Ruth. *Feminist Approaches to Science*. New York: Pergamon Press, 1986.

———. *Science and Gender: A Critique of Biology and Its Theories on Women*. New York: Pergamon Press, 1984.

Bloch, Ruth H. "Untangling the Roots of Modern Sex Roles: A Survey of Four Centuries of Change." *Signs* 4 (1978): 237–52.

Bluestone, Natalie Harris. *Women and the Ideal Society: Plato's Republic and Modern Myths of Gender*. Amherst: University of Massachusetts Press, 1987.

Boaistuou, Pierre. *Theatrum mundi. The theatre or rule of the world, wherin may be seene the running race & course of every mans life . . .* Englished by John Alday. London, 1581.

Bono, Barbara J. "Mixed Genre in Shakespeare's *As You Like It.*" *Renaissance Genres: Essays in Theory, History, and Interpretation*, ed. Barbara K. Lewalski. (Harvard English Studies 14) Cambridge: Harvard University Press, 1986: 189–212.

Booth, Stephen. *King Lear, Macbeth, Indefinition, and Tragedy*. New Haven: Yale University Press, 1983.

Boose, Lynda E. "The Family in Shakespeare Studies, or—Studies in the Family of Shakespeareans; or—The Politics of Politics." (See Chojnacki.) *RQ* 40 (1987): 707–42.

———. "The Father and the Bride In Shakespeare." *PMLA* 97 (1982): 325–47.

Bouwsma, William. *Concordia Mundi: The Career and Thought of Guillaume Postel*. Cambridge: Harvard University Press, 1957.

Boyette, Purvis E. "Milton's Eve and the Neoplatonic Graces." *RQ* 10 (1967): 341–44.

———. "Milton and the Sacred Fire: Sex Symbolism in *Paradise Lost.*" *Literary Monographs 5*, ed. Eric Rothstein. Madison, WI: University of Wisconsin Press, 1973: 63–138.

———. "Sexual Metaphor in Milton's Cosmogony, Physics, and Ontology." *Renaissance Papers*, 1967: 93–103.

———. "Something More about the Erotic Motive in *Paradise Lost.*" *Tulane Studies in English* 15 (1967): 19–30.

Bradley, A. C. *Shakespearean Tragedy: Lectures on "Hamlet," "Othello," "King Lear," "Macbeth."* London: MacMillan, 1904.

Brailow, David C. "Prospero's 'Old Brain': The Old Man as Metaphor in *The Tempest.*" *Shakespeare Studies* 14 (1981): 285–302.

Brake, Mike, ed. *Human Sexual Relations: Towards a Redefinition of Sexual Politics*. New York: Pantheon Books, 1982.

Breton, Nicholas. *Breton's Praise of virtuous ladies* (1606), ed. Sir Egerton Brydges. Kent, England, 1815.

Briggs, K. M. *Fairies in English Tradition and Literature*. Chicago: University of Chicago Press, 1967.

———. *Pale Hecate's Team: An Example of Beliefs on Witchcraft and Magic among Shakespeare's Contemporaries and His Immediate Successors*. New York: Humanities Press, 1962.

Bristol, Michael D. *Carnival and Theater: Plebian Culture and the Structure of Authority in Renaissance England*. New York, London: Methuen, 1985.

Brodwin, Leonora. *Elizabethan Love Tragedy, 1587–1965*. New York: New York University Press, 1971.

Brooks, Cleanth. *The Well Wrought Urn*. New York: Harcourt Brace (Harvester), 1947.

Brown, Steve. "' . . . and his ingle at home': Notes on Gender in Jonson's *Epiceone.*" Paper, Renaissance Society of America. Philadelphia, March 21, 1986.

———. "The Boyhood of Shakespeare's Heroines: Notes on Gender Ambiguity in the Sixteenth Century." Paper, Shakespeare Society of America. Boston, March 27, 1986. (To appear in *SEL*, Spring 1990.)

Bruno, Giordano. *The Expulsion of the Triumphant Beast*, trans., intro., notes

Arthur D. Imerti. New Brunswick, NJ: Rutgers University Press, 1964.

———. *The Heroic Frenzies*, trans., intro., notes Paul Eugene Memmo Jr. Chapel Hill: University of North Carolina Press, 1964.

Brustein, Robert. "The Monstrous Regiment of Women." *Renaissance and Modern Essays: Presented to Vivian de Sola Pinto*, ed. G. R. Hibbard with the assistance of George A. Panichas and Allan Rodway. London: Routledge & Kegan Paul, 1966: 35–50.

Bryant, J. A., Jr. *Shakespeare and the Uses of Comedy*. Lexington: University of Kentucky Press, 1986.

Bryskett, Lodowick. *A discourse of civill life*. London, 1606.

Buoni, Tommaso. *Problems of beautie and all humane affections, trans. into English by S. L(ennard)*. London, 1606.

Burghley, William Cecil, 1st Baron. *The Lord Treasurer Burghleigh's Advice to Queen Elizabeth, in matters of religion and state. Somers Tracts* (2nd ed.) 1 (1809): 164–70.

———. *Precepts, or, Directions for the well ordering and carriage of a mans life . . . In two books*. London, 1636.

Burke, John G. "Hermeticism as a Renaissance World View." *The Darker Vision of the Renaissance: Beyond the Fields of Reason*, ed. Robert S. Kinsman. Berkeley: University of California Press, 1974: 95–117.

Bush, Geoffrey. *Shakespeare and the Natural Condition*. Cambridge: Harvard University Press, 1956.

Busst, A. J. L. "The Image of the Androgyne in the Nineteenth Century." *Romantic Mythologies*, ed. Ian Fletcher. London: Routledge & Kegan Paul, 1967: 1–95.

Butler, E. M. *The Myth of the Magus*. Cambridge: Cambridge University Press, 1948.

———. *Ritual Magic* (1949). New York: Noonday, 1959.

Bynum, Caroline Walker. "The Body of Christ in the Later Middle Ages: A Reply to Leo Steinberg." *RQ* 39 (1986): 399–439.

———. *Holy Feast and Holy Fast: The Religious Significance of Food to Medieval Woman*. Berkeley: University of California Press, 1987.

Calhoun, Thomas O. *Henry Vaughan: The Achievement of "Silex Scintillans"*. Newark: University of Delaware Press, 1981.

Camden, Carroll. *The Elizabethan Woman*. Houston: Elsevier Press, 1952.

Camden, William. *Remains concerning Britain* (1657), ed. R. D. Dunn. Toronto: University of Toronto Press, 1984.

Campbell, Joseph. *The Hero With a Thousand Faces*. Princeton: Princeton University Press, 1949, 1968.

———. *Masks of God*. New York: Viking, 1969.

Campbell, Joseph, assisted by M. J. Abadie. *The Mythic Image*. Princeton: Princeton University Press, 1974.

Carroll, William C. *The Metamorphoses of Shakespearean Comedy*. Princeton: Princeton University Press, 1985.

Caspari, Fritz. *Humanism and the Social Order in Tudor England*. Chicago: University of Chicago Press, 1954.

Cassirer, Ernst. *An Essay on Man: An Introduction to a Philosophy of Human*

Culture. New Haven, London: Yale University Press, 1944.

———. *The Individual and the Cosmos in Renaissance Philosophy* (1926), trans. Mario Domandi. Oxford: Basil Blackwell, 1963.

———. *The Platonic Renaissance in England* (1932), trans. J. P. Pettegrove. Austin: University of Texas Press, 1953.

Cassirer, Ernst, Paul Oskar Kristeller, John Herman Randall Jr., eds. *The Renaissance Philosophy of Man*. Chicago: University of Chicago Press, 1948.

Chaudhuri, Sukanta. *Infirm Glory: Shakespeare and the Renaissance Image of Man*. Oxford: Oxford University Press, 1981.

Cheney, Donald. "Spenser's Hermaphrodite and the 1590 *Faerie Queene*." *PMLA* 87 (1972): 192–200.

Chojnacki, Stanley, ed. "*Recent Trends in Renaissance Studies*: The Family, Marriage and Sex" (intro., three essays, comment, bibliog). *RQ* 40 (1987): 660–751.

Cirillo, Albert R. "The Fair Hermaphrodite: Love-Union in the Poetry of Donne and Spenser." *SEL* 9 (1969): 81–95.

———. "*As You Like It*: Pastoralism Gone Awry." *ELH* 38 (1971): 19–39.

Clapham, David, trans. *A treatise of the nobilitie and excellency of woman Kynde*. (Agrippa, *De Nobilitae E. Praecellentia Foeminei Sexus*, 1529.) London, 1542.

Clark, Alice. *Working Life of Women in the Seventeenth Century*. London: Cass, 1919.

Clulee, Nicholas H. "Astrology, Magic, and Optics: Facets of John Dee's Early Natural Philosophy." *RQ* 30 (1977): 632–80.

Cohen, Derek. *Shakespearean Motives*. New York: St. Martin's, 1988.

Coleridge, S. T. *The Table Talk and Omniana of Samuel Taylor Coleridge*, ed. T. Ashe. London: George Bell and Sons, 1888.

Colet, John. See O'Kelly; Lochman.

Colie, Rosalie L. *Paradoxia Epidemica: The Renaissance Tradition of Paradox*. Princeton: Princeton University Press, 1966.

———. *Shakespeare's Living Art*. Princeton: Princeton University Press, 1974.

Colie, Rosalie L., ed. *Some Facets of "King Lear": Essays in Prismatic Criticism*. Toronto: University of Toronto Press, 1974.

Comito, Terry. "Caliban's Dream: The Topography of Some Shakespeare Gardens." *Shakespeare Studies* 14 (1981): 23–53.

Cope, Jackson I. *The Theater and the Dream: From Metaphor to Form in Renaissance Drama*. Baltimore, London: The Johns Hopkins University Press, 1973.

Copenhaver, Brian P. "Scholastic Philosophy and Renaissance Magic in the *De vita* of Marsilio Ficino." *RQ* 37 (1984): 523–54.

———. *Symphorien Champier and the Reception of the Occultist Tradition in Renaissance France*. The Hague, New York: Mouton, 1978.

Corpus Hermeticum: The Divine Pymander and Other Writings of Hermes Trismegistus, trans. John D. Chambers. New York: Samuel Weiser, 1975.

Corpus Hermeticum, trans. A. D. Nock and A. J. Festugiere. 2nd ed., 4 vols. Paris: Société d'Edition "Les Belles Lettres," 1960.

Cottrell, Robert D. *Sexuality/Textuality: A Study of the Fabric of Montaigne's "Essays"*. Columbus: Ohio State University Press, 1981.

Coursen, H. R. *The Compensatory Psyche: A Jungian Approach to Shakespeare.* Lanham, MD: University Press of America, 1986.

Craig, D. H. "A Hybrid Growth: Sidney's Theory of Poetry in *An Apology for Poetry*." *English Literary Renaissance* 10 (1980): 183–201.

Craig, Hardin. *The Enchanted Glass: The Elizabethan Mind in Literature* (1936). Oxford: Blackwell, 1952.

Cressy, D. *Literacy and the Social Order: Reading and Writing in Tudor and Stuart England.* Cambridge: Cambridge University Press, 1980.

Crewe, Jonathan. *Hidden Designs: The Critical Profession and Renaissance Literature.* New York, London: Methuen, 1986.

Curry, Walter Clyde. *Shakespeare's Philosophical Patterns.* Baton Rouge: Louisiana State University Press, 1937.

Curtius, E. R. *European Literature and the Latin Middle Ages* (1948), trans. Willard R. Trask. Princeton: Princeton University Press, 1953.

Daigle, Lennet J. "*Venus and Adonis*: Some Critical Contexts." *Shakespeare Studies* 13 (1980): 31–46.

D'Amico, Jack. *Knowledge and Power in the Renaissance.* Washington, DC: University Press of America, 1977.

Danby, John F. *Shakespeare's Doctrine of Nature: A Study of "King Lear."* London: Faber and Faber, 1949.

Danson, Lawrence, ed. *On "King Lear"*. Princeton: Princeton University Press, 1981.

Dash, Irene. *Wooing, Wedding, and Power: Women in Shakespeare's Plays.* New York: Columbia University Press, 1981.

Davies, Stevie. *The Idea of Woman in Renaissance Literature: The Feminine Reclaimed.* Sussex: Harvester, 1986.

Davies, Stevie, ed. *Renaissance Views of Man.* Manchester: Manchester University Press, 1978.

De Armas, Frederick A. *The Return of Astraea: An Astral-Imperial Myth in Calderon.* Lexington: University of Kentucky Press, 1986.

Deats, Sara Munson. "*Edward II*: A Study in Androgyny." *Ball State University Forum* 22 (1981): 30–41.

Debus, Allen G. *The Chemical Philosophy: Paracelsian Science and Medicine in the Sixteenth and Seventeenth Centuries.* 2 vols. New York: Science History Publications (Neale Watson Academic Publications), 1977.

———. *Man and Nature in the Renaissance.* Cambridge: Cambridge University Press, 1979.

Dee, John. *John Dee: Essential Readings*, ed., intro. Gerald Suster. Wellingborough: Crucible, 1986.

———. *John Dee on Astronomy: "Propaedeumata Aphoristica" (1558 and 1568), Latin and English*, ed., trans., notes Wayne Shumaker. (Introductory essay, J. L. Heilbron, "Dee and the Scientific Revolution.") Berkeley: University of California Press, 1978.

Delcourt, Marie. *Hermaphrodite: Myths and Rites of the Bisexual Figure in Classical Antiquity* (1956), trans. from French by Jennifer Nicholson. London: Studio Books, 1961.

Dinnerstein, Dorothy. *The Mermaid and the Minotaur: Sexual Arrangements and*

Human Malaise. New York: Harper and Row, 1976.

Dollimore, Jonathan. *Radical Tragedy: Religion, Ideology and Power in the Drama of Shakespeare and his Contemporaries*. Chicago: University of Chicago Press, 1984.

Dollimore, Jonathan and Alan Sinfield, eds. *Political Shakespeare: New Essays in Cultural Materialism*. Manchester: Manchester University Press, 1985.

Donawerth, Jane. *Shakespeare and the Sixteenth-Century Study of Language*. Urbana, Chicago: University of Illinois Press, 1984.

Doran, Madeleine. *Endeavors of Art: A Study of Form in Elizabethan Drama*. Madison: University of Wisconsin Press, 1954.

Dowling, Maria. *Humanism in the Age of Henry VIII*. London, Wolfboro, NH: Croom Helm, 1986.

Drakakis, J., ed. *Alternative Shakespeares*. London: Methuen, 1985.

Dreher, Diane Elizabeth. *Domination and Defiance: Fathers and Daughters in Shakespeare*. Lexington: University of Kentucky Press, 1986.

Driscoll, James P. *Identity in Shakespearean Drama*. Lewisburg, PA: Bucknell University Press, 1983.

Dubrow, Heather. *Captive Victors: Shakespeare's Narrative Poems and Sonnets*. Ithaca, London: Cornell University Press, 1987.

Duerr, Hans Peter. *Dreamtime: Concerning the Boundary Between Wilderness and Civilization*. New York: Basil Blackwell, 1985.

Dundas, Judith. *The Spider and the Bee: The Artistry of Spenser's "Faerie Queene"*. Urbana: University of Illinois Press, 1985.

Dunn, Catherine M. "The Changing Image of Women in Renaissance Society and Literature." *What Manner of Woman: Essays in English and American Life and Literature*, ed. Marlene Springer. New York: New York University Press, 1977: 15–38.

Dusinberre, Juliet. *Shakespeare and the Nature of Women*. London: Macmillan, 1975.

Eagleton, Terence. *Shakespeare and Society: Critical Studies in Shakespearean Drama*. New York: Schocken, 1967.

Easlea, Brian. *Witch Hunting, Magic, and the New Philosophy: An Introduction to the Debates of the Scientific Revolution, 1450–1750*. Atlantic Highlands, NJ: Humanities Press, 1980.

Easton, Sara J. "Presentations of Women in the English Popular Press." *Ambiguous Realities: Women in the Middle Ages and Renaissance*, ed. Carole Levin and Jeanie Watson. Detroit: Wayne State University Press, 1987: 165–83.

Ebreo, Leone. *The Philosophy of Love (Dialoghi d'Amore)*, trans. F. Friedeberg-Selley and Jean H. Barnes; intro. Cecil Roth. London: The Soncino Press, 1937.

Egan, Robert. *Drama Within Drama: Shakespeare's Sense of His Art in "King Lear," "The Winter's Tale" and "The Tempest."* New York: Columbia University Press, 1975.

Eisenstein, Elizabeth. *The Printing Press as an Agent of Change*. 2 vols. Cambridge: Cambridge University Press, 1979.

Eisenstein, Zillah. *The Radical Future of Liberal Feminism*. New York: Longman, 1981.

Elam, K. *Shakespeare's Universe of Discourse: Language-Games in the Comedies.* London: Cambridge University Press, 1984.

Eliade, Mircea. *The Myth of the Eternal Return* (Bollingen Series 46). New York: Pantheon Books, 1954.

———. *Myths, Dreams and Mysteries.* New York: Harper & Row, 1967.

Elton, William R. *"King Lear" and the Gods.* San Marino, CA: Huntington Library, 1968.

Elyot, Sir Thomas. *The boke named The gouernour*, ed. H. H. S. Croft (1883). 2 vols. New York: B. Franklin, 1967.

———. *The Defence of Good Woman*, ed. Edwin Johnstone Howard. Oxford, OH: Anchor Press, 1940.

Engels, Frederick. *The Origin of the Family, Private Property and the State* (1884), intro. Evelyn Reed. New York: Pathfinder Press, 1972.

Epstein, Perle S. *The Private Labyrinth of Malcolm Lowry: "Under the Volcano" and the Cabbala.* New York: Holt, Rinehart & Winston, 1969.

Erickson, Peter. *Patriarchal Structures in Shakespeare's Drama.* Berkeley: University of California Press, 1985.

———. "Review of Marilyn French, *Shakespeare's Division of Experience*," *Women's Studies* 9 (1982): 189–202.

Erickson, Peter and Coppélia Kahn, eds. *Shakespeare's "Rough Magic": Renaissance Essays in Honor of C. L. Barber.* Newark: University of Delaware Press, 1985.

Eriksen, Roy T. "Mnemonics and Giordano Bruno's Magical Art of Composition." *Cahiers Elisabéthains* 20 (1981): 3–10.

Evans, Malcolm. *Signifying Nothing: Truth's True Contents in Shakespeare's Text.* Sussex: Harvester, 1986.

Everett, Barbara. "*Much Ado About Nothing.*" *The Critical Quarterly* 3 (1961): 319–35.

Everie Woman in her humor. London, 1609.

Ewbank, Inga-Stina. "The Fiend-like Queen: A Note on 'Macbeth' and Seneca's 'Medea'," *Shakespeare Survey* 19 (1966): 82–94.

Faas, Ekbert. *Shakespeare's Poetics.* Cambridge: Cambridge University Press, 1986.

Faber, M. D., ed. *The Design Within: Psychoanalytic Approaches to Shakespeare.* New York: Science House, 1970.

Fabricius, Johannes. *Alchemy: The Medieval Alchemists and Their Royal Art.* Copenhagen: Rosenkilde and Bagger, 1976.

Fallon, Francis T. *The Enthronement of Sabaoth: Jewish Elements in Gnostic Creation Myths.* Leiden: E. J. Brill, 1978.

Farrell, Kirby. *Shakespeare's Creation: The Language of Magic and Play.* Amherst: University of Massachusetts Press, 1975.

Farwell, Marilyn R. "Eve, the Separation Scene, and the Renaissance Idea of Androgyny." *Milton Studies* 16 (1982): 3–20.

Fausto-Sterling, Anne. *Myths of Gender: Biological Theories about Women and Men.* New York: Basic Books Inc, 1985.

Febvre, Lucien. *The Problem of Unbelief in the Sixteenth Century: The Religion of Rabelais* (1942), trans. Beatrice Gottlieb. Cambridge: Harvard University Press, 1982.

Felperin, Howard. *Shakespearean Representation: Mimesis and Modernity in Elizabethan Tragedy*. Princeton: Princeton University Press, 1978.

Fenton, Geoffrey. *Monophylo drawne into English by Geffray Fenton: A philosophical discourse & division of love*. London, 1572.

Ferguson, Ann. "Androgyny As an Ideal for Human Development." *Feminism and Philosophy, Part II: Sex Roles and Gender*, ed. Mary Vetterling-Braggin, Frederick A. Elliston, Jane English. Totowa, NJ: Rowman and Littlefield, 1977: 45–69.

Ferguson, Arthur B. "Humanism as a Mode of Perception: The Case of England." *Medieval and Renaissance Studies* 9 (1982): 221–46.

Ferguson, Margaret, Maureen Quilligan, and Nancy J. Vickers, eds. *Rewriting the Renaissance: The Discourses of Sexual Difference in Early Modern Europe*. Chicago: University of Chicago Press, 1986.

Ferrante, Joan M. *Woman As Image in Medieval Literature: From the Twelfth Century to Dante*. New York: Columbia University Press, 1975.

Fiedler, Leslie. *Freaks: Myths and Images of the Secret Self*. New York: Simon and Schuster, 1978.

———. *The Stranger in Shakespeare*. New York: Stein and Day, 1972.

Fineman, Joel. *Shakespeare's Perjured Eye: The Invention of Poetic Subjectivity in the Sonnets*. Berkeley: University of California Press, 1986.

Fisher, Elizabeth. *Woman's Creation: Sexual Evolution and the Shaping of Society*. New York: Anchor/Doubleday, 1979.

Fitz [Woodbridge], L. T. "Egyptian Queens and Male Reviewers: Sexist Attitudes in *Antony and Cleopatra* Criticism." *SQ* 28 (1977): 297–316.

———. "'What Says the Married Woman?': Marriage Theory and Feminism in the English Renaissance." *Mosaic* 13 (1980): 1–22.

Fly, Richard. *Shakespeare's Mediated World*. Amherst: University of Massachusetts Press, 1976.

Forster, Leonard, *The Icy Fire: Five Studies in European Petrarchism*. London: Cambridge University Press, 1969.

Fox, Alice. "How Many Pregnancies Had Lady Macbeth." *University of Dayton Review* 14 (1979–80): 33–7.

———. "Obstetrics and Gynecology in *Macbeth*." *Shakespeare Studies* 12 (1979): 127–41.

Fox, Alistair and John Guy. *Reassessing the Henrician Age: Humanism, Politics and Reform 1500–1550*. New York: Basil Blackwell, 1986.

Fraser, Russell, *The Dark Ages & the Age of Gold*. Princeton: Princeton University Press, 1973.

———. *The Language of Adam: On the Limits and Systems of Discourse*. New York: Columbia University Press, 1977.

Fraunce, Abraham. *The Lawyer's Logic* (1588). Menston, England: The Scolar Press Limited, 1969.

Freccero, Carla. "The Other and the Same: The Image of the Hermaphrodite in Rablais." *Rewriting the Renaissance: The Discourses of Sexual Difference in Early Modern Europe*, ed. M. Ferguson et al. (Chicago: University of Chicago Press, 1986): 145–58.

Freeburg, Victor Oscar. *Disguise Plots in Elizabethan Drama: A Study in Stage Tradition* (1915). New York: Blom, 1965.

French, Marilyn. *Shakespeare's Division of Experience*. New York: Summit Books, 1981.

French, Peter. *John Dee: The World of an Elizabethan Magus*. London: Routledge & Kegan Paul, 1972.

Friedman, Alan. *Hermaphrodeity: The Autobiography of a Poet*. New York: Alfred A. Knopf, 1972.

Friedman, Jerome. *The Most Ancient Testimony: Sixteenth-Century Christian-Hebraica in the Age of Renaissance Nostalgia*. Athens: Ohio University Press, 1983.

Friedman, Susan Stanford. "'Remembering Shakespeare Always, But Remembering Him Differently': H. D.'s *By Avon River*." *Sagetrieb* 2 (1983): 45–70.

Friedrich, Paul. *The Meaning of Aphrodite*. Chicago: University of Chicago Press, 1978.

Frost, Robert. *The Complete Poems*. New York: Holt, Rinehart and Winston, 1949.

Frye, Northrop. *A Natural Perspective: The Development of Shakespearean Comedy and Romance*. New York: Columbia University Press, 1965.

Funkenstein, Amos. *Theology and the Scientific Imagination from the Middle Ages to the Seventeenth Century*. Princeton: Princeton University Press, 1986.

Furnivall, F. J., ed. *The glasse of godley love*. *New Shakespeare Society* 6 (1876): 177–90.

Gagen, Jean E. *The New Woman: Her Emergence in English Drama (1600–1730)*. New York: Twayne Publishers, 1954.

Garber, Marjorie, ed. *Cannibals, Witches, and Divorce: Estranging the Renaissance*. Selected Papers, English Institute, 1985. Baltimore and London: Johns Hopkins University Press, 1987.

Garber, Marjorie B. *Coming of Age in Shakespeare*. London: Methuen, 1981.

———. *Dream in Shakespeare: From Metaphor to Metamorphosis*. New Haven: Yale University Press, 1974.

———. *Shakespeare's Ghost Writers: Literature as Uncanny Causality*. New York, London: Methuen, 1987.

Garin, Eugenio. *Astrology in the Renaissance: The Zodiac of Life*, trans. Carolyn Jackson, June Allen, Clare Robertson. London, Boston: Routledge & Kegan Paul, 1983.

———. *Science and Civic Life in the Italian Renaissance*, trans. Peter Munz. New York: Anchor, 1969.

Gascoigne, George. *Certaine Notes of Instruction (1575)*. *The Renaissance in England*, ed. Hyder Rollins and Herschel Baker. Boston: Heath, 1954.

Gent, Lucy. *Picture and Poetry 1560–1620: Relations between Literature and the Visual Arts in the English Renaissance*. Leamington Spa, Warwickshire: James Hall Publishing Limited, 1981.

Gilbert, Sir Humphrey. *Queene Elizabethes Achademy* (1583), ed. F. J. Furnivall. *Early English Text Society* 8. London, 1869.

Gilman, Ernest B. "'All eyes': Prospero's Inverted Masque." *RQ* 33 (1980): 214–30.

Ginzburg, Carlo. *The Cheese and the Worm: The Cosmos of a Sixteenth Century Miller*, trans. John and Anne Tedeschi. Baltimore: The Johns Hopkins University Press, 1980.

———. *The Night Battles: Witchcraft and Agrarian Cults in the Sixteenth and*

Seventeeth Centuries (1966), trans. John and Anne Tedeschi. Baltimore: Johns Hopkins University Press, 1983.

Goddard, Harold. *The Meaning of Shakespeare*. 2 vols. Chicago: University of Chicago Press, 1951.

Goldberg, Jonathan. *Endlesse Worke: Spenser and the Structures of Discourse*. Baltimore, London: Johns Hopkins University Press, 1981.

———. *James I and the Politics of Literature: Jonson, Shakespeare, Donne, and Their Contemporaries*. Baltimore: Johns Hopkins University Press, 1983.

———. *Voice Terminal Echo: Postmodernism and English Texts*. New York: Methuen, 1986.

Goldman, Michael. *Acting and Action in Shakespearean Tragedy*. Princeton: Princeton University Press, 1985.

———. *The Actor's Freedom: Toward a Theory of Drama*. New York: Viking, 1975.

———. *Shakespeare and the Energies of Drama*. Princeton: Princeton University Press, 1972.

Gombrich, E. H. "*Icones Symbolicae*: Philosophies of Symbolism and Their Bearing on Art," *Symbolic Images: Studies in the Art of the Renaissance*. London: Phaidon Press, 1972: 123–95.

Gourlay, Patricia S. "'O my most sacred lady': Female Metaphor in *The Winter's Tale*," *English Literary Renaissance* 5 (1975): 375–95.

Goy, Robert W. and Bruce S. McEwen. *Sexual Differentiation of the Brain*. Cambridge, MA: MIT Press, 1980.

Grafton, Anthony and Lisa Jardine. *From Humanism to the Humanities: Education and the Liberal Arts in Fifteenth- and Sixteenth-Century Europe*. Cambridge: Harvard University Press, 1986.

Grant, Patrick. *Images and Ideas in Literature of the English Renaissance*. London, Basingstoke: Macmillan, 1979.

———. *Literature and the Discovery of Method in the English Renaissance*. Athens: University of Georgia Press, 1986.

———. "Hermetic Philosophy and the Nature of Man in Vaughan's *Silex Scintillans*." *JEGP* 67 (1968): 406–22.

Grazia, Margreta de. "Shakespeare's View of Language: An Historical Perspective," *SQ* 29 (1978): 374–88.

———. "*The Tempest*: Gratuitous Movement or Action Without Kibes and Pinches." *Shakespeare Studies* 14 (1981): 249–65.

Greene, Gayle and Carolyn Ruth Swift, eds. *Feminist Criticism of Shakespeare*. A double issue of *Women's Studies* 9 (1981): 1–217.

Greene, Gayle and Coppélia Kahn. "The Social Construction of Woman." *Making a Difference: Feminist Literary Criticism*, ed. Gayle Greene and Coppélia Kahn. London: Methuen, 1985.

Greene, Thomas M. *The Light in Troy: Imitation and Discovery in Renaissance Poetry*. New Haven: Yale University Press, 1982.

———. "Magic and Festivity at the Renaissance Court" (The Josephine Waters Bennett Lecture, Renaissance Society of America, 1987). *RQ* 40 (1987): 636–59.

Greenblatt, Stephen, ed. *The Power of Forms in the English Renaissance*. Norman, OK: Pilgrim, 1982.

Greenblatt, Stephen. *Renaissance Self-Fashioning: From More to Shakespeare*. Chicago,

London: University of Chicago Press, 1981.

Greenblatt, Stephen, ed. *Representing the English Renaissance*. Berkeley: University of California Press, 1988.

Grassi, Ernesto. *Heidegger and the Question of Renaissance Humanism*. Binghamton, NY: Medieval and Renaissance Texts and Studies for SUNY, 1983.

Greer, Germaine. *Shakespeare*. Oxford, New York: Oxford University Press, 1986.

Griffiths, T. R. "'This island's mine': Caliban and Colonialism." *Yearbook of English Studies* 13 (1983): 159–80.

Gros Louis, Kenneth R. R. "The Triumph and Death of Orpheus in the English Renaissance." *SEL* 9 (1969): 63–80.

Gross, Kenneth. *Spenserian Poetics: Idolatry, Iconoclasm, and Magic*. Ithaca, London: Cornell University Press, 1985.

Grosseteste, Robert. *On Light*, trans. Clare C. Riedle. Milwaukee, WI: Marquette University Press, 1942.

Grudin, Robert. *Mighty Opposites: Shakespeare and Renaissance Contrariety*. Berkeley, Los Angeles: University of California Press, 1979.

Guarino, Guido A. *The Albertis of Florence: Leon Battista Alberti's "Della Famiglia."* Lewisburg: Bucknell University Press, 1971.

Guazzo, Stefano. *The ciuile conuersation of M. Stephen Guazzo*. London: T. East, 1586.

H. D. [Hilda Doolittle.] *By Avon River*. New York: Macmillan, 1949.

Halio, Jay L. "The Metaphor of Conception and Elizabethan Theories of the Imagination." *Neophilologus* 50 (1966): 454–61.

Hamilton, A. C. "Sidney and Agrippa." *Review of English Studies* 7 (1956): 151–57.

Hamilton, Roberta. *The Liberation of Women: A Study of Patriarchy and Capitalism*. London, Boston: G. Allen & Unwin, 1978.

Hanning, Robert W. and David Rosand, eds. *Castiglione: The Ideal and the Real in Renaissance Culture*. New Haven: Yale University Press, 1983.

Harbage, Alfred. *Shakespeare and the Rival Traditions*. New York: Macmillan, 1952.

———. *William Shakespeare: A Reader's Guide*. New York: Noonday, 1963.

Harding, Sandra and Jean F. O'Barr, eds. *Sex and Scientific Inquiry*. Chicago: University of Illinois Press, 1987.

Harper, Ralph. *Human Love—Existential and Mystical*. Baltimore: Johns Hopkins University Press, 1966.

Harrie, Jeanne. "Duplessis-Mornay, Foix-Candale and the Hermetic Religion of the World." *RQ* 31 (1978): 499–514.

Harris, Anthony. *Night's Black Agents: Witchcraft and Magic in Seventeenth-Century English Drama*. Manchester: Manchester University Press, 1980.

Haselkorn, Anne M. *Prostitution in Elizabethan and Jacobean Comedy*. Troy, NY: The Whitston Publishing Company, 1983.

Hattaway, Michael. *Elizabethan Popular Theater: Plays in Performance*. London: Routledge & Kegan Paul, 1982.

Hay, Dennis. "England and the Humanities in the Fifteenth Century." *Itinerarium Italicum: The Profile of the Italian Renaissance in the Mirror of Its European*

Transformations, ed. Heiko A. Oberman with Thomas Bradley Jr. Leiden: E. J. Brill, 1975.

Hayles, Nancy. "Sexual Disguise in *As You Like It* and *Twelfth Night*." *Shakespeare Survey* 32 (1979): 63–72.

———. "Sexual Disguise in *Cymbelina*." *Modern Language Quarterly* 41 (1980): 231–47.

Heilbrun, Carolyn. *Reinventing Womanhood*. New York: Norton, 1979.

———. *Toward a Recognition of Androgyny* (1973). New York: Harper Colophon, 1974.

Heller, Thomas C., Morton Sosna, and David E. Wellberry, eds. *Reconstructing Individualism: Autonomy, Individuality and the Self in Western Thought*. Stanford: Stanford University Press, 1986.

Heltzel, Virgil B. *A Check List of Courtesy Books in the Newberry Library*. Chicago: The Newberry Library, 1942.

Henderson, Katharine Usher and Barbara F. McManus. *Half Humankind: Contexts and Texts of the Controversy about Women in England, 1540–1640*. Urbana: University of Illinois Press, 1985.

Heninger, S. K., Jr. *The Cosmolographical Glass: Renaissance Diagrams of the Universe*. San Marino: The Huntington Library, 1977.

———. *A Handbook of Renaissance Meteorology; with Particular Reference to Elizabethan and Jacobean Literature*. New York: Greenwood, 1968.

———. *Touches of Sweet Harmony: Pythagorean Cosmology and Renaissance Poetics*. San Marino: The Huntington Library, 1974.

Hieatt, A. Kent. *Chaucer, Spenser, Milton: Mythopoeic Continuities and Transformations*. Montreal, London: McGill-Queen's University Press, 1975.

Hoby, Sir Thomas. *The book of the courtier . . . 1561*, intro. Walter Raleigh, 1900. New York: AMS Press, 1967.

Hodges, Devon L. *Renaissance Fictions of Anatomy*. Amherst: University of Massachusetts Press, 1985.

Hogrefe, Pearl. *The Life and Times of Sir Thomas Elyot, Englishman*. Ames: Iowa State University Press, 1967.

———. *Tudor Women: Commoners and Queens*. Ames: Iowa State University Press, 1975.

———. *Women of Action in Tudor England: Nine Biographical Sketches*. Ames: Iowa State University Press, 1977.

Holderness, Graham, Nick Potter, and John Turner. *Shakespeare, The Play of History*. Iowa City: University of Iowa Press, 1987.

Hole, Christina. *A Mirror of Witchcraft*. London: Chatto & Windus, 1957.

Holland, Norman. "Caliban's Dream." *The Design Within*, ed. M. D. Faber. New York: Science House, 1970: 521–37.

Holm, Janis Butler. "The Myth of a Feminist Humanism: Thomas Salter's *The Mirrhor of Modestie*." *Ambiguous Realities: Women in the Middle Ages and Renaissance*, eds. Carole Levin and Jeanie Watson. Detroit: Wayne State University Press, 1987: 197–218.

Honigmann, E. A. J. *Shakespeare's Impact on His Contempories*. London: Basingstoke:

Macmillan, 1982.

Hopkins, Jasper. *A Concise Introduction to the Philosophy of Nicholas of Cusa.* Minneapolis: University of Minnesota Press, 1948.

———. *Nicholas of Cusa's Dialectical Mysticism.* Minneapolis: The A. J. Banning Press, 1985.

Horowitz, Daniel. *Shakespeare: An Existential View.* London: Tavistock, 1965.

Horwich, Richard. "Integrity in *Macbeth*: The Search for the 'Single State of Man'." *SQ* 29 (1978): 365–73.

Houston, John Porter. *The Rhetoric of Poetry in the Renaissance and Seventeenth Century.* Baton Rouge: Louisiana State University Press, 1983.

Howard, Jean E. *Shakespeare's Art of Orchestration: Stage Technique and Audience Response.* Urbana: University of Illinois Press, 1984.

Howe, James Robinson. *Marlowe, Tamburlaine, and Magic.* Athens: Ohio University Press, 1976.

Hubbard, Ruth and Marian Lowe. *Genes and Gender II: Pitfalls in Research on Sex and Gender.* New York: Gordian Press, 1979.

Huizinga, Johan. *Men and Ideas: History, the Middle Ages, the Renaissance*, trans. James S. Holmes and Hans van Marle. Princeton: Princeton University Press, 1959, 1984.

Hull, Suzanne W. *Chaste, Silent and Obedient: English Books for Women, 1475–1640.* San Marino: The Huntington Library, 1982.

Hulse, Clark. *Metamorphic Verse: The Elizabethan Minor Epic.* Princeton: Princeton University Press, 1981.

Hunter, G. K. *John Lyly: The Humanist as Courtier.* London: Routledge & Kegan Paul, 1962.

Hunter, Robert Grams. *Shakespeare and the Comedy of Forgiveness.* New York: Columbia University Press, 1965.

Huston, Dennis J. *Shakespeare's Comedies of Play.* New York: Columbia University Press, 1981.

Hurstfield, Joel. *The Queen's Wards: Wardship and Marriage under Elizabeth I.* London, New York: Longman, Green, 1958.

Hutchinson, J. B., ed. *Biological Determinants of Sexual Behavior.* New York: John Wiley and Sons, 1978.

Hyde, Thomas. *The Poetic Theology of Love: Cupid in Renaissance Literature.* Newark: University of Delaware Press, 1986.

Ide, Richard. "The Theatre of the Mind: An Essay on *Macbeth.*" *English Literary Renaissance* 42 (1975): 338–61.

Illich, Ivan. *Gender.* New York: Pantheon, 1982.

Jacobi, Jolande, ed.; trans. Norman Guterma. *Parcelsus: Selected Writings.* (Bollingen Series 28.) New York: Pantheon, 1958.

James, D. G. *The Dream of Learning: An Essay on "The Advancement of Learning," "Hamlet," and "King Lear."* Oxford: Clarendon Press, 1951.

———. *The Dream of Prospero.* Oxford: Clarendon, 1967.

Jardine, Lisa. "Cultural Confusion and Shakespeare's Learned Heroines: 'These are old paradoxes'." *SQ* 38 (1987): 1–18.

———. *Still Harping on Daughters: Women and Drama in the Age of Shakespeare.* Sussex: Harvester, 1983.

Jayne, Sears Reynolds. *Marsilio Ficino's Commentary on Plato's Symposium: The Text and a Translation, with an Introduction.* Columbia: *University of Missouri Studies* 19 (1944).

Johnson, Paul. *Elizabeth I: A Study in Power and Intellect.* London: Weidenfeld and Nicolson, 1974.

Jordan, Constance. "Woman's Rule in Sixteenth-Century British Political Thought." *RQ* 40 (1987): 421–51.

———. "Feminism and the Humanists: The Case of Sir Thomas Elyot's *Defence of Good Women.*" *RQ* 36 (1983): 181–201.

Jordan, June. *Living Room.* New York: Thunder's Mouth Press, 1985.

Jorgensen, Paul A. *Lear's Self-Discovery.* Berkeley, Los Angeles: University of California Press, 1967.

———. *Our Naked Frailties: Sensational Art and Meaning in "Macbeth".* Berkeley: University of California Press, 1971.

Jung, Carl. *Memories, Dreams, Reflections.* New York: Pantheon Books, 1963.

Kahn, Coppélia. "'Magic of bounty': *Timon of Athens*, Jacobean Patronage, and Maternal Power." *SQ* 38 (1987): 34–57.

———. *Man's Estate: Masculine Identity in Shakespeare.* Berkeley: University of California Press, 1981.

Kahn, Victoria. *Rhetoric, Prudence, and Skepticism in the Renaissance.* Ithaca: Cornell University Press, 1985.

Kaplan, Alexandra G. and Joan P. Bean. *Beyond Sex-Role Stereotypes: Readings Toward a Psychology of Androgyny.* Boston: Little, Brown, 1976.

Keach, William. *Elizabethan Erotic Narratives: Irony and Pathos in the Ovidian Poetry of Shakespeare, Marlowe, and Their Contemporaries.* New Brunswick, NJ: Rutgers University Press, 1977.

Keats, John. *Selected Poems and Letters*, ed. Douglas Bush. Cambridge, MA: Riverside, 1959.

Keller, Evelyn Fox. *Reflections on Gender and Science.* New Haven: Yale University Press, 1985.

Kelly-Gadol, Joan. "Did Women Have a Renaissance?" *Becoming Visible: Women in European History*, ed. Renate Bridenthal and Claudia Koonz. Boston: Houghton-Miflin, 1977: 137–64.

Kelso, Ruth. *Doctrine for the Lady of the Renaissance.* Urbana: University of Illinois Press, 1965.

Kemp, Martin. *Leonardo da Vinci: The Marvellous Works of Nature and Man.* Cambridge: Harvard University Press, 1981.

Kermode, Frank, ed. *The Tempest* (Arden). Cambridge: Harvard University Press, 1954, 1958.

Kernan, Alvin B., ed. *The Alchemist.* New Haven: Yale University Press, 1974.

Kernan, Alvin B. *The Playwright as Magician: Shakespeare's Image of the Poet in the English Public Theater.* New Haven, London: Yale University Press, 1979.

Kessler, Suzanne J. and Wendy McKenna. *Gender: An Ethnomethodological*

Approach. Chicago: University of Chicago Press, 1978.

Kimbrough, Robert. "Androgyny, Old and New." *The Western Humanities Review* 35 (1981): 197–215.

———. "Macbeth: The Prisoner of Gender." *Shakespeare Studies* 16 (1983): 175–90.

———. "Shakespeare's Androgyny Seen Through Disguise." *SQ* 33 (1982): 17–33.

———. *Shakespeare's "Troilus and Cressida" and Its Setting*. Cambridge: Harvard University Press, 1964.

———. *Sir Philip Sidney*. New York: Twayne, 1971.

King, John N. *English Reformation Literature: The Tudor Origins of the Protestant Tradition*. Princeton: Princeton University Press, 1982.

———. "The Goodly Woman in Elizabethan Iconography." *RQ* 38 (1985): 41–84.

Kingdon, Robert M., ed. *Transition and Revolution*. Minneapolis: Burgess Pub. Co., 1974.

Kinney, Arthur F. *Humanist Poetics: Thought, Rhetoric and Fiction in Sixteenth-Century England*. Amherst: University of Massachusetts Press, 1986.

Kinney, Arthur F. and Kirby Farrell, eds. *Women in the Renaissance*. Special issue, *English Literary Renaissance* 14 (1984): 253–439.

Kirik, Kathy L. "An Inquiry into Misogyny in *King Lear*: The Making of an Androgyny." *Journal of Evolutionary Psychology*. Pittsburgh, PA, 1979: 13–28.

Kirsch, Arthur. "The Emotional Landscape of *King Lear*." *SQ* 39 (1988): 154–70.

———. *Shakespeare and the Experience of Love*. Cambridge: Cambridge University Press, 1981.

Klein, Joan Larsen. "Lady Macbeth: 'Infirm of purpose'." *The Woman's Part: Feminist Criticism of Shakespeare*, ed. Lenz, et al. Urbana: University of Illinois Press, 1980: 240–55.

Knapp, Bettina L. *Theatre and Alchemy*. Detroit: Wayne State University Press, 1980.

Knecht, Robert J. *Francis I*. Cambridge: Cambridge University Press, 1982.

Knight, G. Wilson. *The Crown of Life: Essays in Interpretation of Shakespeare's Final Plays*. London, New York, Toronto: Oxford University Press, 1947.

———. *The Imperial Theme: Further Interpretations of Shakespeare's Tragedies Including the Roman Plays*. London: Oxford University Press, 1931.

———. *The Mutual Flame: On Shakespeare's "Sonnets" and "The Phoenix and the Turtle*." London: Methuen, 1955.

Knox, John. *The First Blast of the Trumpet Against the Monstrous Regiment of Women* (1558), ed. E. Arber. English Scholar's Library, no. 2. London, 1878.

Koenigsberger, Dorothy. *Renaissance Man and Creative Thinking: A History of Concepts of Harmony 1400–1700*. Atlantic Highlands, NJ: Humanities Press, 1979.

Kott, Jan. *Shakespeare: Our Contemporary* (1964), trans. Boleslaw Taborski. Garden City, NY: Anchor/Doubleday, 1966.

Koyré, Alexandre. *The Astronomical Revolution: Copernicus, Kepler, Borelli* (1961), trans. R. E. W. Maddison. Ithaca: Cornell University Press, 1973.

Kristeller, Paul Oskar. *Renaissance Thought: The Classic, Scholastic, and Humanistic Strains*. New York: Harper Torchbooks, 1961.

———. *Renaissance Thought and Its Sources*, ed. Michael Mooney. New York: Columbia University Press, 1979.

Kuhn, Maura Slattery. "Much Virtue in *If*." *SQ* 28 (1977): 40–50.

Kuhn, Thomas. *The Essential Tension: Selected Studies in Scientific Tradition and Change*. Chicago, London: University of Chicago Press, 1977.

Kuntz, Marion L. *Guillaume Postel, Prophet of the Restitution of All Things: His Life and Thought*. (*International Archives of the History of Ideas* 98.) The Hague, Boston: Martinus Nijhoff, 1981.

LaBalme, Patricia H. *Beyond Their Sex: Learned Women of the European Past*. New York: New York University Press, 1981.

LaBelle, Jenijoy. "'A Strange Infirmity': Lady Macbeth's Amenorrhea." *SQ* 31 (1980): 381–86.

Labrizzi, Charles G. "*Macbeth* and the 'Milk of Human Kindness': A Note." *Massachusetts Studies in English* 5 (1978): 29–31.

La Guardia, Eric. *Nature Redeemed: The Imitation of Order in Three Renaissance Poems*. (Studies in English Literature, 31) New York: Humanities Press; The Hague: Mouton, 1966.

Lambert, Helen H. "Viewpoint: Biology and Equality: A Perspective on Sex Differences." *Signs* 4 (1978): 97–117.

Lanham, Richard A. *The Motives of Eloquence: Literary Rhetoric in the Renaissance*. New Haven: Yale University Press, 1976.

LaPrimaudaye, Pierre de. *The French Academie newly trans. into English by T[homas] B[arnes]*. London, 1586.

Laslett, Peter. *Family Life and Illicit Love in Earlier Generations: Essays in Historical Sociology*. Cambridge: Cambridge University Press, 1977.

———. *The World We Have Lost*. New York: Scribner, 1965.

Latham, Jacqueline E. "The Magic Banquet in *The Tempest*." *Shakespeare Studies* 12 (1979): 215–27.

LaTorre, Ronald A. *Sexual Identity*. Chicago: Nelson-Hall, 1979.

LeComte, Edward. *Milton and Sex*. New York: Columbia University Press, 1978.

Leech, Clifford. "Venus and Her Nun: Portraits of Women in Love by Shakespeare and Marlowe." *SEL* 5 (1965): 247–68.

Leggatt, Alexander. *Shakespeare's Comedy of Love*. New York: Barnes & Noble, Harper & Row, 1974.

Lenz, Carolyn Ruth Swift, Gayle Greene, Carol Thomas Neely, eds. *The Women's Part: Feminist Criticism of Shakespeare*. Urbana: University of Illinois Press, 1980.

Lerner, Gerda. *The Creation of Patriarchy*. New York, Oxford: Oxford University Press, 1986.

Levao, Ronald. *Renaissance Minds and Their Fictions: Cusanus, Sidney, Shakespeare*. Berkeley: University of California Press, 1985.

Leverenz, David. "The Woman in Hamlet: An Interpersonal View." *Representing Shakespeare*, ed. Murray M. Schwartz and Coppélia Kahn. Baltimore: Johns Hopkins University Press, 1980: 110–28.

Levin, Carole and Jeanie Watson, eds. *Ambiguous Realities: Women in the Middle Ages and Renaissance*. Detroit: Wayne State University Press, 1987.

Levin, Harry. *The Myth of the Golden Age in the Renaissance*. Bloomington: Indiana University Press, 1969.

Levin, Richard. "Feminist Thematics and Shakespearean Tragedy." *PMLA* 103 (1988): 125–36.

———. "Sexual Equations in the Elizabethan Double Plot." *Literature and Psychology* 16 (1966): 2–14.

Levin, Richard A. *Love and Society in Shakespearean Comedy: A Study of Dramatic Form and Content*. Newark: University of Delaware Press, 1985.

Lewalski, Barbara. *Protestant Poetics and the Seventeenth Century Religious Lyric*. Princeton: Princeton University Press, 1979.

Lindberg, David C. *Roger Bacon's Philosophy of Nature*. Oxford: Clarendon; New York: Oxford University Press, 1983.

———. *Theories of Vision from al-Kindī to Kepler*. Chicago: University of Chicago Press, 1976.

Linden, Stanton J. "The Breaking of the Alembic: Patterns and Alchemical Imagery in English Renaissance Poetry." *Wascana Review* (Renaissance Issue) 9 (1974): 105–13.

Lindenbaum, Peter. "Prospero's Anger." *Massachusetts Review* 25 (1984): 161–71.

Lindheim, Nancy. *The Structures of Sidney's "Arcadia."* Toronto, Buffalo, London: University of Toronto Press, 1981.

Lull, Ramon. *Selected Works of Ramon Llull (1232–1316)*, ed., trans. Anthony Bonner. 2 vols. Princeton: Princeton University Press, 1985.

Lochman, Daniel Thomas. *The Ecstatic Embrace: Form and Content in the Major Works of John Colet*. Ph.D. Thesis. Madison: University of Wisconsin, 1983.

Lockerd, Benjamin G., Jr. *The Sacred Marriage: Psychic Integration in "The Faerie Queene."* Lewisburg, PA: Bucknell University Press, 1987.

Long, Michael. *The Unnatural Scene: A Study in Shakespearean Tragedy*. London: Methuen, 1976.

Lowe, Marian. "Viewpoint: Sociobiology and Sex Differences." *Signs* 4 (1978): 118–25.

Luyster, Robert W. *Hamlet and Man's Being: The Phenomenology of Nausea*. Lanham, MD: University Press of America, 1984.

Lynch, Stephen J. "Sin, Suffering, and Redemption in *Leir* and *Lear*." *Shakespeare Studies* 18 (1986): 161–74.

Lyons, Charles R. *Shakespeare and the Ambiguity of Love's Triumph*. The Hague, Paris: Mouton, 1971.

MacCary, W. Thomas. *Friends and Lovers: The Phenomenology of Desire in Shakespearean Comedy*. New York: Columbia University Press, 1985.

Macfarlane, Alan. *Marriage and Love in England: Modes of Reproduction 1300–1840*. New York: B. Blackwell, 1986.

———. *Witchcraft in Tudor and Stuart England: A Regional and Comparative Study*. New York: Harper & Row, 1970.

Mack, Maynard. *"King Lear" in Our Time*. London: Methuen, 1966.

Mackinnon, Lachlan. *Shakespeare the Asthete: An Explanation of Literary Theory*. New York: St. Martin's Press, 1987.

Maclean, Ian. *The Renaissance Notion of Woman: A Study in the Fortunes of*

Scholasticism and Medical Science in European Intellectual Life. Cambridge: Cambridge University Press, 1980.

Mahoney, Edward P., ed. *Philosophy and Humanism: Renaissance Essays in Honor of Paul Oskar Kristeller*. New York: Columbia University Press, 1976.

Mancinus, Dominicus. *The mirrour of good manners . . . trans. into English by Alexander Barclay*. London, 1570.

Mandrou, Robert. *From Humanism to Science 1480–1700*, trans. Brian Pearce. Atlantic Highlands, NJ: Humanities Press, 1979.

Marcotte, Paul J. *Priapus Unbound: Shakespeare's Concept of Love Inferred from Six Early Works*. Ottawa: University of Ottawa Press, 1971.

Marcus, Leah S. *The Politics of Mirth: Jonson, Herrick, Milton, Marvell, and the Defense of Old Holiday Pastimes*. Chicago: University of Chicago Press, 1986.

———. "Shakespeare's Comic Heroines, Elizabeth I, and the Political Uses of Androgyny." *Women in the Middle Ages and the Renaissance*, ed. M. B. Rose. Syracuse: Syracuse University Press, 1986: 135–53.

Marlowe, Christopher. *The Works*, ed. C. F. Tucker Brooke. Oxford: Clarendon, 1910.

Marsh, Derick R. C. *Passion Lends Them Power: A Study of Shakespeare's Love Tragedies*. Manchester: Manchester University Press; New York: Barnes & Noble, 1976.

Martz, Louis. "Shakespeare's Humanist Enterprise: *The Winter's Tale*." *English Renaissance Studies, Presented to Dame Helen Gardner in Honour of her Seventieth Birthday*, ed. John Carey. Oxford: Clarendon, 1980.

Mason, H. A. *Humanism and Poetry in the Early Tudor Period: An Essay*. London: Routledge & Kegan Paul, 1959.

———. *Shakespeare's Tragedies of Love*. London: Chatto & Windus, 1970.

Mason, Philip. *Prospero's Magic: Some Thoughts on Class and Race*. London: Oxford University Press, 1962.

May, Robert. *Sex and Fantasy: Patterns of Male and Female Development*. New York: Norton, 1980.

May, Rollo. *Love and Will*. New York: W. W. Norton, 1969.

McFarland, Thomas. *Shakespeare's Pastoral Comedy*. Chapel Hill: University of North Carolina Press, 1972.

McFarlane, I. D. "Montaigne and the Concept of the Imagination." *The French Renaissance and Its Heritage: Essays Presented to Alan M. Boase*, ed. D. R. Haggis, S. Jones, F. W. Leakey, E. G. Taylor, G. M. Sutherland. London: Methuen, 1968.

McGuire, Philip C. *Speechless Dialect: Shakespeare's Open Silences*. Berkeley: University of California Press, 1985.

McLuskie, Kathleen. "The Patriarchal Bard: Feminist Criticism and Shakespeare—*King Lear* and *Measure for Measure*." *Political Shakespeare: New Essays in Cultural Materialism*, ed. Dollimore and Sinfield. Manchester: University of Manchester Press, 1985: 88–108.

Mebane, John S. *Renaissance Magic and the Return of the Golden Age: The Occult Tradition and Marlowe, Jonson, and Shakespeare*. Lincoln and London: University of Nebraska Press, 1989.

———. "Renaissance Magic and the Return of the Golden Age: Utopianism and Religious Enthusiasm in *The Alchemist*." *Renaissance Drama* 10 (1979): 117–39.

Merchant, Carolyn. *The Death of Nature: Women, Ecology, and the Scientific Revolution*. San Francisco: Harper, 1980.

Merchant, W. Moelwyn. "His Fiend-like Queen." *Shakespeare Survey* 19 (1966): 75–81.

Merivale, Patricia. *Pan, the Goat-God: His Myth in Modern Times*. Cambridge: Harvard University Press, 1969.

Meyer, Russell, J. "'Fixt in heauens hight': Spenser, Astronomy, and the Date of the *Cantos of Mutabilitie*." *Spenser Studies* 4 (1983): 115–29.

Meyerholf, Barbara. "The Older Woman as Androgyne." (Special issue on androgyny.) *Parabola: Myth and the Quest for Meaning* 3 (1978): 74–89.

Midelfort, H. C. Erick. "Witchcraft, Magic, and the Occult." *Reformation Europe: A Guide to Research*, ed. Steven E. Ozment. St. Louis: Center for Reformation Research, 1982: 183–209.

Miller, Robert P. "The Myth of Mars' Hot Minion in *Venus and Adonis*." *ELH* 26 (1959): 470–81.

Molho, Anthony and John A. Tedeschi. *Renaissance Studies in Honor of Hans Baron*. DeKalb: Northern Illinois University Press, 1971.

Mollenkott, Virginia Ramey. *The Divine Feminine: The Biblical Imagery of God as Female*. New York: Crossroad, 1984.

———. "John Donne and the Limitations of Androgyny." *JEGP* 80 (1981): 22–38.

———. "Some Implications of Milton's Androgynous Muse." *Women, Literature, Criticism*, ed. Harry R. Garvin. *Bucknell Review* 24 (1978): 27–36.

Monegal, E. R. "The Metamorphoses of Caliban." *Diacritics* 7 (1977): 78–83.

Money, John. *Love & Love Sickness: The Science of Sex, Gender Difference, and Pair-Bonding*. Baltimore: Johns Hopkins University Press, 1980.

Money, John and Patricia Tucker. *Sexual Signatures: On Being a Man or a Woman*. Boston: Little, Brown, 1975.

Montaigne, Michael de. *An Apology for Raymond Sebond*, ed., trans., intro., notes M. A. Screech. London: Penguin, 1987.

Montano, Rocco. *Shakespeare's Concept of Tragedy: The Bard As Anti-Elizabethan*. Chicago: Regnery Gateway, 1986.

Monter, William. *Ritual, Myth, and Magic in Early Modern Europe*. Athens: Ohio University Press, 1984.

Montreux, Nicolas de. *Honours academie. Done into English by R. T.* London: Th. Creede, 1610.

Montrose, Louis A. "'Eliza, Queene of Shepheardes' and the Pastoral of Power." *English Literary Renaissance* 10 (1980): 153–82.

———. "The Elizabethan Subject and the Spenserian Text." *Literary Theory/ Renaissance Text*, ed. Patricia Parker and David Quint. Baltimore: Johns Hopkins University Press, 1985: 303–340.

———. "'Shaping Fantasies': Figurations of Gender and Power in Elizabethan Culture." *Representations* 2 (1983): 61–94.

More, Henry. *Conjectura Cabbalistica. Or, a Conjectural Essay of Interpreting the minde of Moses, according to a Threefold Caballa*. London, 1653.

Morgan, John. *Godly Learning: Puritan Attitudes towards Reason, Learning, and Education*. Cambridge: Cambridge University Press, 1986.

Morris, Harry. *Last Things in Shakespeare*. Tallahassee: Florida State University Press, 1985.

Mowat, Barbara. *The Dramaturgy of Shakespeare's Romances*. Athens: University of Georgia Press, 1976.

———. "Prospero, Agrippa, and Hocus Pocus." *English Literary Renaissance* 11 (1981): 281–303.

Muir, Kenneth, Jay L. Halio, and D. J. Palmer, ed. *Shakespeare, Man of the Theater: Proceedings of the Second Congress of the International Shakespeare Association*. Newark: University of Delaware Press, 1981.

Mulcaster, Richard. *Positions wherein those primitive circumstances be examined which are necessary for the training up of children*. London, 1581.

Mullaney, Steven. *The Place of the Stage: License, Play, and Power in Renaissance England*. Chicago: University of Chicago Press, 1987.

Murrin, Michael. *The Veil of Allegory: Some Notes Toward a Theory of Allegorical Rhetoric in the English Renaissance*. Chicago: University of Chicago Press, 1969.

Murstein, Bernard I. *Love, Sex, and Marriage Through the Ages*. New York: Springer, 1974.

Nauert, Charles G., Jr. *Agrippa and the Crisis of Renaissance Thought*. Urbana: University of Illinois Press, 1965.

Needler, Howard I. "Of Truly Gargantuan Proportions: From the Abbey of Thélème to the Androgynous Self." *University of Toronto Quarterly* 51 (1982): 221–47.

Neely, Carol Thomas. *Broken Nuptials in Shakespeare's Plays*. New Haven, London: Yale University Press, 1985.

Nelson, John C. *Renaissance Theory of Love: The Context of Giordano Bruno's "Eroici Furori."* New York: Columbia University Press, 1958.

Nelson, William. *The Poetry of Edmund Spenser*. New York, London: Columbia University Press, 1963.

Nenna, Giovanni Battistee. *Nennio; or, A treatise of nobility . . . Done into English by William Jones*. London, 1595.

Nestrick, William V. "Spenser and the Renaissance Mythology of Love." *Literary Monographs 6*, ed. Eric Rothstein and Joseph A. Wittreich Jr. Madison: University of Wisconsin Press, 1975: 35–70.

Neumann, Erich. *The Great Mother: An Analysis of the Archetype*, trans. Ralph Manheim. London: Routledge & Kegan Paul, 1963.

Nevo, Ruth. *Comic Transformations in Shakespeare*. London: Methuen, 1980.

Newman, Karen. "Portia's Ring: Unruly Women and Structures of Exchange in *The Merchant of Venice*." *SQ* 38 (1987): 19–33.

———. *Shakespeare's Rhetoric of Comic Character: Dramatic Convention in Classical and Renaissance Comedy*. New York, London: Methuen, 1985.

Niccholes, Alexander. *A discourse of marriage and wiving . . . London, 1615. The Harleian Miscel.* 2 (1809): 156–82.

Nicholl, Charles. *The Chemical Theatre*. London: Routledge & Kegan Paul, 1980.

Nicholson, Marjorie Hope. *The Breaking of the Circle: Studies in the Effect of the "New Science" upon Seventeenth-century Thought*. Rev. ed. New York, London: Columbia University Press, 1962.

Nohrnberg, James. *The Analogy of "The Faerie Queene."* Princeton: Princeton University Press, 1977.

Noonan, John T., Jr. *Contraception: A History of Its Treatment by the Catholic Theologians and Canonists.* Cambridge: Harvard University Press, 1966.

Norbrook, David. *Poetry and Politics in the English Renaissance.* Boston, London: Routledge & Kegan Paul, 1984.

Novarr, David. *The Disinterred Muse: Donne's Texts and Contexts.* Ithaca, London: Cornell University Press, 1980.

Novy, Marianne L. *Love's Argument: Gender Relations in Shakespeare.* Chapel Hill: University of North Carolina Press, 1984.

Oberman, Heiko A. and Charles Trinkaus, eds. *The Pursuit of Holiness in Late Medieval and Renaissance Religion.* Leiden: Brill, 1974.

O'Flaherty, Wendy Doniger. *Women, Androgynes, and Other Mythical Beasts.* Chicago, London: University of Chicago Press, 1980.

O'Kelly, Bernard and Catherine A. L. Jarrott. *John Colet's Commentary on First Corinthians: A New Edition of the Latin Text, with Translation, Annotations, and Introduction.* Binghamton, NY: Medieval and Renaissance Text and Studies, SUNY, 1985.

Orgel, Stephen. *The Illusion of Power: Political Theater in the English Renaissance.* Berkeley: University of California Press, 1975.

———. "New Uses of Adversity: Tragic Experience in *The Tempest.*" *In Defense of Reading*, ed. Reuben Brower and Richard Poirier. New York: Dutton, 1963.

———. "Nobody's Perfect, or Why Did the English Stage Take Boys for Women?" *South Atlantic Quarterly* 88 (1989): 7–29.

———. "Prospero's Wife." *Representing the English Renaissance*, ed. Stephen Greenblatt. Berkeley, Los Angeles, London: University of California Press, 1988: 217–29.

Orgel, Stephen, ed. *The Tempest* (The Oxford Shakespeare). Oxford: Clarendon, 1987.

Ornstein, Robert. *Shakespeare's Comedies: From Roman Farce to Romantic Mystery.* Newark: University of Delaware Press, 1986.

Ortner, Sherry B. and Harriet Whitehead, eds. *Sexual Meanings: The Cultural Construction of Gender and Sexuality.* Cambridge: Cambridge University Press, 1981.

Ozment, Steven E. *Homo Spiritualis: A Comparative Study of the Anthropology of Johannes Tauler, Jean Gerson, and Martin Luther (1509–16) in the Context of Their Theological Thought.* Leiden: Brill, 1969.

Pagel, Walter. *Paracelsus: An Introduction to Philosophical Medicine in the Era of the Renaissance.* Basel: S. Karger, 1958.

Pagels, Elaine. *The Gnostic Gospels.* New York: Random House, 1979.

Paglia, Camille A. "The Apollonian Androgyne and *The Faerie Queene.*" *English Literary Renaissance* 9 (1979): 42–63.

Palingenius, Marcellus. *The Zodiake of Life*, trans., Barnabe Googe. Intro. Rosemond Tuve. New York: Scholar's Facsimile Reprints, 1947.

Panofsky, Erwin. *Renaissance and Renascences in Western Art* (1960). New York: Harper (Icon), 1970.

———. *Studies in Iconology: Humanistic Themes in the Art of the Renaissance* (1939). New York: Harper Torchbooks, 1962.

Paracelsus. *Works*, trans. Robert Turner. London: Askin Publishers, 1975.

Parker, Barbara L. *A Precious Seeing: Love and Reason in Shakespeare's Plays*. New York, London: New York University Press, 1987.

Parker, Patricia and David Quint, eds. *Literary Theory/Renaissance Texts*. Baltimore: Johns Hopkins University Press, 1986.

Parker, Patricia and Geoffrey Hartman, eds. *Shakespeare and the Question of Theory*. New York: Methuen, 1985.

Parsons, Jacquelynne. *The Psychobiology of Sex Differences and Sex Roles*. New York: McGraw-Hill, 1980.

Partrides, C. A., ed. *The Cambridge Platonists* (1970). New York: Cambridge University Press, 1980.

Patrides, C. A. *Premises and Motifs in Renaissance Thought and Literature*. Princeton: Princeton University Press, 1982.

Pearson, D'Orsay W. "'Unless I Be Reliev'd by Prayer': *The Tempest* in Perspective." *Shakespeare Studies* 7 (1974): 253–82.

———. "Witchcraft in *The Winter's Tale*: Paulina as 'Alcahueta y vn Poquito Hechizera'." *Shakespeare Studies* 12 (1979): 195–213.

Pequigney, Joseph. *Such Is My Love: A Study of Shakespeare's Sonnets*. Chicago: University of Chicago Press, 1985.

Perella, Nicolas J. *The Kiss Sacred and Profane: An Interpretative History of Kiss Symbolism and Related Religio-Erotic Themes*. Berkeley: University of California Press, 1969.

Perrot, Jean. *Mythe et littérature sous le signe des Jumeaux*. (Collection "Sup") Paris: Presses Universitaires de France, 1976.

Perry, Anthony T. *Erotic Spirituality: The Integrative Tradition from Leone Ebero to John Donne*. Tuscaloosa: University of Alabama Press, 1980.

Peterson, Richard S. *Imitation and Praise in the Poetry of Ben Jonson*. New Haven: Yale University Press, 1981.

Petrarch. *The Remedies and Uses of Fortune*, trans. T. Twyne. London, 1579.

Pitkin, Hannah Fenichel. *Fortune Is a Woman: Gender and Politics in the Thought of Niccolo Machiavelli*. Berkeley: University of California Press, 1984.

Pitt, Angela. *Shakespeare's Women*. New York: Barnes and Noble, 1981.

Pleck, Joseph H. *The Myth of Masculinity*. Cambridge: MIT Press, 1981.

Plessis de Mornay, Philippe du. *A Woorke concerning the trewnesse of the Christian Religion, written in French*, trans. Sir Philip Sidney and Arthur Golding (London, 1587). *The Prose Works of Sir Philip Sidney*, ed. Albert Feuillerat. 4 vols. Cambridge: Cambridge University Press, 1963. 3: 187–307.

Plowden, Alison. *Marriage with My Kingdom: The Courtships of Elizabeth I*. New York: Stein & Day, 1977.

———. *Tudor Women: Queens and Commoners*. New York: Atheneum, 1979.

Pomeroy, Sarah B. *Goddesses, Whores, Wives, and Slaves: Women in Classical Antiquity*. New York: Schocken Books, 1975.

Prior, Mary, ed. *Women in English Society: 1500–1800*. London: Methuen, 1985.

Putnam, Maxine. "A Glimpse into the Lives of English Women during the Renaissance." *Florida State University Studies* 5 (1952): 67–78.

Pyke, Sandra W. and J. Martin Graham. "Gender Scheme Theory and Androgyny: A Critique and Elaboration." *International Journal of Women's Studies* 6 (1983): 3–17.

Quilligan, Maureen. *Milton's Spenser: The Politics of Reading*. Ithaca: Cornell University Press, 1983.

Rabil, Albert, Jr., ed. *Renaissance Humanism: Foundations, Forms, and Legacy*. 3 Vols. Philadelphia: University of Pennsylvania Press, 1988.

Rabkin, Norman. *Shakespeare and the Common Understanding*. London: Collier-Macmillan, 1967.

———. *Shakespeare and the Problem of Meaning*. Chicago: University of Chicago Press, 1981.

Rackin, Phyllis. "Shakespeare's Boy Cleopatra, the Decorum of Nature, and the Golden World of Poetry." *PMLA* 87 (1972): 201–12.

———. "Androgyny, Mimesis, and the Marriage of the Boy Heroine on the English Renaissance Stage." *PMLA* 102 (1987): 29–41.

Raitiere, Martin N. "The Unity of Sidney's *Apology for Poetry*." *SEL* 21 (1981): 37–57.

Ranald, Margaret Loftus. *Shakespeare and His Social Context: Essays in Osmotic Knowledge and Literary Interpretation*. New York: AMS Press, 1987.

Raymond, Janice G. *The Transsexual Empire: The Making of the She-Male*. Boston: Beacon Press, 1979.

Read, John. *Prelude to Chemistry: An Outline of Alchemy, Its Literature and Relationships*. New York: Macmillan, 1937.

Reed, Robert R. *The Occult on the Tudor and Stuart Stage*. Boston: Christopher, 1965.

Regosin, Richard L. *The Matter of My Book: Montaigne's "Essais" as the Book of the Self*. Berkeley: University of California Press, 1977.

Reuchlin, Johann. *On the Art of the Kabbalah* (1517), trans. Martin and Sarah Goodman; intro. G. Lloyd Jones. New York: Abaris Books, 1983.

Richlin, Amy. *The Garden of Priapus: Sexuality and Aggression in Roman Humor*. New Haven: Yale University Press, 1983.

Ringler, Richard N. "The Faunus Episode." *Modern Philology* 63 (1965): 12–19.

Roberts, Josephine A. *Architectonic Knowledge in the "New Arcadia"*. Baton Rouge: Louisiana State University Press, 1978.

Robinson, J. T. "Man, Morals and Meta-evolution." *Central Issues in Anthropology* 2 (1980): 69–87.

Rogers, Katherine M. *The Troublesome Helpmate: A History of Misogyny in Literature*. Seattle: University of Washington Press, 1966.

Rose, Mark. *Shakespearean Design*. Cambridge: Harvard University Press, 1972.

———. *Heroic Love: Studies in Sidney and Spenser*. Cambridge: Harvard University Press, 1968.

———. "Sidney's Womanish Man." *Review of English Studies* 15 (1964): 353–65.

Rose, Mary Beth, ed. *Women in the Middle Ages and the Renaissance: Literary and*

Historical Perspectives. Syracuse, NY: Syracuse University Press, 1986.

Rossi, Paolo. *Francis Bacon: From Magic to Science*, trans. Sacha Rabinovitch. Chicago: University of Chicago Press, 1968.

———. "Hermeticism, Rationality, and the Scientific Revolution." *Reason, Experiment, and Mysticism in the Scientific Revolution*, ed. M. L. Righini Bonelli and W. R. Shea. New York: Science History Publications, 1975: 247–73.

Rossky, William. "Imagination in the English Renaissance: Psychology and Poetic." *Studies in the Renaissance* 5 (1957): 49–73.

Rougement, Denis de. *Love in the Western World*. New York: Harcourt, Brace, 1940.

Rowe, J. G. and W. H. Stockdale, eds. *Florilegium Historiale: Essays Presented to Wallace K. Ferguson*. Toronto: University of Toronto Press, 1971.

Rubinstein, Frankie. *A Dictionary of Shakespeare's Sexual Puns and Their Significance*. London: Macmillan, 1984.

Saccio, Peter. *The Court Comedies of John Lyly: A Study in Allegorical Dramaturgy*. Princeton: Princeton University Press, 1969.

Salter, Thomas. *A mirrhor mete for all mothers, matrons, and maidens, intituled the Mirrhor of modestie . . . London, 1579*, ed. Collier. London: *Illustrations of Old English Literature* (Green Series 1), 1866.

Sanday, Peggy Reeves. *Female Power and Male Dominance: On the Origins of Sexual Inequality*. Cambridge: Cambridge University Press, 1981.

Saslow, James M. *Ganymede in the Renaissance: Homosexuality in Art and Society*. New Haven: Yale University Press, 1986.

Schaffer, Kay F. *Sex-Role Issues in Mental Health*. Reading, MA: Addison-Wesley, 1979.

Schaya, Leo. *The Universal Meaning of the Kabbalah* (1958), trans. Nancy Pearson. London: George Allen & Unwin, 1971.

Schmitt, Charles. *John Case and Aristotelianism in Renaissance England*. Kingston, Ont.: McGill-Queen's University Press, 1983.

Schneider, Laurie. "Ms. Medusa: Transformations of a Bisexual Image." *The Psychoanalytic Study of Society* 91 (1981): 105–33.

Scholem, Gershom. *Major Trends in Jewish Mysticism*. Jerusalem: Schocken Publishing House, 1941.

Schotz, Myra Glazen. "The Great Unwritten Story: Mothers and Daughters in Shakespeare." *The Lost Tradition: Mothers and Daughters in Literature*, ed. Cathy N. Davidson and E. M. Brona. New York: F. Unger, 1980: 44–54.

Schwartz, Jerome. "Aspects of Androgyny in the Renaissance." *Human Sexuality in the Middle Ages and Renaissance*, ed. Douglas Radcliffe-Umstead. University of Pittsburgh Publications on Middle Ages and Renaissance 4. Pittsburgh: Center for Medieval and Renaissance Studies, University of Pittsburgh Press, 1978: 121–31.

Schwartz, Murray M. and Coppélia Kahn, eds. *Representing Shakespeare: New Psychoanalytic Essays*. Baltimore, MD: Johns Hopkins University Press, 1980.

Scoular, Kitty W. *Natural Magic: Studies in the Presentation of Nature in English Poetry from Spenser to Marvell*. Oxford: Clarendon, 1965.

Screech, Michael A. "The Illusion of Postel's Feminism." *Journal of the Warburg and Courtauld Institutes* 16 (1953): 162–70.

———. *The Rabelaisian Marriage*. London: Arnold, 1958.

Secor, Cynthia. "The Androgyny Papers." (Special issue on androgyny, ed. Secor.) *Women's Studies* 2 (1974): 139–41.

Secret, François. *Les Kabbalistes Chrétiens de la Renaissance*. Paris: Mouton, 1964.

———. *Postelliana*. Nieuwkoop: B. DeGraaf, 1981.

Seltzer, Daniel. "The Actors and Staging." *A New Companion to Shakespeare Studies*, ed. Kenneth Muir and S. Schoenbaum. Cambridge: Cambridge University Press, 1971: 35–54.

———. "The Staging of the Last Plays," *Stratford-Upon-Avon Studies 8: The Dark Comedies to the Last Plays*. New York: St. Martin's, 1967: 127–65.

Seung, T. K. *Cultural Thematics: The Formation of the Faustian Ethos*. New Haven, London: Yale University Press, 1976.

Seward, John P. and Georgene H. Seward. *Sex Differences: Mental and Temperamental*. Lexington, MA: Lexington Books, 1980.

Seznec, Jean. *Survival of the Pagan Gods*, trans. Barbara F. Sessions. New York: Pantheon Books, 1953.

Shakespeare, William. *The Complete Pelican Shakespeare*, ed. Alfred Harbage (1969). New York: Viking, 1977.

Shapiro, Michael. *Children of the Revels: The Boy Companies of Shakespeare's Time and their Plays*. New York: Columbia University Press, 1977.

———. "Role-Playing, Reflexivity and Metadrama in Recent Shakespearean Criticism." *Renaissance Drama* 12 (1981): 145–61.

Shepherd, Simon. *Marlowe and the Politics of Elizabethan Theatre*. New York: St. Martin's, 1986.

Sherman, Julia A. *Sex-Related Cognitive Differences: An Essay on Theory and Evidence*. Springfield, IL: Charles C. Thomas, 1978.

Sherwood, Terry G. *Fulfilling the Circle: A Study of John Donne's Thought*. Buffalo, Toronto: Toronto University Press, 1984.

Shorter, Edward. *The Making of the Modern Family*. New York: Basic Books, 1975.

Showalter, Elaine. "Virginia Woolf and the Flight into Androgyny." *A Literature of Their Own: British Women Novelists From Brontë to Lessing*. Princeton: Princeton University Press, 1976. Chap. X, 263–97.

Shulman, Jeff. "At the Crossroads of Myth. The Hermeneutics of Hercules from Ovid to Shakespeare." *ELH* 50 (1983): 83–106.

Shumaker, Wayne. *The Occult Sciences in the Renaissance: A Study in Intellectual Patterns*. Berkeley: University of California Press, 1972.

———. *Renaissance Curiosa: John Dee's Conversations with Angels; Girolamo Cardano's Horoscope of Christ; Johannes Trithemius and Cryptography; George Dalgarno's Universal Language*. Binghamton: Medieval and Renaissance Texts and Studies, SUNY, 1982.

Sidney, Sir Philip. *A Defence of Poetry. Miscellaneous Prose of Sir Philip Sidney*, ed. Katherine Duncan-Jones and Jan Van Dorsten. Oxford: Clarendon, 1973: 73–121.

———. *New Arcadia*, ed. Victor Skretrowicz. Oxford: Clarendon, 1987.

———. *Old Arcadia*, ed. Jean Robertson. Oxford: Clarendon, 1973.

———. *The Poems*, ed. William Ringler. Oxford: Clarendon, 1962.

Siegel, Paul N. *Shakespeare's English and Roman History Plays: A Marxist Approach*. Cranbury, NJ: Associated University Presses, 1986.

Siemon, James R. *Shakespearean Iconoclasm*. Berkeley: University of California Press, 1985.

Silberman, Lauren. "Singing Unsung Heroines: Androgynous Discourse in Book 3 of *The Faerie Queene*." *Rewriting the Renaissance: The Discourses of Sexual Difference in Early Modern Europe*, ed. Margaret Ferguson, Maureen Quilligan, Nancy J. Vickers. Chicago: University of Chicago Press, 1986: 259–71.

Sinfield, Alan. *Literature in Protestant England 1560–1660*. London: Croom Helm, 1982.

Singer, Irving. *The Nature of Love: Plato to Luther*. New York: Random House, 1966.

Singer, June. *Androgyny: Toward a New History of Sexuality*. Garden City, NY: Anchor/Doubleday, 1976.

Slater, Philip. *The Glory of Hera*. Boston: Beacon, 1968.

Slights, William W. E. "Maid and Man in *Twelfth Night*." *Journal of English and Germanic Philology* 80 (1981): 327–48.

Sloane, Thomas O. *Donne, Milton, and the End of Humanist Rhetoric*. Berkeley: University of California Press, 1985.

Smith, A. J. *The Metaphysics of Love: Studies in Renaissance Love Poetry from Dante to Milton*. Cambridge, New York: Cambridge University Press, 1985.

Smith, Hallet. *Shakespeare's Romances: A Study of Some Ways of the Imagination*. San Marino, CA: Huntington, 1972.

Smith, Marion B. "Shakespeare and Polarity of Love," *Humanities Association Bulletin* 16 (1975): 7–18.

Smith, Morton. *Clement of Alexandria and a Secret Gospel of Mark*. Cambridge: Cambridge University Press, 1973.

Snyder, Susan. *The Comic Matrix of Shakespeare's Tragedies: "Romeo and Juliet," "Hamlet," "Othello," and "King Lear."* Princeton: Princeton University Press, 1979.

Southern, John. *Pandora* (1584). New York: Columbia University Press, 1938.

Speaight, Robert. *Nature in Shakespearian Tragedy*. London: Hollis and Carter, 1955.

Spencer, Theodore. *Shakespeare and the Nature of Man*. New York: Macmillan, 1942; 1949, 2nd ed.

Spenser, Edmund. *The Poetical Works*, ed. J. C. Smith and E. De Selincourt. London: Oxford University Press, 1912, 1948.

Stanley, Thomas. "A Platonic Discourse upon Love." *The Poems and Translations of Thomas Stanley*, ed. G. M. Crump. Oxford: Clarendon, 1962.

Stansbury, Joan. "Characterization of the Four Young Lovers in *A Midsummer Night's Dream*." *Shakespeare Survey* 35 (1982): 57–63.

Staton, Shirley F. "Reading Spenser's *Faerie Queene*—In a Different Voice." *Ambiguous Realities: Women in the Middle Ages and Renaissance*, ed. Carole Levin and Jeanie Watson. Detroit: Wayne State University Press, 1987: 145–62.

Steadman, John M. *Nature into Myth*. Pittsburgh: Duquesne University Press, 1978.

Stein, Arnold. "On Elizabethan Wit." *SEL* 1 (1961): 75–91.

Stevenson, D. L. *Love Game Comedy*. New York: Columbia University Press, 1946.

Stone, Lawrence. *The Crisis of the Aristocracy, 1558–1641*. Oxford University Press, 1965.

———. *The Family, Sex and Marriage in England 1500–1800*. New York: Harper & Row, 1977.

Strong, Roy. *The Cult of Elizabeth: Elizabethan Portraiture and Pageantry*. Wallop, Hampshire: Thomas Hudson, 1977.

Struever, Nancy S. *The Language of History in the Renaissance: Rhetoric and Historical Consciousness in Florentine Humanism*. Princeton: Princeton University Press, 1970.

Stuever, R. H., ed. *Historical and Philosophical Perspectives of Science. Minnesota Studies in Philosophy of Science* 5 (1970).

Summers, David. *Michelangelo and the Language of Art*. Princeton: Princeton University Press, 1981.

Summers, Joseph. "'Look There, Look There!' The Ending of *King Lear*." *English Renaissance Studies, Presented to Dame Helen Gardner in Honour of Her Seventieth Birthday*, ed. John Carey. Oxford: Clarendon, 1980: 74–93.

———. *Dreams of Love and Power: On Shakespeare's Plays*. Oxford: Clarendon, 1984.

Sundelson, David. *Shakespeare's Restorations of the Father*. New Brunswick, NJ: Rutgers University Press, 1983.

Swetnam, Joseph. *The arraignment of lewd, idle, froward, and unconstant women: or the vanitie of them, choose you whether. With a commendation of wise, virtuous and honest women* . . . London, 1615.

Swietlicki, Catherine. *Spanish Christian Cabala: The Works of Luis de Leon, Santa Teresa de Jesus, and San Juan de la Cruz*. Columbia: University of Missouri Press, 1986.

Tanner, Nancy. *On Becoming Human*. Cambridge: Cambridge University Press, 1981.

Tayler, Edward William. *Nature and Art in Renaissance Literature*. New York: Columbia University Press, 1964.

Teilhard de Chardin, Pierre. *The Phenomenon of Man*. New York: Harper, 1956.

Thomas, Keith. *Religion and the Decline of Magic: Studies in Popular Beliefs in Sixteenth- and Seventeenth-Century England*. London: Weidenfeld and Nicolson, 1971.

Thompson, William Irwin. *The Time Falling Bodies Take to Light: Mythology, Sexuality, and the Origins of Culture*. New York: St. Martin's, 1981.

Thorndike, L. *A History of Magic and Experimental Science*. 8 vols. New York: Macmillan, 1929–34.

Thorne, William Barry. "*Cymbeline*: 'Lopp'd Branches' and the Concept of Regeneration." *SQ* 20 (1969): 143–59.

Todd, Janet, ed. *Gender and Literary Voice*. New York: Holmes and Meier, 1980.

Torshell, Samuel. *The womens glorie: the 2nd ed., enl.* London, 1650.

Tracy, James D. "Humanism and the Reformation." *Reformation Europe: A Guide to Research*, ed. Steven E. Ozment. St. Louis: Center for Reformation Research, 1982: 42–47.

Traister, Barbara Howard. *Heavenly Necromancers. The Magician in English Renaissance Drama*. Columbia: University of Missouri Press, 1984.

Travitsky, Betty, ed. and compiler. *The Paradise of Women: Writings by Englishwomen of the Renaissance*. Westport, CT, and London: Greenwood, 1981.

Trebilcot, Joyce. "Two Forms of Androgynism." *Feminism and Philosophy, Part II: Sex Roles and Gender*, ed. Mary Vetterling-Braggin, Frederick A. Elliston, Jane English. Totowa, NJ: Rowman and Littlefield, 1977: 70–78.

Trinkaus, Charles. "Humanism, Religion, Society: Concepts and Motivations of Some Recent Studies." *RQ* 29 (1976): 676–713.

———. *In Our Image and Likeness: Humanity and Divinity in Italian Humanist Thought*. 2 vols. Chicago: University of Chicago Press, 1970.

———. "Marsilio Ficino and the Ideal of Human Autonomy." *Ficino and Renaissance Neoplatonism*, ed. Konrad Eisenbichler and Olga Zorzi Pugliese. (University of Toronto Italian Studies 1.) Ottawa: Dovehouse Editions Canada, 1986: 141–53.

———. *The Scope of Renaissance Humanism*. Ann Arbor: University of Michigan Press, 1983.

Trousdale, Marion. *Shakespeare and the Rhetoricians*. Chapel Hill: University of North Carolina Press, 1982.

Tuberville, George. *The noble art of venerie*. London, 1611.

Tuve, Rosemond. *Allegorical Imagery: Some Medieval Books and Their Posterity*. Princeton: Princeton University Press, 1966.

———. *Elizabethan and Metaphysical Imagery: Renaissance Poetic and Twentieth-Century Critics*. Chicago: University of Chicago Press, 1947.

Tuveson, Ernest Lee. *The Avatars of Thrice Great Hermes: An Approach to Romanticism*. Lewisburg, PA: Bucknell University Press, 1982.

Utley, F. L. *The Crooked Rib: An Analytical Index to the Argument about Women in English and Scots Literature to the End of the Year 1586*. Columbus: Ohio State University Press, 1944.

Van den Berg, Kent T. *Playhouse and Cosmos: Shakespearean Theater as Metaphor*. Newark: University of Delaware Press, 1985.

Van Laan, Thomas P. *Role-playing in Shakespeare*. Toronto, Buffalo: University of Toronto Press, 1978.

Vaughter, Reesa M. "Psychology: Review Essay." *Signs* 2 (1976): 120–46.

Veeder, William. *Mary Shelley & Frankenstein: The Fate of Androgyny*. Chicago: University of Chicago Press, 1984.

Vetterling-Braggin, Mary, ed. *"Femininity," "Masculinity," and "Androgyny": A Modern Philosophical Discussion*. Totowa, NJ: Rowman & Littlefield, 1982.

Vickers, Brian. "Frances Yates and the Writing of History." *Journal of Modern History* 51 (1979): 287–316.

Vickers, Brian, ed. *Occult and Scientific Mentalities in the Renaissance*. Cambridge, New York: Cambridge University Press, 1984.

Vives, Jean Luis. *The Instruction of a Christian Woman*, trans. Richard Hyrde. London: Thomas Berthelet, 1540.

Voldben, A. *After Nostradamus*, trans. Gavin Gibbons. London: Mayflower Books, 1975.

Wagner, David L., ed. *The Seven Liberal Arts*. Bloomington: Indiana University Press, 1983.

Waite, Arthur Edward. *The Holy Kabbalah*. Hyde Park, NY: University Books, 1960.

Waite, Arthur Edward, ed. *Paracelsus* (1894). 2 vols. Berkeley: Shambhala Publishers, 1976.

Walker, D. P. *The Ancient Theology: Studies in Christian Platonism from the Fifteenth to the Eighteenth Century*. London: Duckworth, 1972.

———. *The Decline of Hell: Seventeenth-Century Discussions of Eternal Torment*. Chicago: University of Chicago Press, 1964.

———. *Music, Spirit and Language in the Renaissance*. London: Variorum Reprints, 1985.

———. *Spiritual and Demonic Magic from Ficino to Campanella*. London: Warburg Institute, University of London, 1958.

———. *Studies in Musical Science in the Late Renaissance*. London: Warburg Institute, University of London; Leiden: E. J. Brill, 1978.

———. *Unclean Spirits: Possession and Exorcism in France and England in the Late Sixteenth and early Seventeenth Centuries*. Philadelphia: University of Pennsylvania Press, 1981.

Wallace, Karl R. *Francis Bacon on the Nature of Man; The Faculties of Man's Soul: Understanding, Reason, Imagination, Memory, Will, and Appetite*. Urbana: University of Illinois Press, 1967.

Warner, Marina. *Joan of Arc: The Image of Female Heroism*. New York: Knopf, 1981.

Warren, Michael. "*King Lear*, IV. vi. 83: The Case For 'Crying'." *SQ* 35 (1984): 319–21.

Watson, Robert N. *Shakespeare and the Hazards of Ambition*. Cambridge, London: Harvard University Press, 1984.

Watson, Thomas. *Holsome and catholyke doctrine*. London, 1558.

Watts, Pauline Moffitt. *Nicolaus Cusanus: A Fifteenth-Century Vision of Man*. Leiden: Brill, 1982.

Weil, Andrew. *The Marriage of the Sun and Moon: A Quest for Unity in Consciousness*. Boston: Houghton Mifflin, 1980.

Weimann, Robert. *Shakespeare and the Popular Tradition in the Theater: Studies in the Social Dimension of Dramatic Form and Function*, ed. Robert Schwartz. Baltimore: Johns Hopkins University Press, 1978.

Weiner, Andrew D. *Sir Philip Sidney and the Poetics of Protestantism: A Study of Contexts*. Minneapolis: University of Minnesota Press, 1978.

Weisheipl, James A., ed. *Albertus Magnus and the Sciences: Commentary Essays, 1980*. Leiden: Brill, 1980.

Weitz, Shirley. *Sex Roles: Biological, Psychological, and Social Foundations*. New York: Oxford University Press, 1977.

Weld, John. *Meaning in Comedy: Studies in Elizabethan Romantic Comedy*. Albany: SUNY Press, 1975.

Wells, Robin Headlam. *Shakespeare, Politics and the State*. Atlantic Highlands, NJ: Humanities Press, 1986.

———. *Spenser's "Faerie Queene" and the Cult of Elizabeth*. London, Canberra: Barnes and Noble, 1983.

West, Robert Hunter. *The Invisible World: A Study of Pneumatology in Elizabethan Drama*. Athens: University of Georgia Press, 1939.

Westman, Robert S. and J. E. McGuire, eds. *Hermeticism and the Scientific Revolution*. Los Angeles: William Andrews Clark Memorial Library, 1977.

Westlund, Joseph. *Shakespeare's Reparative Comedies: A Psychoanalytic View of the Middle Plays*. Chicago: University of Chicago Press, 1984.

Westermarck, E. A. *The History of Human Marriage*. 5th ed., rewritten. New York: The Allerton Book Company, 1922.

Whateley, William. *A bride-bush. Or A direction for married persons* . . . London, 1623.

———. *A care-cloth: or, A treatise of the cumbers and troubles of marriage* . . . London, 1624.

Wheeler, Richard P. *Shakespeare's Development and the Problem Comedies: Turn and Counter-Turn*. Berkeley, Los Angeles, London: University of California Press, 1981.

Whetstone, George. *The English Mirror: a regard wherin al estates may behold the conquests of enuy*. London, 1586.

Whitaker, Virgil K. *The Mirror up to Nature: The Technique of Shakespeare's Tragedies*. San Marino, CA: The Huntington Library, 1965.

———. *Shakespeare's Use of Learning: An Inquiry into the Growth of his Mind & Art*. San Marino, CA: The Huntington Library, 1953.

Whittier, Gayle. "Falstaff as a Welshwoman: Uncomic Androgyny." *Ball State University Forum* 20 (1979): 23–35.

Wikander, Mathew H. "As Secret as Maidenhead: The Profession of the Boy-Actress in *Twelfth Night*." *Comparative Drama* 20 (1986–87): 149–63.

Willeford, William. *The Fool and his Scepter: A Study of Clowns and Jesters and their Audience*. Evanston: Northwestern University Press, 1969.

Willet, Andrew. *A treatise of Salomons marriage* . . . London, 1612.

Williams, Arnold. *The Common Expositor: An Account of the Commentaries on Genesis, 1527–1633*. Chapel Hill: University of North Carolina Press, 1948.

Williamson, Marilyn L. *The Patriarchy of Shakespeare's Comedies*. Detroit: Wayne State University Press, 1986.

Wilshire, Bruce. *Role Playing and Identity: The Limits of Theatre as Metaphor*. Bloomington: Indiana University Press, 1982.

Wind, Edgar. *Pagan Mysteries in the Renaissance* (1938; rev. 1958; enlarged 1968). New York: Norton, 1968.

Wing, John. *The crowne conjugall, or the spouse royal*. London, 1632.

Witt, Ronald G. *Hercules at the Crossroads: The Life, Works, and Thought of Coluccio Salutati*. Durham. NC: Duke University Press, 1983.

Wittig, Michele Andrisin and Anne C. Petersen, eds. *Sex-Related Differences in Cognitive Functioning: Developmental Issues*. New York: Academic Press, 1979.

Wolkstein, Diane, ed., and Samuel Noah Kramer, trans. *Inanna, Queen of Heaven and Earth: Her Stories and Hymns from Sumer*. New York: Harper and Row, 1983.

Woodbridge [Fitz], Linda. *Women and the English Renaissance; Literature and the Nature of Womankind, 1540–1620*. Champaign: University of Illinois Press, 1984.

Woodman, Leonora. *Stanza My Stone: Wallace Stevens and the Hermetic Tradition.* West Lafayette, IN: Purdue University Press, 1983.

Woolf, Virginia. *A Room of One's Own.* (1929). New York: Harcourt, Brace & World, 1957.

Worthen, William B. *The Idea of the Actor: Drama and the Ethics of Performance.* Princeton: Princeton University Press, 1984.

Wren, Robert M. "The 'Hideous Trumpet' and Sexual Transformation in Macbeth." *Forum* 4 (1967): 18–21.

Yates, Frances. *The Art of Memory.* Chicago: University of Chicago Press, 1966.

———. *The Art of Ramon Lull: An Approach to It through Lull's Theory of the Elements.* (JWCI 17 [1954].) Worcester, London: Baglis and Sons, Trinity Press, 1954.

———. *Astraea: The Imperial Theme in the Sixteenth Century.* London, Boston: Routledge & Kegan Paul, 1975.

———. *Giordano Bruno and the Hermetic Tradition.* Chicago: University of Chicago Press, 1964.

———. *Ideas and Ideals in the North European Renaissance.* London, Boston: Routledge & Kegan Paul, 1984.

———. *Lull and Bruno: Collected Essays.* London, Boston: Routledge & Kegan Paul, 1982.

———. *The Occult Philosophy in the Elizabethan Age.* London: Routledge & Kegan Paul, 1979.

———. *Renaissance and Reform: The Italian Contribution.* London, Boston: Routledge & Kegan Paul, 1983.

———. *The Rosicrucian Enlightenment.* Boston, London: Routledge & Kegan Paul, 1972.

———. *Shakespeare's Last Plays: A New Approach.* London: Routledge & Kegan Paul, 1975.

———. *Theatre of the World.* Chicago: University of Chicago Press, 1969.

Young, David P. *The Heart's Forest: A Study of Shakespeare's Pastoral Plays.* New Haven: Yale University Press, 1972.

———. *The Art of "A Midsummer Night's Dream."* New Haven: Yale University Press, 1966.

Zika, Charles. "Reuchlin and Erasmus: Humanism and Occult Philosophy." *Journal of Religious History* 9 (1977): 223–46.

Zolla, Elémire. *The Androgyne: Reconciliation of Male and Female.* New York: Crossroad, 1981.

Index

(Pages in bold face indicate passage of detailed analysis.)